SHE WHO TELLS A STORY

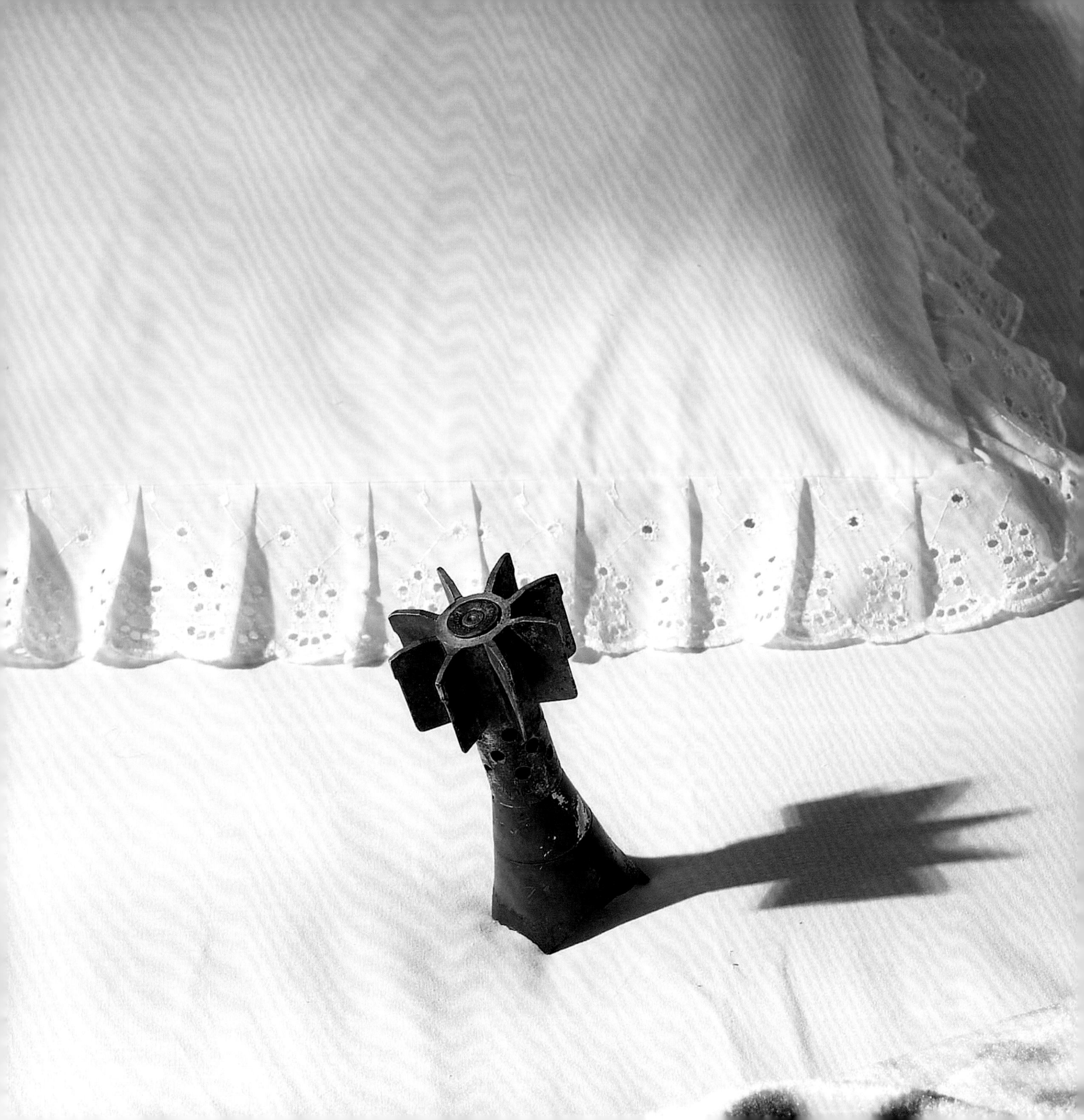

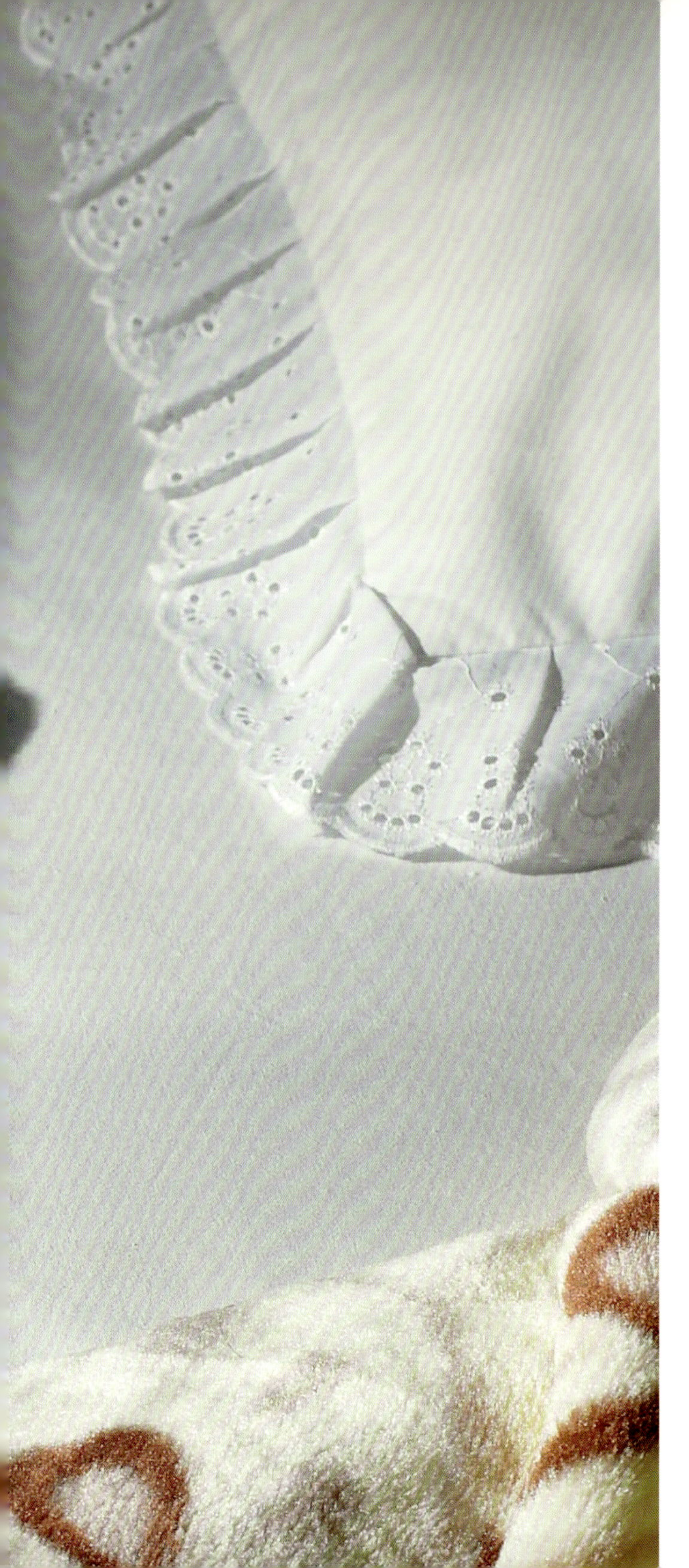

SHE WHO TELLS A STORY

راوية

WOMEN PHOTOGRAPHERS FROM IRAN AND THE ARAB WORLD

KRISTEN GRESH

Foreword by Michket Krifa

MFA PUBLICATIONS | **MUSEUM OF FINE ARTS, BOSTON**

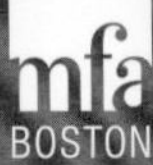

mfa
BOSTON

MFA Publications
Museum of Fine Arts, Boston
465 Huntington Avenue
Boston, Massachusetts 02115
www.mfa.org/publications

Published in conjunction with the exhibition
*She Who Tells a Story: Women Photographers
from Iran and the Arab World*, organized by the
Museum of Fine Arts, Boston, from August 27,
2013, to January 12, 2014

The exhibition was generously supported
by the Robert Mapplethorpe Foundation, with
additional support from the Barbara Jane
Anderson Fund.

Generous support for this publication
was provided by the Andrew W. Mellon
Publications Fund, wtih additional support
from the Barbara Lee Family Foundation.

ISBN 978-0-87846-804-1
Library of Congress Control Number:
2013938797

The Museum of Fine Arts, Boston, is a
nonprofit institution devoted to the promotion
and appreciation of the creative arts. The
Museum endeavors to respect the copyrights
of all authors and creators in a manner
consistent with its nonprofit educational
mission. If you feel any material has been
included in this publication improperly, please
contact the Department of Rights and
Licensing at 617 267 9300, or by mail at the
above address.

While the objects in this publication necessarily represent only a small portion of
the MFA's holdings, the Museum is proud to
be a leader within the American museum
community in sharing the objects in its collection via its website. Currently, information
about more than 330,000 objects is available
to the public worldwide. To learn more
about the MFA's collections, including prove-
nance, publication, and exhibition history,
kindly visit *www.mfa.org/collections*.

For a complete listing of MFA publications,
please contact the publisher at the above
address, or call (617 369 3438).

Edited by Lucy Flint and Jennifer Snodgrass
Proofread by Kathryn Blatt
Designed by Lucinda Hitchcock
Typeset by Matt Mayerchak
Production by Terry McAweeney
Production assistance by Anna Barnet
Printed on 150 gsm Gardamatt and bound at
Graphicom, Verona, Italy

Available through ARTBOOK | D.A.P.
155 Sixth Avenue, 2nd floor
New York, New York 10013
tel: 212 627 1999   fax: 212 627 9484
www.artbook.com

Front cover: plate 62 (detail)
Back cover: plate 39 (detail)

SECOND PRINTING
Printed and bound in Italy
This book was printed on acid-free paper.

CONTENTS

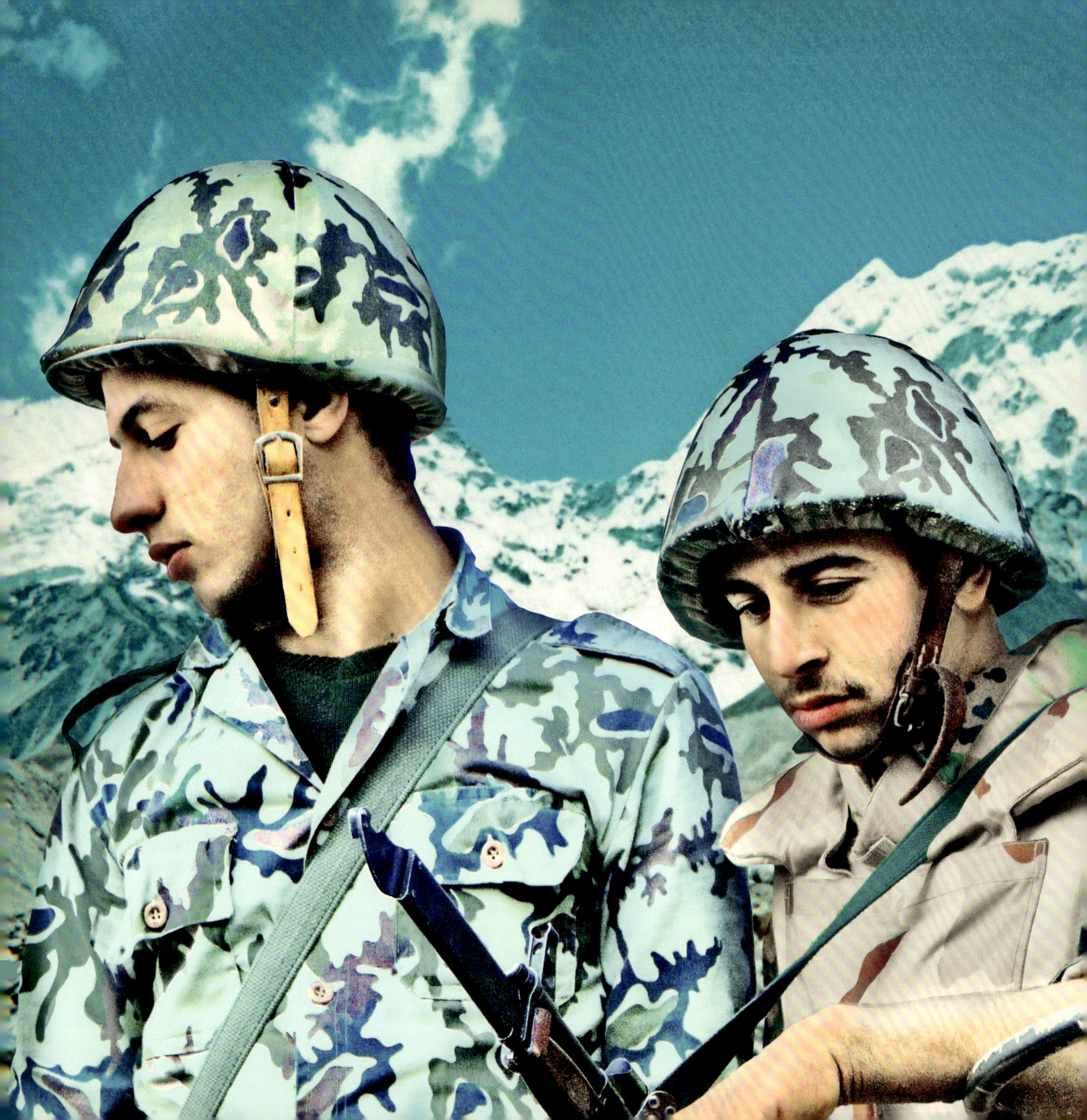

DIRECTOR'S FOREWORD

A good photograph is one that tells a story and helps us see, as Goethe once observed, what is hardest to see — namely, what is in front of our eyes. *She Who Tells a Story*, the first major exhibition and publication of its kind in the United States, brings together extraordinary photographs by twelve exceptional artists from Iran and the Arab world. Their photographs and videos, ranging from fine art to documentary, tell stories that touch our hearts, challenge our misperceptions, and help us see with fresh eyes a vibrant, complex, and exciting Middle East. It is our hope that these powerful visual narratives will inspire curiosity about the region and open a cultural dialogue about the art of Iran and the Arab world, led by these pioneering artists.

We are delighted to announce that this project has also led to significant acquisitions for the MFA's permanent collection. We extend our gratitude to lenders to the exhibition, in particular to the Los Angeles County Museum of Art and the Smithsonian Freer and Sackler Galleries of Art, as well as to generous private collectors, galleries, and the artists themselves. We are also thankful for the generous financial support provided for the exhibition by the Robert Mapplethorpe Foundation, and the additional support of the Barbara Jane Anderson Fund. This publication was made possible with generous support from the Andrew W. Mellon Publications Fund, with additional support from the Barbara Lee Family Foundation.

Great museums are the living repository of stories of the past, present, and future. We hope the compelling narratives embodied in the images in *She Who Tells a Story* will inspire viewers and readers to discover the energy and variety of contemporary art arising from a rapidly changing region of our world.

Malcolm Rogers

*Ann and Graham Gund Director
Museum of Fine Arts, Boston*

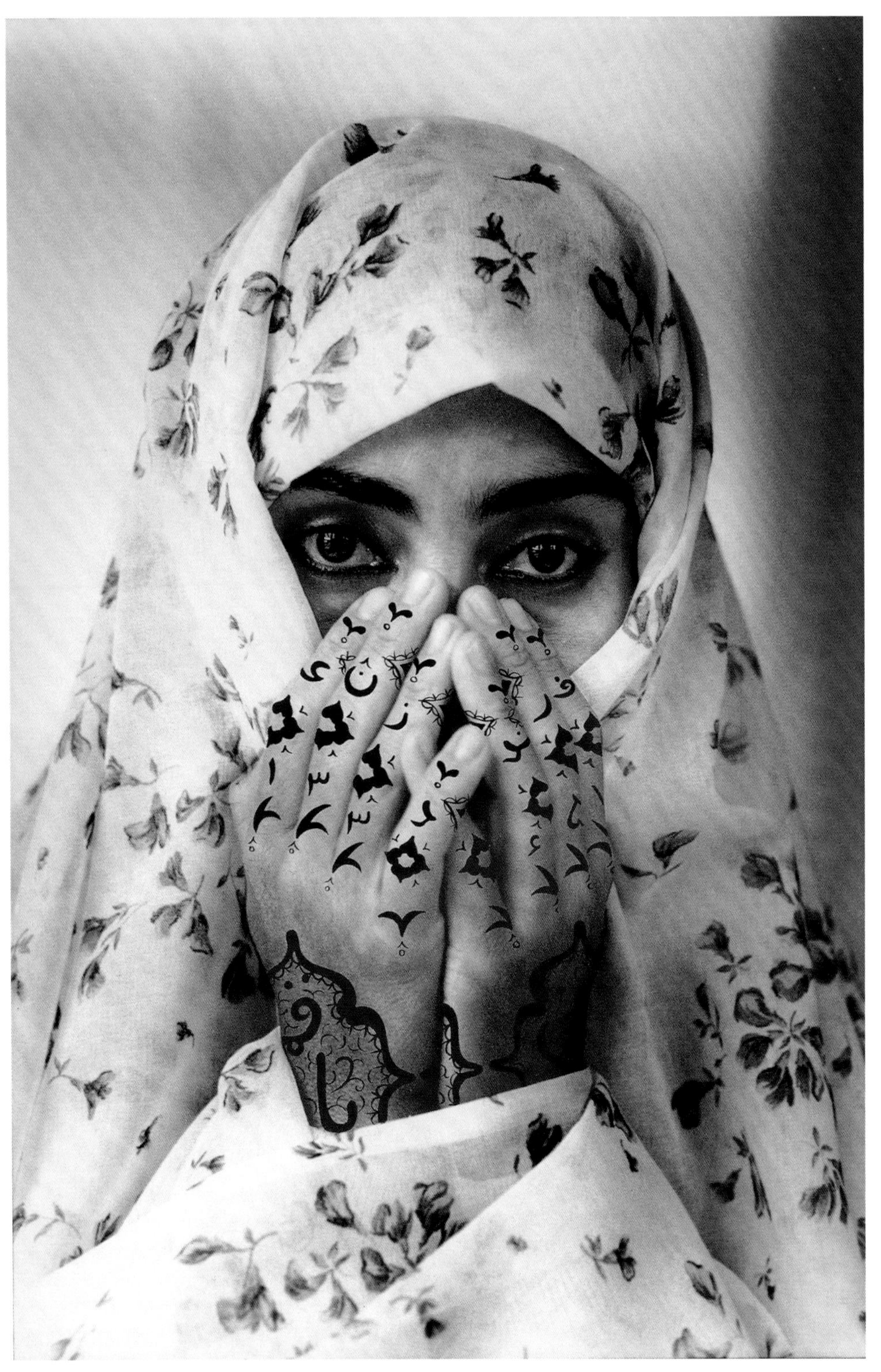

At a time when artists are sought out from every corner of the world, many eyes have turned toward the countries of the Middle East and North Africa. The emerging art scene in the region is served by many national and international institutions: museums, festivals, fairs, art biennales. These make it possible to show artists who had generally exhibited only in private institutions and galleries. In addition, contemporary art, long neglected, has become a government priority in some countries of the region—for example, in the nations of the Persian Gulf, in Morocco, and in Algeria. These governments have finally come to understand that art can be an excellent investment, as well as a means of promotion and communication. Thus the Art Dubai International Fair, the Sharjah Biennial, the Mathaf (Arab Museum of Modern Art) in Qatar, the Museum of Modern and Contemporary Art (MAMA) in Algiers, the Istanbul Biennial, the Cairo Biennale, and the Marrakech Art Fair have become gathering places for the international art world. Private galleries and art centers are also multiplying, and artists have organized collectives that form a network throughout the region.

Interest in work by artists, and especially women artists, from this part of the globe has increased again since 2011, when the Arab revolts that began shaking several countries raised consciousness about the issues of freedom of expression and gender equality. Artists took part in these movements in large numbers, and they are now redefining their spaces of creativity under changed circumstances. They are striving to break free of the censorship that has often forced them to express themselves through circumvention. Women, who were just as active as men during these insurrections, are fighting to acquire or redefine their rights and to achieve a status that is constantly threatened by radical Islamist movements. Most of these radical discourses and activities are crystallized in and projected onto the female body, the eternal object of identity-based fantasy. As a result, women artists are at the forefront of a battle waged on two fronts: one for their creative and intellectual freedom, and the other against discrimination.

Since the advent of political and social debates on the Islamic veil (the *hijab* or the more extensive *niqab*)—the site of a modern mythology on the clash of civilizations—not a day goes by when the media does not report acts of sexual discrimination against Muslim women, violence they have suffered, or their uneasy place in society. Secular society tends to understand the veil, especially the *niqab*, in symbolic terms, as the supreme emblem of confinement and subjection to an identity and as an object of

Michket Krifa

1. Shirin Neshat
Identified, 1995
From *Women of Allah* series
Framed: 132.1 x 88.9 cm (52 x 35 in.)

frustration and exclusion. The condition of women is becoming one of the major issues in the battle for civil and democratic rights in Muslim countries. Politicians, leaders, and thinkers on all sides claim the right to engage in discourse and reflection on behalf of women, while insisting that women model particular behaviors and modes of life. In theory, all decisions contribute to the improvement of women's lot, and concern about their position is discussed in every parliamentary and televised debate and even in sermons in the mosques. The situation of women is analyzed, judged, pitied, and used as a political instrument. Moderates in the "Orient" brandish a map of reforms related to women's status, often implemented in dribs and drabs in exchange for what is perceived as good female behavior within a modern civil society. For conservatives, women can only be a disembodied subject—in the best case, the model of a society's purity, and in the worst, that of its decline. And so, from one day to the next, the escalation of the phantasmagoria inscribed on the female body continues.

Fortunately, women themselves have formed feminist movements, citizen associations, and media networks to parry these ideological manipulations. They are raising their voices and making demands. As for the women artists of the region, they operate on the margins of the discourse and controversy that instrumentalize them. Far from being trapped by the images—the phantasmagoria—they co-opt bits and pieces of these projections, dismantle them, twist them, and send them back reinterpreted in sublimated forms. In identifying the walls of archetypal images that confine them, these women tear them down. They begin by refusing to belong to an unindividuated group, demanding a singularity that is unusual in countries where the "I" is almost taboo.

The individual demands a strictly personal history and vision. These women belong only to themselves. Peering into their deepest, most intimate selves, they bring forth their multiple identities and diverse expressions. They integrate cultural strata, play on death-dealing borderlines, and subvert soul-killing social expectations. They create hybrid forms remote from male conflicts and open themselves to a new way of belonging that they define as uniquely their own. Since no single definition of femininity persists, they engage in a sort of role-playing or cross-dressing, trying on the conflicted identities wrought by war and gender roles, to accentuate the absurdity of labels that highlight difference and conceal resemblance. The metamorphosis of the body through violence and the anonymity of the modern city takes these women to a different realm, that of the individual caught in an urban jungle and dominated by the power relations of fragmented or shattered societies. Their side-glances penetrate the strangest and most clandestine places, gathering up bits of stories, often secret, from which decent society generally averts its gaze. They reinvent the gestures and rituals of apparently deserted places and lost habits. They journey freely through time and space, covering the entire expanse of their world. Only recently objects of fantasy, held fast in hidebound imaginations, they have now become nomads of the imaginary. Through the image, which they now control, they amuse themselves, sowing confusion and shrewdly violating the rules of representation. They have successfully eluded the crude reflections that presented them with a doctored image of themselves by becoming "women of images" (*femmes d'images*) themselves.[1]

In the last twenty years, women have been extremely productive in art worldwide. Even though the richness of women's creativity runs counter to gender prejudices in the Arab world and Iran, this area has witnessed a corresponding emergence of a large number of prolific women visual artists and photographers. The variety of expressive forms they adopt invites us to exercise restraint in characterizing them. Little by little, the evolution that has occurred in the region and its consciousness has eclipsed geographical classification in favor of singular approaches to the artists.

The mid-1990s were marked by enormous upheavals in the Middle East and North Africa. For many artists, these sounded the death knell of nationalism-based ideologies. All that remained were human beings assailed by doubts and weakness. So it was that, on the ashes of national causes, the nature of the individual arose as a question in these societies. Male and female artists at the time approached their artistic experiments via their own lives. Photography, which until then had generally consisted of reportage, entered the private realm. Paradoxically, women were the first to seize on the medium to delve deeper into identity and representation, often personally embodying their investigation. Mona Hatoum, a Palestinian, and Shirin Neshat, an Iranian, were the first to imprint the repercussions of political and sociological tragedies on their own flesh in videos and photographs (plate 1). They eloquently expressed the fractured identity and dispossession of "women's being." Very quickly, Shirin Neshat's photographs prompted Western art critics to search for an aesthetics of the veil, often with a desire to see her works solely as a critique of the Iranian regime and, more broadly, of Islam. This view extended to the pernicious suggestion that she was using the Western pictorial language to cast a negative eye on her native country and culture. In amalgamating the artist's personal and sometimes sublimated expression with the reductive and redundant discourse on the media, they distorted her artistic singularity into an anthropological curiosity. The art critic Samuel Herzog has commented on the rather cynical paradox that "though we define Western artists by their individuality, we define others by their cultural, social, or political identity. Even while seeking to be global, therefore, and to bring everyone together under the roof of contemporary art, we sacralize an insurmountable difference."[2]

Over time, nevertheless, Shirin Neshat and Mona Hatoum came to be recognized as major artists on the international art scene no longer reduced to their cultural identity.

In the next generation, artists of mixed heritage such as Jananne Al-Ani (Irish and Iraqi), Zineb Sedira (Franco-Algerian), and Raeda Saadeh (Palestinian-Arab citizen of Israel) came on the scene. They exposed the ambivalence and uncertainty of their identity by dressing in the contradictory remnants of their multiple origins, claiming the territory of their own bodies as the site of representation.[3] All three women subtly elude neo-Orientalist approaches through a subversive and unexpected use of the veil and of unveiling. They propose a representation, composed of gesture and the transformation of ritual, that rejects any form of symbolism or iconolatry. In response to (political and sexual) reductions of their identity, they reappropriate their bodies—the space of their creation and the affirmation of their individuality—in subtly theatricalized series of self-portraits that poetically address the marks left on their beings.

The French-born Zineb Sedira gives expression to Algeria, her culture of origin, that of the formerly colonized. It is a culture of shadow, which corresponds to the racial discrimination currently experienced by Maghrebi immigrants. In photographing parts of women's bodies and their full shadows projected onto walls, she also speaks of another form of exile, the more insidious experience of alterity, the inability to find an intact image of oneself in the other's gaze (see her *Self-Portrait or the Virgin Mary*, 2000). That amputation, the extinguishing of the light on a denigrated identity, is an assault on the very definition of the body and its contours.

In all her studies, Jananne Al-Ani inquires into her dual identity through explorations of the familial body. Having begun by tracking the representation of the Arab woman in the European imaginary, she then surveys all of Orientalist iconography,

while transposing and interrogating it. In two images from 1996, she surrounds
herself with her sisters and mother to play on the subterfuge of the desire for the
Orient (plates 2–3). In the first print, the subtle gradation of light in the photographs
unveils what is visible of the women's bare legs, a progression that parallels the
incremental veiling of their faces. In the second, the degree of veiling is reversed
among the women, who are themselves reversed in order. In another untitled series
from 1998, composed as a diptych, the same family members pose in traditional Arab
dress in one of the photographs and in Western clothing in the other. Installed side
by side, the images create the impression of a dress-up session. It is as if the women
had agreed to rewrite a part of their painful history, a shared version that allows the
family to recompose itself into a single body. The fragmented body of each woman
is part of a movement of synchronization leading to the advent of the familial body.

In very private performances, the Palestinian Raeda Saadeh has herself photographed onstage dressed as a bride. Impeccably coiffed and made up, she
assumes languorous poses in a diffusely lit setting, evoking Hollywood glamour or
classical Western painting. Yet what ought to be among the happiest moments in life
is transformed into a nightmare. The black veil worn by the bride, otherwise dressed
in white, tightens around her neck to the point of strangulation. The loving partner
she engages in a dance on an empty dance floor is a skeleton (*Black Veil* and *Dance
with a Skeleton*, both 1998). Her body cries out against the straitjacket of women's
traditional roles: spouse, housewife, or seductress. But there is also the sensation
of suffocation and implosion in a being whose private space is devoured by the daily
violation of geographical territory.

In the *Great Masters* series (2007), Saadeh theatricalizes the portrait. She photographs herself simulating the great classical female figures of painting—the Mona
Lisa, Vermeer's milkmaid, Diana the Huntress—replicating their postures, movements, and clothing within the Palestinian countryside and hence against the background of colonization and destruction. This absurd disconnect accentuates the mental
and geographical imprisonment that a state of occupation daily imposes. Rarely has
occupation been represented in such a disturbing manner: it is the occupation of the
inside of a body, which, for lack of living space, turns rigid.

In Iran, where the art scene has been notable for its quality throughout the
last fifteen years, many young women have come to the fore, including the young

2–3. Jananne Al-Ani
Untitled, 1996
Each: 122 x 182 cm (48 x 71 ⅝ in.)

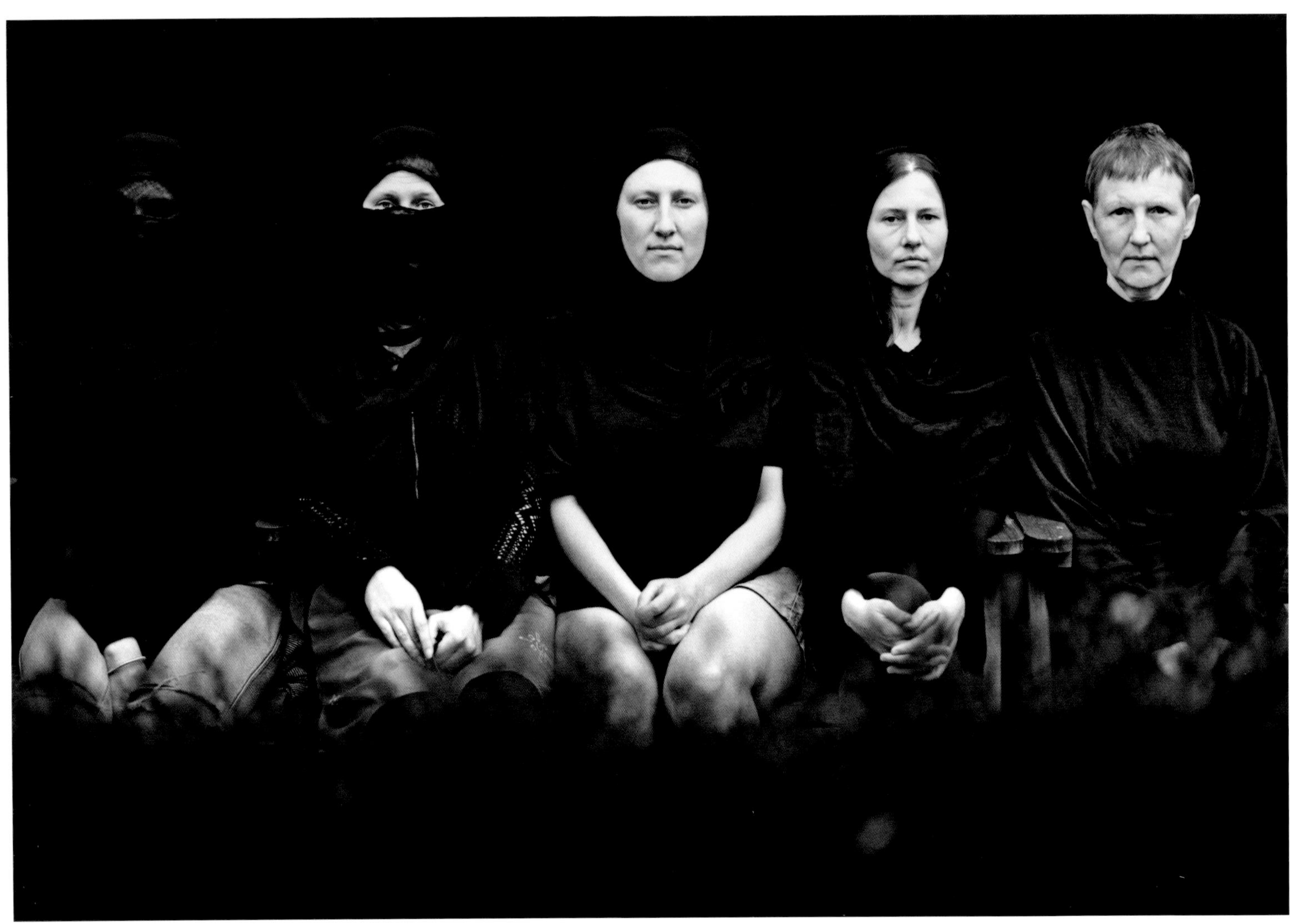

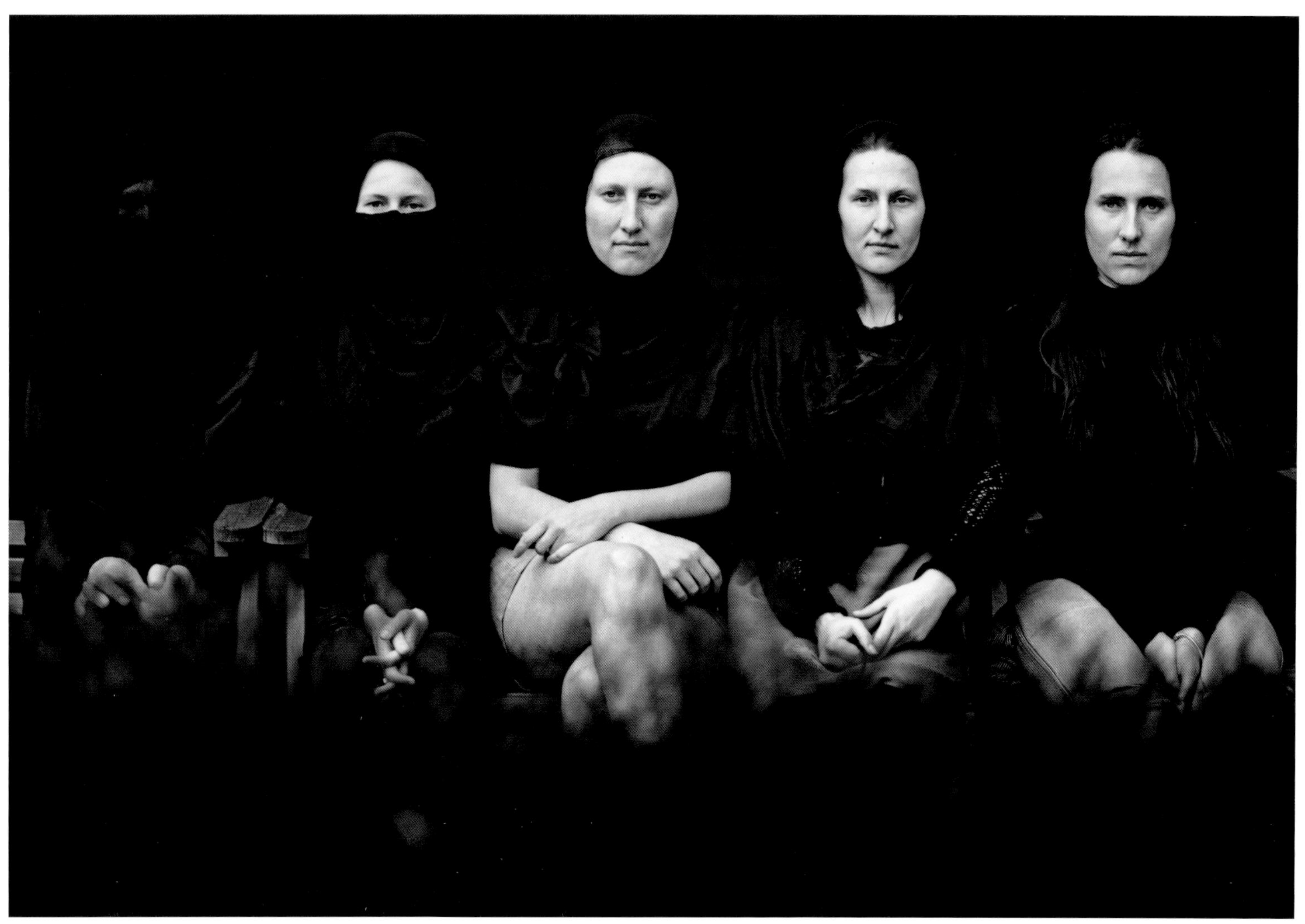

photographer Shadi Ghadirian. She enjoyed international success with her *Qajar* series (1998), which combines figures posed in historical studio settings with deliberately anachronistic youthful accessories that for years were officially banned: a motorcycle helmet, a Pepsi can, a bicycle, a portable radio (plate 4; see plates 6–9). In a second series, *Like Every Day* (2001–2), Ghadirian uses humor and panache to denounce the conditions of housewives, who can come to identify with their tasks: rather than a face, her subjects have a household utensil—a grater, a clothes iron, a broom, a saucepan, or, more dangerously, a knife. Ghadirian plays subtly with codes and the limits of their transgression. Through her depictions of daily life in Tehran and other works that reflect her social concerns, Ghadirian demystifies the reductive, monolithic images that outsiders may harbor.

In *Nil, Nil* and *White Square*, she denounces the intrusion of war into the daily lives of Iranian people. Scarred by more than eight years of conflict with Iraq, surrounded by countries at war and threatened daily by imminent conflict, young Iranians have learned how to deal with the culture of war. Ghadirian has grown up with the glorification of martyrs and of "relics" brought back by young soldiers. In *White Square*, she lovingly surrounds used helmets, waist belts, and strings of bullets with a red silk ribbon and photographs them as if they were still lifes. In *Nil, Nil*, weapons have completely besieged familial intimacy and invaded the household, such as a hand grenade in the fruit dish or a gas mask in a child's bedroom (see plates 53–58).

Through these *mises en scène* of daily life in Tehran, intimately linked to her social concerns, Ghadirian contributes to the demystification of simplistic visions one might have from one side or another. She opens the door to new understanding by creating visionary art works that are part of a vibrant and complex reality with multiple connotations.

Various incursions into the feminine universe have taken a more documentary approach, including those of, notably, the photographers Rula Halawani, Zohra Bensemra, Reem Al Faisal, Rana El Nemr, Laura Boushnak, Newsha Tavakolian, Tanya Habjouqa, among many other equally talented women. These photographers declare no intention other than to offer a wider panorama of images of Arab and Iranian women, seen from the "inside" and by the women themselves. The endogenous glimpses they provide privilege the plurality and complexity of representations of the feminine. They are an invitation to revise all preconceptions since, as Fatima Mernissi

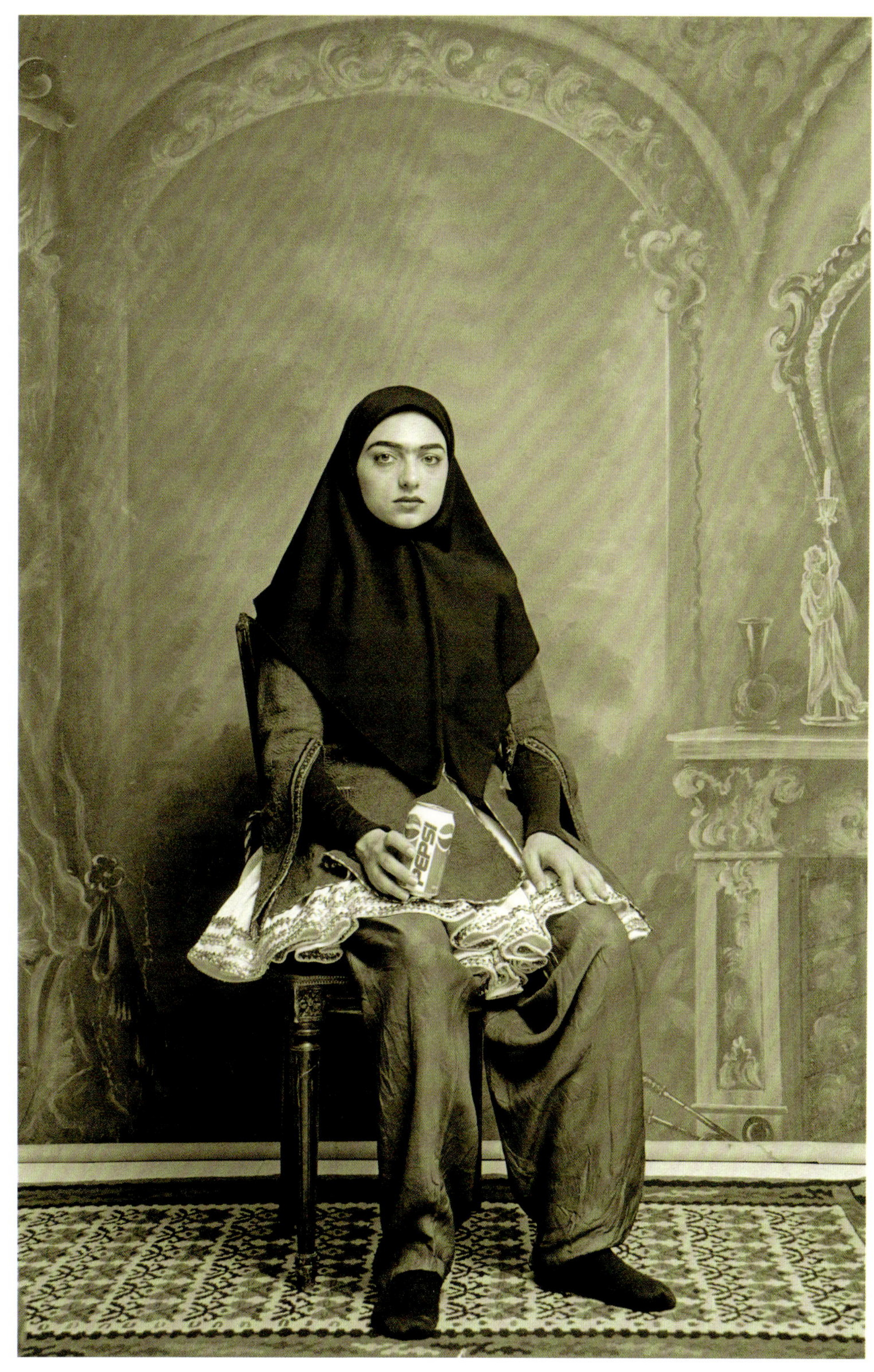

4. Shadi Ghadirian
From *Qajar* series, 1998
40 x 30 cm (about 16 x 12 in.)

writes, "A foreigner's most precious baggage is his or her difference. If you focus on the dissimilar and the different, you can receive illuminations, or *lawami*."[4] Thus, we need the other to achieve our emotional plenitude; we need to dismantle the stereotypes to begin a dialogue.

Each of these women has provided a vision or an interpretation of the world she has witnessed. The documentary gaze of Zohra Bensemra allows us to see, through her reportage, the diversity of women in Algeria pursuing everyday lives. Reem Al Faisal is the only woman (and a Saudi besides) who was able to photograph the pilgrimage to Mecca when she did. The Palestinian Rula Halawani brings into sharp focus her displacement to blood-spent geopolitical surroundings (see plates 78–84). And Rana El Nemr's series *The Metro* (2003) evokes the pressures on women in an urban environment (see plates 65–71). Women's interest in the new documentary photography has also been expressed through the creation of the collective Rawiya, composed of young female photographers from the Middle East who combine a documentary approach to their subject with a self-expressive attention to aesthetic forms. Among them, Newsha Tavakolian and Tanya Habjouqa have both studied loss and grief: loss of a brother, husband, or son. In *Mothers of Martyrs* (2005), consisting of *mises en abîme*, Tavakolian presents, in a rather painterly way, women posing in front of the camera with a portrait of a man lost at war. Tanya Habjouqa's documentary series *Wives of the Syrian Revolution* (2012) comprises a personal photographic journal documenting female Syrian refugees in Jordan as they attempt to provide a normal life for their children under tragic conditions.

The formal liberties these photographers take reflect the scope of the artistic field they are exploring, while the variety of their narrative choices provide a range of possible guideposts that humanity might find in a chaotic world.

It is important to note that most of the photographers from this region who are working on formal questions of representation are women. Whether through dramatic depictions of daily life, self-portraits, or products of the artist's imagination, these vignettes insist on subjectivity as one of the determining elements of their narration. Each of these women recounts bits of stories she has imagined or interpreted, whether or not they are her own. Photography, then, functions as a medium that, far from revealing the artist's self, serves to establish that self as an imaginary construction. These "women of images" engage in the play of interpretive ambiguity and reject the play of identification. This leads us to wonder about the forms and investigations their perspectives inspire, and to rejoice at the privilege of penetrating the very particular universe they allow us to glimpse.

The exploration of the space of representation brings us back to the insoluble riddle of reconciling *être* and *paraître* — "being" and "seeming to be," the private and the public. On the characteristics of photography, Roland Barthes noted that the medium originated as an art of the person and of embodiment. The irruption of the private in the public is consummated as such in public. For Barthes, the private is "the absolutely precious, inalienable place where my image is free, it is the condition for an interiority that I believe is indistinguishable from my interiority, or, if you prefer, from the Intractable of which I am made, and I return to it to reconstitute, through a necessary resistance, the division of public and private."[5]

It appears, therefore, that for each of these women photographers, image-making constitutes a sort of personal journal, where fragments of reality, reverie, and engagement provide slices of subjectivity transfigured by elliptical dramatizations open to multiple interpretations.

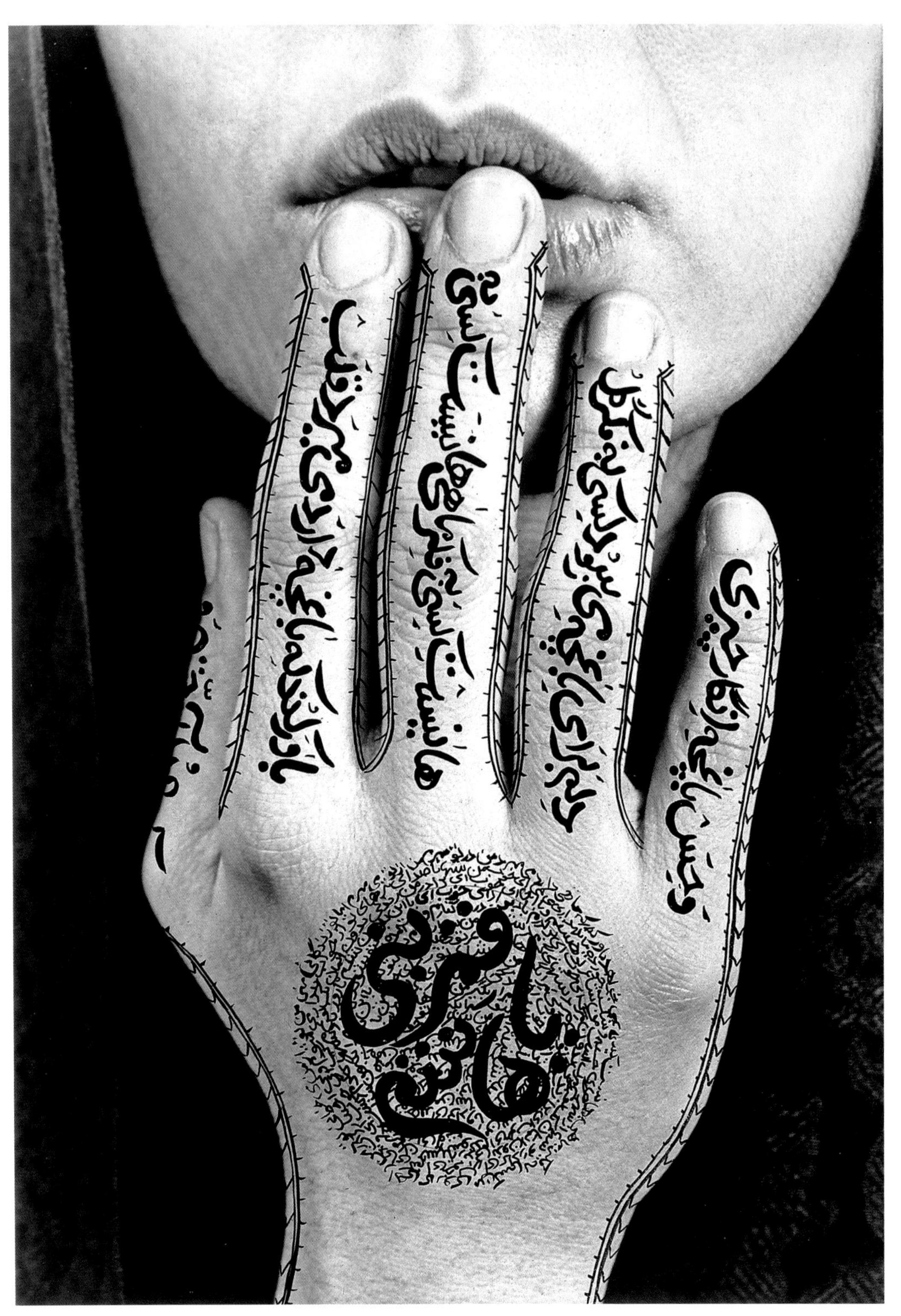

STORIES WE THOUGHT WE KNEW

During this critical time for the Middle East, as national and personal identities are being dismantled and rebuilt, contemporary photography reflects the complexities of unprecedented change.[1] Interest in contemporary art from Iran and the Arab world has exploded since September 11, 2001, and intensified further since the beginning of the Arab Spring.[2] Photography, both fine-art and documentary, can be used as a tool for understanding the intricacies of a region subject to a recurrent reductionism that systematically privileges politics over culture. One of the most significant trends to emerge recently is the work of women photographers, whose remarkable and provocative images provide insights into new cultural landscapes. *She Who Tells a Story* brings together the vital pioneering work of twelve leading artists and invites viewers inside and outside the Middle East to explore these new landscapes and to confront their own preconceptions.

Though these photographers challenge stereotypes, the choice to unite them as a group has been seen by some, ironically, as confirming a stereotype. While attending a recent exhibition in Paris of one of the photographers represented in these pages, an Iranian-born artist expressed the view that the decision to show work by only Arab and Iranian women was "alarming." He argued that women from the region are seen by the outside world as oppressed, and that subsuming them into a group would only reinforce this perception. On the contrary, the work collected here challenges the common belief that women are powerless in these countries. And as observed by the Tunisian-born curator and critic Michket Krifa, and the Iranian gallery owner Anahita Ghabaian Etehadieh, among others, some of the strongest and most significant photographic work in the region today is being made by women.[3]

"She who tells a story" is a translation of the Arabic term *rawiya*, which is also the name of a small collective of female photographers based in the Middle East, founded in 2009.[4] The idea of a woman storyteller is a fitting premise for these photographs, themselves a collection of poignant stories. Far removed from the historical myths and traditional tales of the "Persian" Queen Sheherazade and the "Arabian" *Thousand and One Nights*, these stories are pertinent narratives about contemporary life in Iran and the Arab world. Reflecting on the power of politics and the legacy of war, the selected artists elaborate visions of layered, constructed, fragmented, and staged identities. They explore the dualities of the visible and the invisible, the permissible and the forbidden, the spoken and the silent, and the prosaic and the horrific.

Kristen Gresh

5. Shirin Neshat, Untitled, 1996
From *Women of Allah* series
167.6 x 132.1 cm (66 x 52 in.)

She Who Tells a Story introduces and celebrates work from a region that cannot be defined in a singular territorial, religious, or ethnic way.[5] Associating artistic imagination with geography, or gender, runs the risk of creating a deceptive simplicity that this project aims to avoid. The selection of artists is not an attempt to categorize, ghettoize, segregate, or create false commonalities, but, rather, an effort to show the strength and diversity of some of the most compelling contemporary photography from Iran and the Arab world.

This array of work, ranging in genre from portraiture to documentary, is almost entirely from 2000 or later, with the exception of a few key pieces from the 1990s that provide a historical backdrop. The artists and their work are presented in two categories, not necessarily mutually exclusive: "Constructing Identities" and "New Documentary." Within these divisions, series of visual narratives reveal the richness of each artist's work while allowing for extended glimpses into both the social and political landscapes of Iran and the Arab world.

To understand the contemporary work in *She Who Tells a Story* and explain the urgency of its presentation, it is necessary to consider the history of photography in the Middle East. The iconography has, in the past, consisted largely of images created from an outsider or Western point of view. In the nineteenth century, photographs were generally made in the context of archaeological exploration or commissioned by government agencies and religious organizations.[6] Early photographs of subjects ranging from pyramids and sacred biblical sites to staged harem scenes and belly dancers invariably reflect the European imagination and conception of the East rather than the lived reality of the Middle East. It was only two decades after photography was invented that the first local practitioners began to appear, an example being the court photographer Antoin Sevruguin, who was Persian-born to an Armenian-Georgian family and active from about 1870 to 1925, during the Qajar period.[7]

Twentieth-century photography of the Arab world and Iran emerged mainly from studios operating in Alexandria, Cairo, Beirut, Damascus, Tunis, and Tehran. Many of the photographers in these studios, such as Alban and Van Leo, who worked in Cairo, shared an Armenian background.[8] Despite the rise of press photography over the course of the century, local photojournalism did not develop in the same way it did in other regions of the world. Following independence in the mid-1950s and 1960s, many Arab countries nationalized the media, curtailing photographers' freedom and discouraging the establishment of visual archives.[9] Even so, prominent photojournalists such as Marc Riboud, Micha Bar-Am, David Douglas Duncan, and Abbas produced images of the twentieth-century Middle East that have permeated the Western visual imagination.

To reclaim and understand the region's photographic past and present, the Arab Image Foundation (AIF), founded in Beirut in 1997, collects existing archives of local photographers and provides an intellectual platform and physical site for the promotion of historical research and scholarly study. The Rare Books Library and Special Collections Library of the American University of Cairo, which has also acquired local photographic archives, is another center for research on the history of photography in the area. In Iran, similar efforts have been made to legitimize and contextualize Iranian photography, often in remarkably difficult circumstances. After the Iranian Revolution in 1979, the photographer Bahman Jalali, Iran's first photography historian, was a pioneer in the fight to establish the medium as a fine art.[10]

Since then, both artistic and documentary photography have flourished, and women have been primary contributors to its progress—just as they have played a leading role in social change, as demonstrated in recent protests in Iran and the Arab world. Rose Issa, an independent curator and gallery owner based in London who has showcased art and film from the Middle East since the early 1980s, has pointed to the paradox that her native Iran, a country that supposedly represses women, has generated energetic and outspoken female leaders in many fields.[11] The significant presence of women in the arts and public life contradicts the way much of the outside world perceives Iranian women.[12]

The writer Omid Rouhani has noted that, after the Revolution of 1979, Iranian women artists "began looking for ways of proving and expressing their identity, and did so well before men. This autobiographical, personal vision of collective social and individual issues, both existential and philosophical, was more prominent in work by women. And in this regard a new phase began with the presidential elections of June 2009: beyond questions of self-discovery, feminism and equality, new issues await today's women artists."[13] The Tehran-born-and-based photographer Newsha Tavakolian testifies to the power of contemporary women in Iran, many of whom are highly educated. Women such as Tavakolian exploit the government-imposed requirement that women wear a *hijab* in public as a welcome means to wield autonomy and agency. She explains: "When you see me at work, I always wear a long, long *abaya* and *hijab* [cloak and headscarf], because I have power that way."[14]

While the majority of participants in this exhibition do not wish to be categorized as women photographers, several recognize that their experience is sometimes different, in important ways, from that of their male counterparts. In conversation, the Egyptian photographers Rana El Nemr and Nermine Hammam have both referred to the privileged position of the female photographer, Hammam noting that her series *Upekkha* would be significantly different if the subjects had been reacting to the experience of being photographed by a man rather than a woman.[15]

Constructing Identities

The images in *She Who Tells a Story* not only are made by women with roots in Iran and the Arab world, but are about the people, landscapes, and cultures of the region. Many of the photographers here explore questions of identity through an evolving and shifting set of narratives that must be understood as a response to Orientalism. Historically, "Orientalism" has referred to artistic or literary depictions by European or American artists and writers of the East, including Middle Eastern, North African, and Eastern cultures. In his pioneering study *Orientalism* (1978), the Palestinian-born scholar Edward Said argued that Orientalism aligns Western romanticized visions of the region with the goals of European and American colonialism and imperialism; it is a discourse of power, presenting the "Orient" as culturally inferior. Since the appearance of Said's provocative study, questions surrounding imagery of Middle Eastern, North African, and Asian cultures have been vigorously reconsidered and debated. Regardless of the opinions expressed in these sometimes contentious conversations, Orientalism, and, more specifically, Orientalist painting, is indisputably fundamental to the region's historical visual representation.[16]

Concerning the related issue of gender-based power relations reflected in the portrayal of Middle Eastern women, the Iraqi-born artist Jananne Al-Ani comments particularly on the representation of the veil: "Debate around the veil is one of the remaining subjects which persistently invokes the tired and clichéd binaries of East/West, black/white, male/female."[17] In her writings, Al-Ani uses the fundamental, triangulated relationship between the photographer, stage, and actors to examine historical work with new eyes.[18] In contemporary art practice in the 1990s, both Al-Ani and the Iranian-born

Shirin Neshat simplified this triangulation by staging themselves as performers in *mises-en-scène* that challenge the historically male-dominated representation of Middle Eastern women. Their work, historical now itself, includes Neshat's series *Women of Allah* and Al-Ani's diptych of photographs of female members of her family. By the early 2000s, the Moroccan-born Lalla Essaydi had embarked on an oeuvre that likewise questioned Orientalism.

These three artists, each in her distinctive way, effected far-reaching changes in the history of visual representation and the perception of Orientalist stereotypes. Despite their current geographic distance from their native countries, Neshat, Al-Ani, and Essaydi all produce work that is inspired, directly and indirectly, by the Middle East.[19] Considering and reconsidering Orientalist iconography seems, in fact, particularly compelling for these women, who embody an exilic, expatriate, or bicultural identity.[20]

Neshat's series *Women of Allah* (1993–97) was the outcome of a visit the photographer made to her native Iran fifteen years after the Iranian Revolution and evokes the role that women played in the upheaval. These portraits of female warriors bearing arms, with the words of contemporary Iranian female writers inscribed across their faces and hands, address the paradoxes of "female Islamic militancy" and the precariousness of women's place in Iranian society.[21] Combining the elements of the veil, the gun, the text, and the gaze, Neshat's poetic portraits gained her immediate attention on the contemporary art scene. Frequently deploying the authority of unwavering eye contact, the carefully crafted images break down Orientalist tropes of female submission by showing women's empowerment in the face of opposition. In one untitled image, words written on a woman's hand raised to her mouth give her a voice despite her closed lips (plate 5). *Speechless* portrays a gun barrel beside a woman's cheek, pointing directly at the viewer (plate 10). *I Am Its Secret* shows a veiled woman whose almond-shaped eyes gaze intensely at the viewer amid concentric circles of calligraphy that make her face into a target (plate 11). In *Women of Allah*, the conjoining of guns, the female figure, and Farsi writing makes the body into a battleground for the confrontation of politics and language. The series represented a turning point in the recent history of representation as well as debates about the veil, and inspired new and divergent artistic explorations by other photographers of the region.[22]

Around the same time, Al-Ani questioned the perception of historical narratives and the representation of the "Oriental" woman, with a particular consideration of the

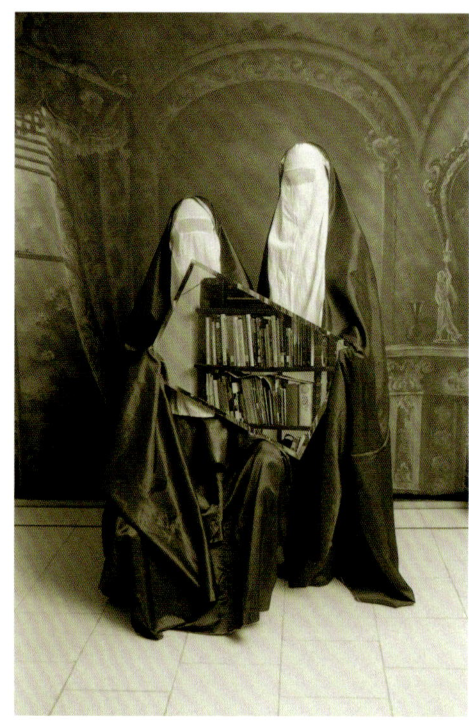

photographic construction of identity through anthropological and ethnographic photography. In her 1996 diptych of two large-format prints, she used herself and the other women in her family to show a progression in veiling (see plates 2–3). Standing between the two prints installed face-to-face, the viewer is trapped between the women's unblinking stares. Al-Ani emphasizes the power of lens-based media—combining forces with physical space—to manipulate the viewer, while exposing Orientalist myths and the "Orientalizing" gaze. This concern with the layering and concealment of identities by the *hijab*, which raged in the 1990s, is now seen as passé by many artists based in Iran and the Arab world today. Others are finding new, provocative ways of representing both the veil and its implications, often within a critical analysis of Orientalism.

Such artists include Lalla Essaydi, who, like Neshat, associates Islamic calligraphy—a sacred and generally male art form—with women's bodies to suggest the complexity of gender roles within Islamic culture. While Neshat writes text on the printed surface of her photographs, Essaydi applies henna calligraphy directly onto her models, their drapery, and their surroundings before photographing the scene. For Essaydi, the presence of text is related to the dominance of the word in Islam: "The word is powerful in our culture because we don't [visually] portray God; our religion is based on the book, and, so, everything is based on the word. That is why a lot of [Muslim] artists work with writing."[23] In her series *Converging Territories* (2003–4), calligraphy fills the image, covering the skin and robes of the women and the wall behind them (see plate 13). Elsewhere, as in *Harem # 1*, Essaydi makes reference to features of Orientalist painting, such as the nineteenth-century odalisque pose or the containment of women within beautifully carved walls of architecture. Here the disparity between the grandeur of the Moroccan architecture and the modest scale of the recess the woman occupies suggests isolation and gendered spatiality; the figure, wrapped in fabric designed by the artist, blends almost entirely with her "habitat."

Such echoes of Orientalism permeate much of the visual representation of the Middle East today, raising questions about insider-versus-outsider and reciprocal stereotyping. From the staged portrait photographs of the nineteenth century to contemporary staged photography, these images offer viewers the possibility of revising preconceived notions.

Like Neshat's and Al-Ani's work from the 1990s, the iconic series *Qajar* (1998) by the Iranian artist Shadi Ghadirian was a point of departure for many contemporary

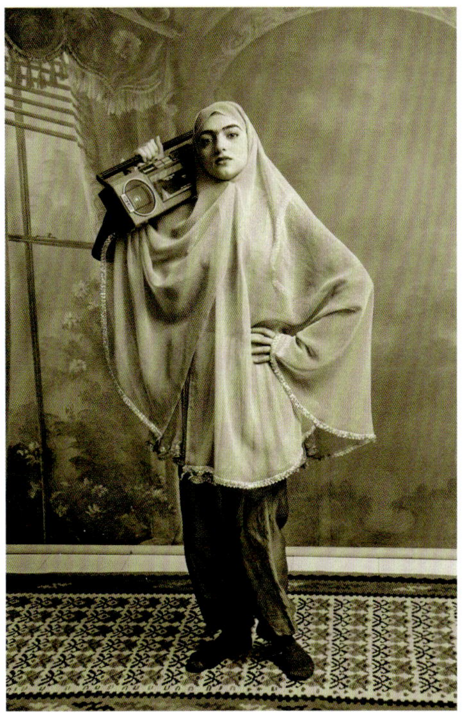

7

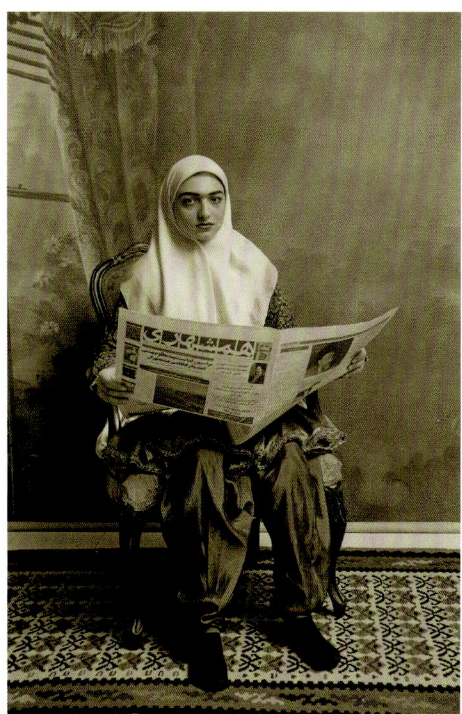

8

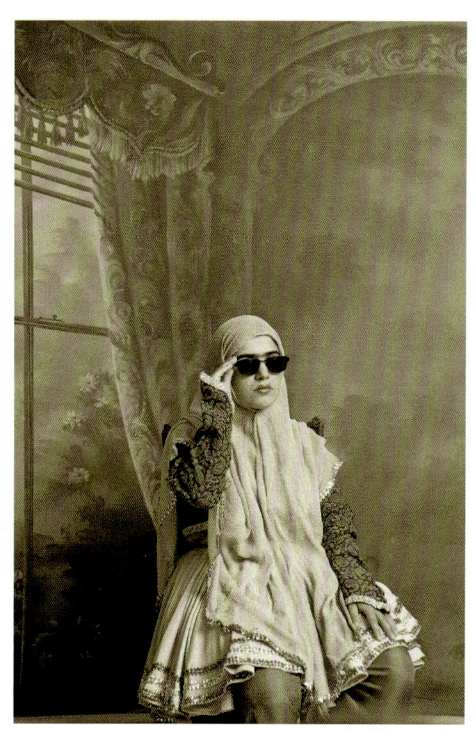

9

photographers (plates 6–9; see plate 4). These humorous pastiches set up a cross-cultural and cross-temporal encounter between a nineteenth-century Persian photographer's European-influenced backdrop and Ghadirian's contemporary studio props. Ghadirian juxtaposes young women in traditional Iranian dress with what she describes as "modern" objects, such as boom boxes, musical instruments, and makeup. The incongruity between the subjects and their attributes suggests a tension between tradition and modernity and between restriction and freedom within the public and private realms. In one image, the object is the regularly banned newspaper *Hamshahri*, for which Ghadirian and her husband once worked; in another, it is a mirror reflecting foreign and banned books, an allusion to the censorship and compromised communication that limited experience in Iran in the 1990s. Now aided by the Internet, Iranians have greater access to the outside world, but until the late 1990s, life was more circumscribed; Ghadirian recalls that specific activities such as playing or listening to music in public, having parties, and wearing makeup were taboo.

Ghadirian's staged portraits of the 1990s laid a conceptual and aesthetic foundation for investigations by later photographers into issues of identity and the realities of being a female Iranian, or Arab, artist. The Yemeni artist Boushra Almutawakel's series *Mother, Daughter, Doll* (2010; plates 16–24) challenges the rise of religious extremism, increasingly pervasive in Yemen and neighboring countries, which calls for the public

6–9. Shadi Ghadirian
From *Qajar* series, 1998
Each: 40 x 30 cm (about 16 x 12 in.)

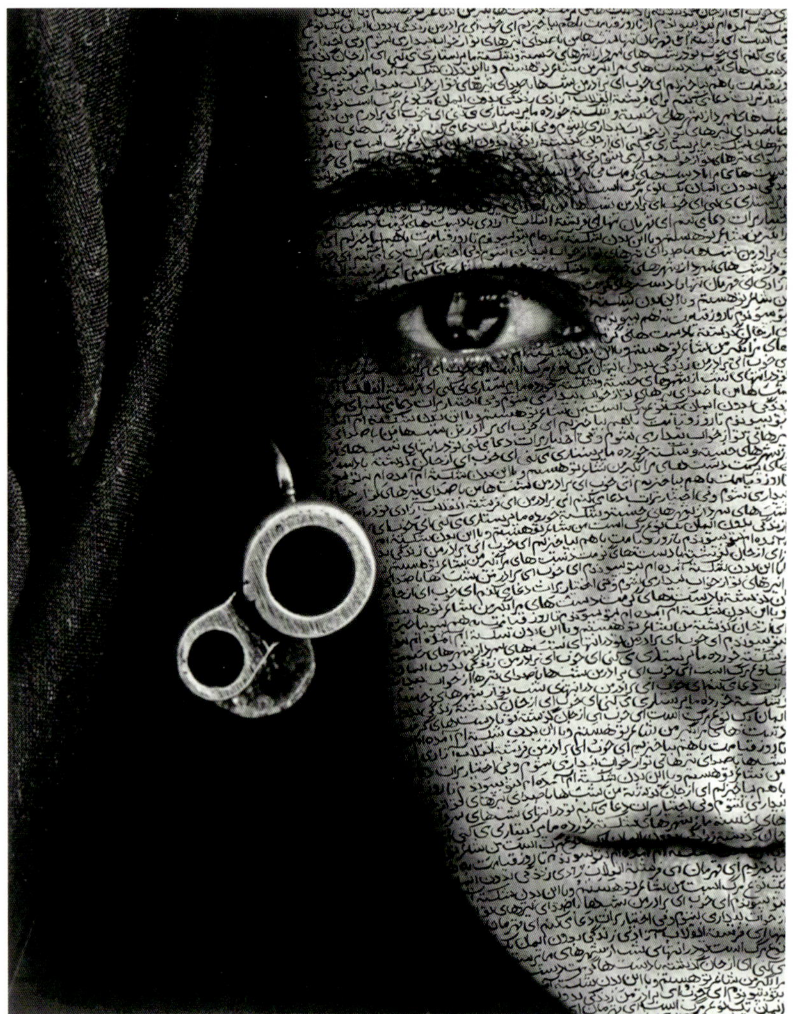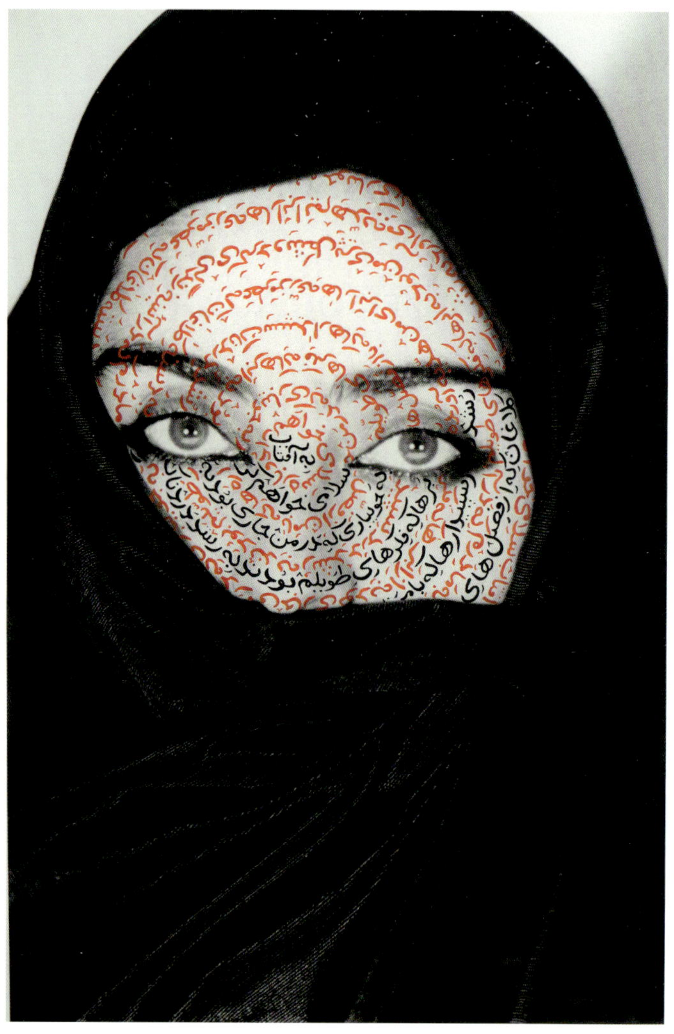

10. Shirin Neshat
Speechless, 1996
From *Women of Allah* series
167.6 x 132.1 cm (66 x 52 in.)

11. Shirin Neshat
I Am Its Secret, 1993
From *Women of Allah* series
33 x 22.9 cm (13 x 9 in.)

concealment of women's, and even young girls', bodies. These staged portraits do not denounce the *hijab*, but visually protest the covering of young females and the trend toward black clothing and covering, particularly the more extensive *niqab*.[24] The fading of the smiles of mother and daughter corresponds to the incremental disappearance of their colorful clothing from one picture to the next; the series ends with the image of an empty pedestal draped in black fabric — mother, daughter, and doll are completely eliminated. Almutawakel uses the veil as a visual device to challenge current social trends and explore the complexities of public appearance, creating this profound statement about the erasure of the individual through dress.

In the intimate portraits that constitute Lebanese-born Rania Matar's series *A Girl and Her Room* (2011; plates 25–30), young women pose comfortably in their bedrooms — their personal havens — in both the Middle East and the United States. Personal and poetic, this documentary exploration of female identity and belongings discloses both regional and more universal human characteristics.

Almutawakel and Matar offer sensitive perspectives on the public and private lives of women, in particular, young women. Their work represents two photographic approaches to the themes of visibility and invisibility, and the inner and outer awareness of self, one highly staged by the artist and the other arranged in an intimate collaboration between the artist and subject.

Other photographers react to more public social and political situations inside or outside their country of origin. The series *Listen* (2010; plates 39–52) by Newsha Tavakolian comprises portraits of professional singers who, as women, are forbidden by Islamic tenets to perform in public or to record CDs in their native country of Iran.[25] Metaphors of music, voice, and expression are also found in Ghadirian's *Qajar* series and in a powerful still called *Mystified* from Neshat's film *Turbulent*, which shows a female singer with a microphone (plate 12).

Tavakolian's singers do not appear with microphones, although each is clearly caught mid-song. The photographer's passion for these women's stories inspired her to create imaginary photographic CD covers that would represent the character of each performer. The accompanying video shows the women emotionally mouthing unheard words, suggesting the idea of an imposed silence. As a former photojournalist, Tavakolian is aware of perceived — and sometimes real — obstacles to photographing in public in Iran, and has turned to fine-art photography to address social issues.

Her childhood dream was to be a singer, and today her photography provides her, along with her subjects, with an eloquent voice.

Tavakolian represents a generation of empowered, young, postrevolutionary Iranian photographers who are intimately attached to their national identity and are finding ways to creatively pursue their artistic expression. Neshat represents a generation of artists born before the revolution who have left the country, yet continue to draw on their cultural heritage. In her series *Book of Kings* (2012; plates 31–38), whose title is translated from that of the thousand-year-old Persian poem *Shahnameh*, Neshat employs language as forcefully as she did in *Women of Allah*. While the epic poem tells of the heroic deeds of former rulers, the photographic series is inspired by the stories of contemporary participants in the Arab Spring and Iranian protesters representing the Iranian Green Movement in 2009. *Book of Kings* is a metaphorical and lyrical ode to patriotism, nationalism, politics, history, revolt, and heroism in the past and present.

New Documentary

Diversity within contemporary visual media from the Middle East is, in part, a product of the distinct regional identities within Iran and the Arab world. Further variety results from the multiplicity of photographic work, which encompasses documentary, photojournalistic, and fine-art traditions, and expresses the ideals and aesthetics of each photographer. The second category of work assembled here brings artistic imagination to the documentation of real-life experiences to form a new kind of documentary. Themes of war, occupation, protest, and revolt and concerns about photography as a medium all find a place in this new genre.

Contemporary Iranian society and the coexistence of daily life and war is a pervasive subject in the work of Shadi Ghadirian and Gohar Dashti, another photographer of postrevolutionary Iran. This content may be related to their shared experience of growing up during the Iran-Iraq war (1980–88). Ghadirian's *Nil, Nil* (2008; plates 53–58) and Dashti's *Today's Life and War* (2008; plates 59–64) are staged narratives recounting unknown stories of war. Photographic narratives created through staging could be considered what Rose Issa calls "real fictions—a subtle mixture of documentary and fiction that blurs the line between reality and creativity."[26] Although Iranians are no longer at war, wartime stories endure and anxiety about possible future conflicts permeates their consciousness.

Like Ghadirian's early *Qajar* series, the colorful still-life images in *Nil, Nil* present startling juxtapositions, here of distinctly masculine and feminine objects — a soldier's helmet hanging next to a headscarf, worn combat boots and a pair of red high heels — in intimate settings. The series brings to the forefront the experience of women at home during war, invoking untold tales of loss and waiting. *Nil, Nil* is the title of a short story about war by Ghadirian's husband, Peyman Hooshmandzadeh.

The theatrical photographs of a couple pursuing ordinary activities in a fictional battlefield in Dashti's *Today's Life and War* (2008) tell an equally unknown story of daily life amid military paraphernalia. The pictures describe private celebrations and daily domestic routines interrupted by a symbol of war, whether barbed wire, a missile head, or a wall of sandbags. The photographer's portrait of her generation expresses the emotional impact of growing up surrounded by the tragedy of war. Boundaries and barriers, real and metaphorical, recur throughout her surreal scenarios and evoke her own story of growing up near the Iran-Iraq border.

Alternatives to these staged documentaries can be found in the works of the Egyptian Rana El Nemr and the Jordanian Tanya Habjouqa, both of whom directly capture urban stories in photographs that address questions of space, identity, and the sense of belonging.

El Nemr's depictions of her fellow Egyptians in the series *The Metro* (2003; plates 65–71) convey the anonymity of contemporary life in the megalopolis of Cairo. The riders, depicted through lines, patterns, colors, and forms, are very much alone despite living in a crowded city. In the subway car designated for women, El Nemr inconspicuously observes her subjects as they sit or stand, deep in thought, poetically capturing both the displacement and belonging that inform the subtle interactions between people and public space.

Habjouqa's *Women of Gaza* (2009; plates 72–77) records the experience of females in Gaza who, like all residents of the occupied territory, live with limited freedom. The photographs celebrate modest pleasures such as a picnic on the beach, an aerobics class, or a boat ride on the Mediterranean. Connecting intimately with her subjects, Habjouqa gently portrays the bright side of their not-always-so-bright lives.

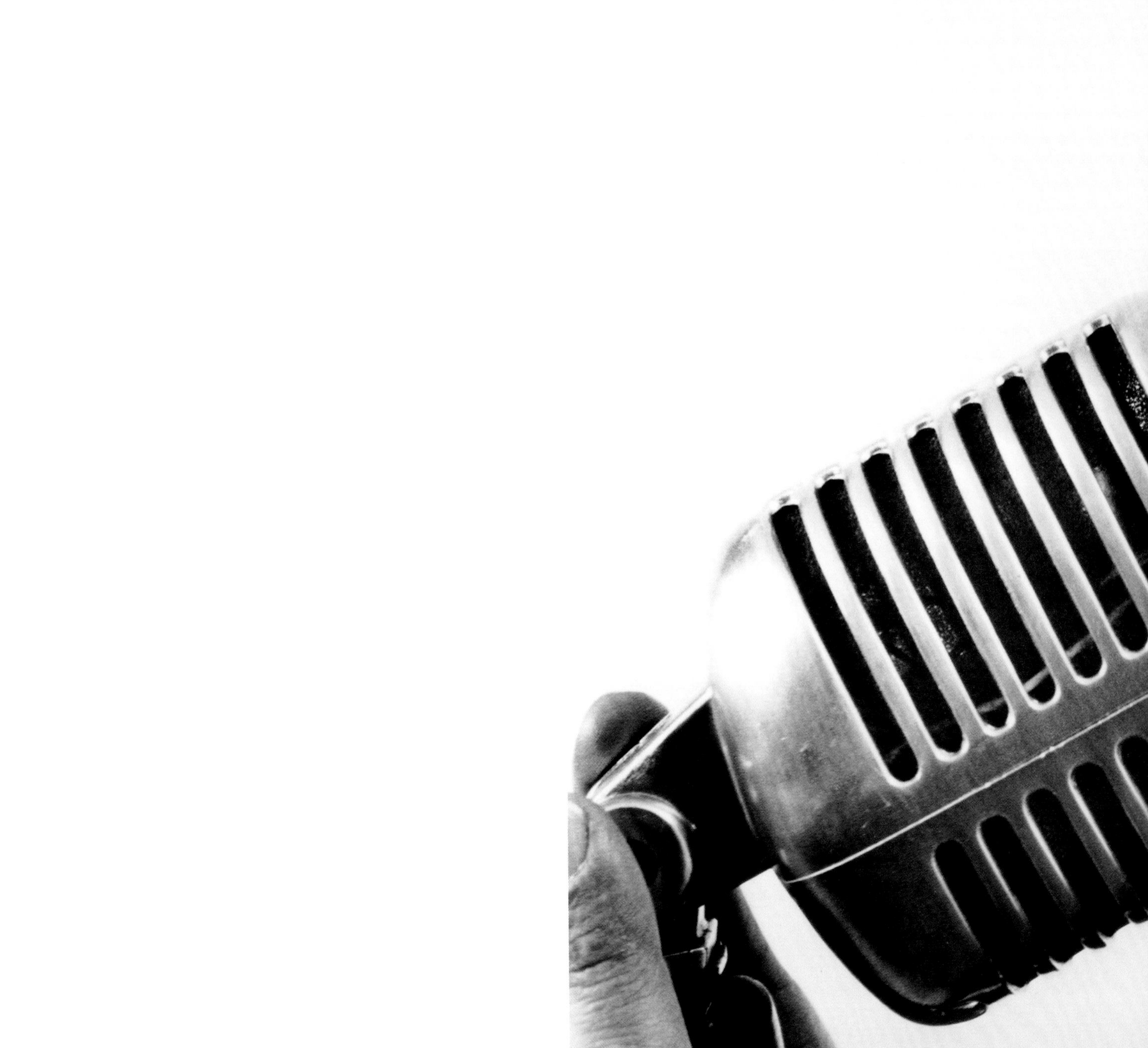

12. Shirin Neshat
Mystified, 1997
From the film *Turbulent*
94 x 139.7 cm (37 x 55 in.)

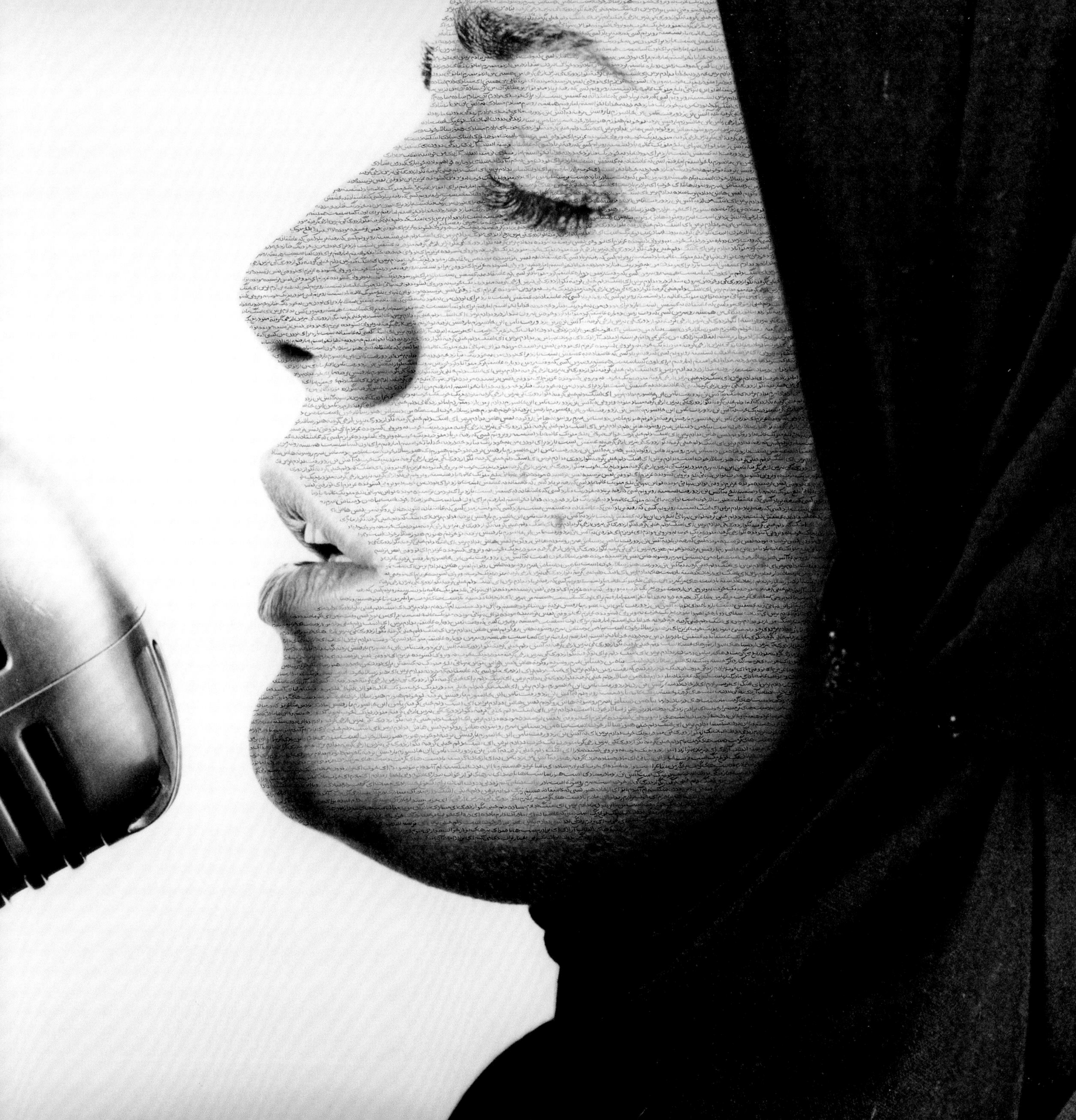

Another area of exploration for Middle Eastern photographers is the medium itself. In a discussion of the convergence of photography and the Middle East, the curator Marta Weiss identifies three categories of "recording, reframing, and resisting."[27] Jananne Al-Ani, Nermine Hammam, and Rula Halawani, with roots in Iraq, Egypt, and Palestine respectively, exploit the recording capability of the photographic medium while pushing its boundaries in new ways, including reframing and resisting. Simultaneously, they challenge the mass media.

In her *Negative Incursions* (2002; plates 78–84), Halawani enlarges and prints negatives without reversing their values, producing the effect of night-vision camera images used for military or scientific purposes. Obscuring the specifics of time and place, the reversed rendering of the Israeli incursion of 2002 increases the dramatic intensity of the compositions. The thick black border around the images imitates the shape of a television screen, conveying Halawani's criticism of the inadequacy of media coverage of Palestinian suffering. Bringing a strong graphic sense to her politically charged situation as a Palestinian living in East Jerusalem, Halawani powerfully addresses the experience of destruction and displacement, as well as the nature of photographic media.

Hammam's series *Cairo Year One* (2011–12; plates 85–97) also muses on the uses of photography. In the first part of the series, *Upekkha*, Hammam embeds photographs of soldiers she took in Tahrir Square during the eighteen-day uprising in January 2011 within the paradisiacal scenery of candy-colored postcards from her personal collection. Like Ghadirian in her *Qajar* series, the photographer plays on images from another era. Hammam's incongruous composites question the media's rendition of a historic event while commenting on the anticlimactic arrival of the army in the square and the surprising fragility of military power.

In *Unfolding* (2012), the second part of *Cairo Year One*, Hammam integrates amateur frame grabs and other reproductions from the media into images of Japanese screens. A particularly vivid work in the series is *Codes of My Kin*, which reproduces the controversial image from the Arab Spring of a woman, later referred to in the press as the Blue Bra Girl, being dragged on the ground by soldiers. The focus in the press and social media on the woman's body and undergarments is particularly disturbing because it ignores the violence being committed.[28] Hammam's use of the image is, in part, a response to the hostility following the uprising that made it impossible for photographers and journalists to photograph freely in the streets.[29] In decontextualizing and recontextualizing existing photographs, Hammam is inspired by the layered identities of her "revolutionized" country and questions about censorship. She pushes against the limitations on artistic and photographic freedom so that she can continue producing provocative work.[30]

As part of a work incorporating both still and moving images called *The Aesthetics of Disappearance: A Land without People*, Al-Ani shot images of the Jordanian landscape from an airplane. Reminiscent of wartime aerial reconnaissance photography, the stills that compose the single-screen video *Shadow Sites II* (2011; plates 98–104) reveal traces of natural and man-made activity in the land below. The video moves from one abstracted aerial view to another in an intentionally disorienting way, with the soundtrack of the roar of an airplane accompanying the dissolving imagery.

Shadow Sites II offers an analogy to the photographic medium itself. Many of the sites Al-Ani photographs are visible only when sunlight projects at a low angle onto the terrain, which, like a light-sensitive photographic surface, yields scenes not visible to the naked eye. With her camera, Al-Ani records these exposures realized by the sun and land. Her innovative coupling of the elements of nature with the technologies of photography and flight provides a provocative reference to the history of photography as well as a means to cast doubt on the veracity of testimony and memory.[31] The revelation of latent images in the landscape brings to the surface latent myths of Middle Eastern identity.

She Who Tells a Story offers a prism through which we can better understand the complex cultural, political, and religious mosaic that makes up the rich and multiple identities of this region in flux. It is intended to break down ideas of a nostalgic, Orientalist, traditional, or exotic world through showing contemporary visual media. These images force Western viewers to examine the way they look at the Middle East, and all viewers to rearticulate our ideas about the stories we thought we knew. The artists shown here use photography to communicate their experiences, desires, wishes, and silences, and to challenge received notions and perceptions. *She Who Tells a Story* is an invitation to discover new photography, to shift our perspective, and to open a cultural dialogue that is not centered on conflict and politics, but begins with the art and interwoven histories of a selection of extraordinary photographers from Iran and the Arab world.

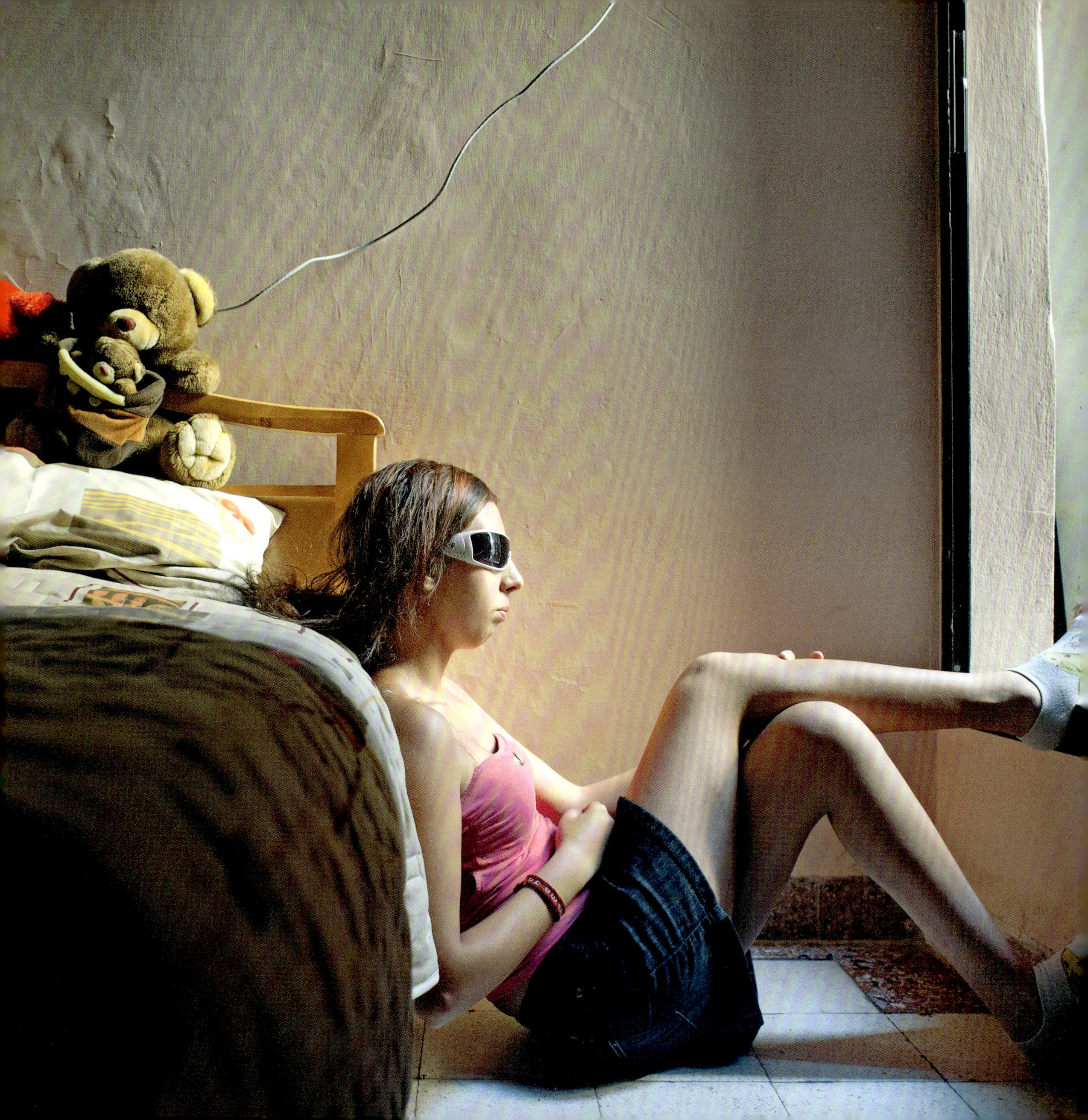

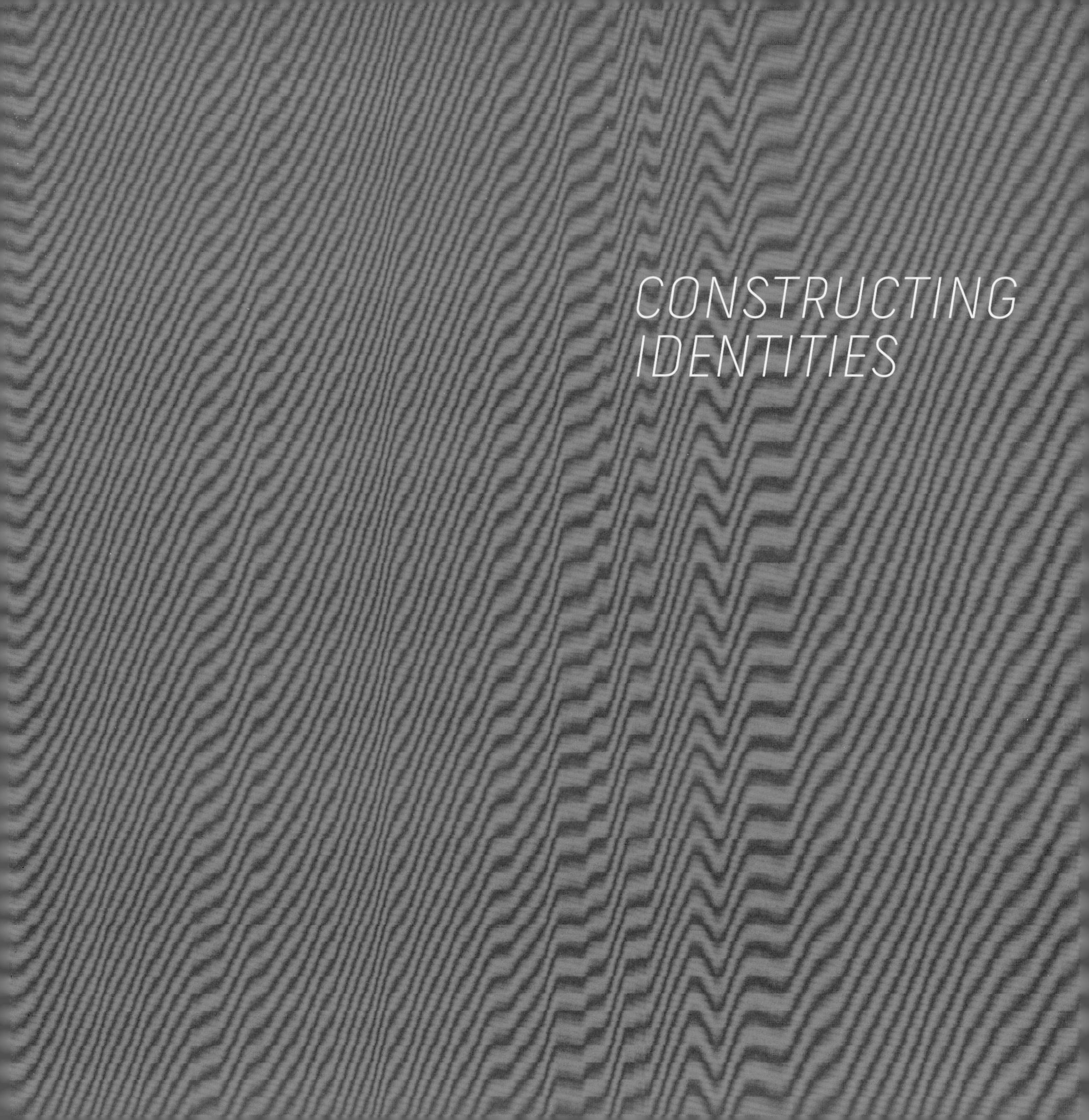

CONSTRUCTING IDENTITIES

13. *Converging Territories #29*, 2004
142.2 x 111.8 cm (56 x 44 in.)

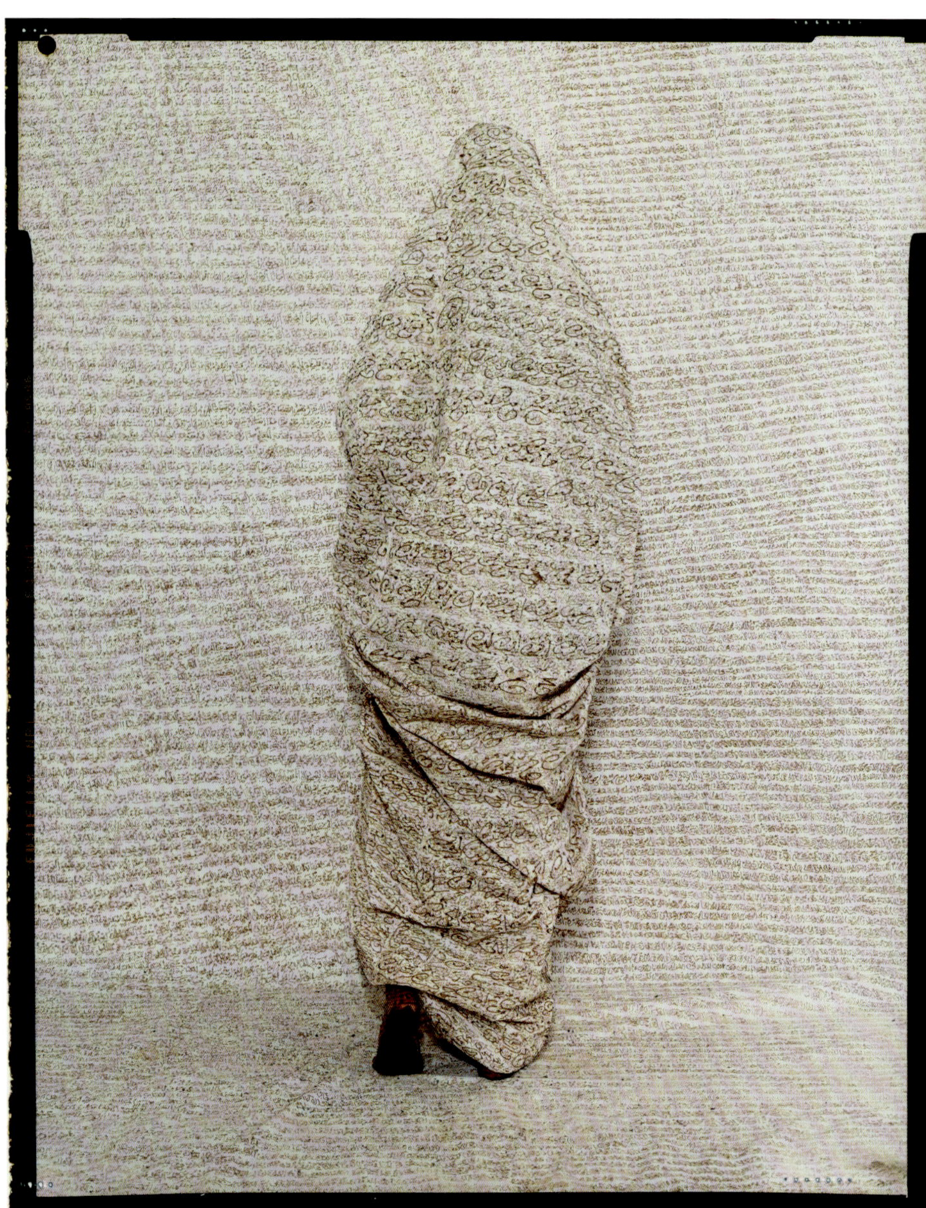

Lalla Essaydi

Born and raised in Morocco, Lalla Essaydi has lived in Saudi Arabia and France and currently divides her time between Morocco and the United States. She received a Master of Fine Arts degree at the School of the Museum of Fine Arts in Boston, which awarded her the SMFA Medal in 2012. Essaydi's photography has been presented internationally in many major exhibitions in the United States, Europe, the Middle East, and North Africa. The Smithsonian National Museum of African Art in Washington, D.C., organized the retrospective *Lalla Essaydi: Revisions* in 2012.

Through her carefully orchestrated performance-based photography, Essaydi provocatively explores Orientalism, emphasizing that it is not just a projection of the West but also affects how Arab culture sees itself. Her work addresses female identity, belonging, loss, space, and isolation with a personal approach related to her childhood in Morocco and her identity as both an insider and outsider in her adopted cultures.

In her large-format photographs, this former painter combines the arts of Islamic calligraphy and architecture with representations of the female body. Using dye from the henna plant, she writes in calligraphy on the drapery and bodies of her subjects. While henna is traditionally applied by women for important celebrations in the life of a Moroccan woman — puberty, marriage, or the birth of a child — calligraphy is a sacred Islamic art generally practiced by men. For Essaydi, then, henna calligraphy is "a veil and an expressive statement" through which women "speak" in her images.[1]

Essaydi's series *Converging Territories* (2003–4) confronts the public and the private, spheres traditionally allocated in Morocco to men and women, respectively. The series was created in a family home, which served as a place of isolation on occasions when she was confined as a girl, for a month at a time, as punishment for being disobedient. Her photographic subjects and their elaborate drapery are covered in lines of calligraphy that also run over the walls, floor, and ceiling. This constricted and undefined space, inspired by the artist's memories, suggests psychological confinement as well as all boundaries imposed on women.

In *Les femmes du Maroc* (*Women of Morocco*, 2005–8), a series staged in Essaydi's studio in Boston, the expatriate photographer appropriates and challenges Orientalist myths related to voyeuristic Western imagery of harems, the veil, and the odalisque pose. The photographs evoke ideas of separation, displacement, and identity, reflecting the artist's expatriate identity. In a later series, *Bullets* (2012), women are covered in and surrounded by golden bullets in decorative patterns, a reference to her fear about growing restrictions on women in a new postrevolutionary era in the Middle East and North Africa.

In *Harem* (2009), women are posed in a traditional Moroccan *riad* (Dar al Basha palace) owned by her family. Replacing calligraphy with the detailed patterns of decorative tiles, in this series the photographer addresses the complexity and meaning of space as, in her words, "actual and metaphorical, remembered and constructed."[2]

The fabric covering the models, designed and made by the artist, responds to the decorative patterns of the architecture, so the women blend into the architecture of their private space the way the women in *Converging Territories* and *Les femmes du Maroc* are unified with their calligraphy-covered surroundings.

The large triptych that opens the narrative, *Harem #1*, features a sumptuous courtyard, with beautifully decorated columns and brightly colored tiles, leading to a framed niche. In the niche, a woman reclines in an odalisque pose. The word *odalisque* has Turkish roots and means "to belong to a place," as this figure literally does. The series makes direct reference to the work of nineteenth-century painters, such as Jean-Léon Gérôme and Jean-Auguste-Dominique Ingres, who often depicted Orientalist subjects such as the harem — a group of women in Muslim culture who live together, generally in polygamous families, in a secluded part of a home that is reached by a series of labyrinth-like hallways and forbidden to men. In this image, the woman is dwarfed by the grand architecture, suggesting a metaphor of the isolation and confinement of women.

The triptych's imagined spaces and Orientalized subject reveal the artist's self-aware and reflexive relation to her art, as do the uncropped borders of the film around the edge of the three images, which evoke the artifice of photography and emphasize the medium's ability to create false realities.

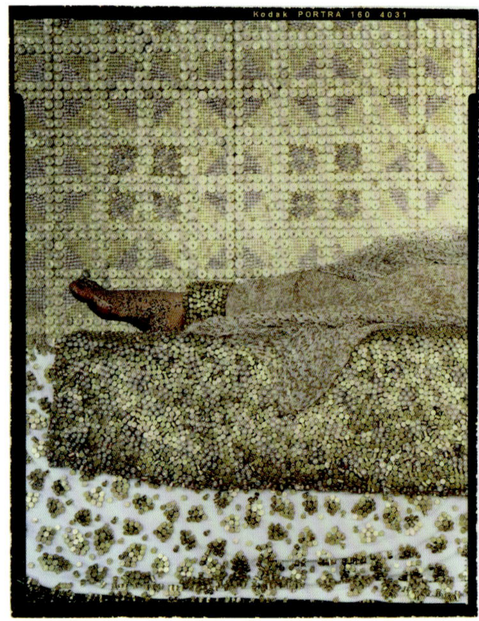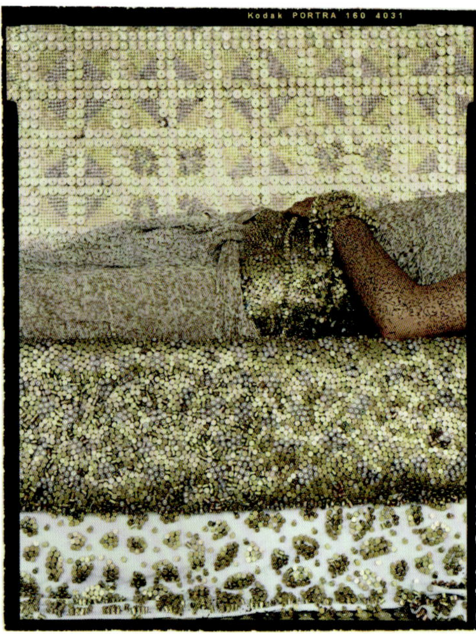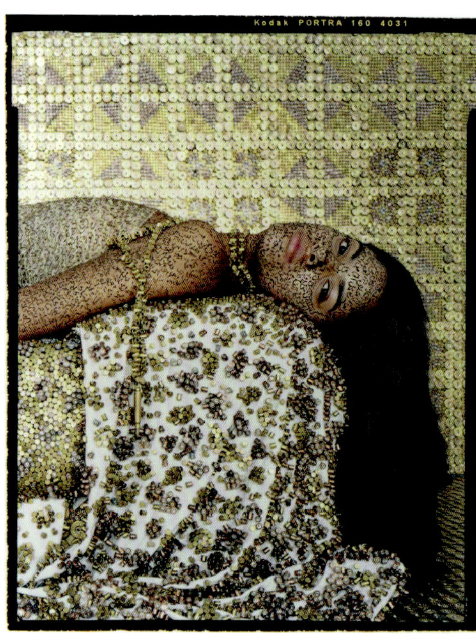

14. *Bullets Revisited #3*, 2012
Overall: 1.68 x 3.81 m (5 ½ x 12 ½ ft)

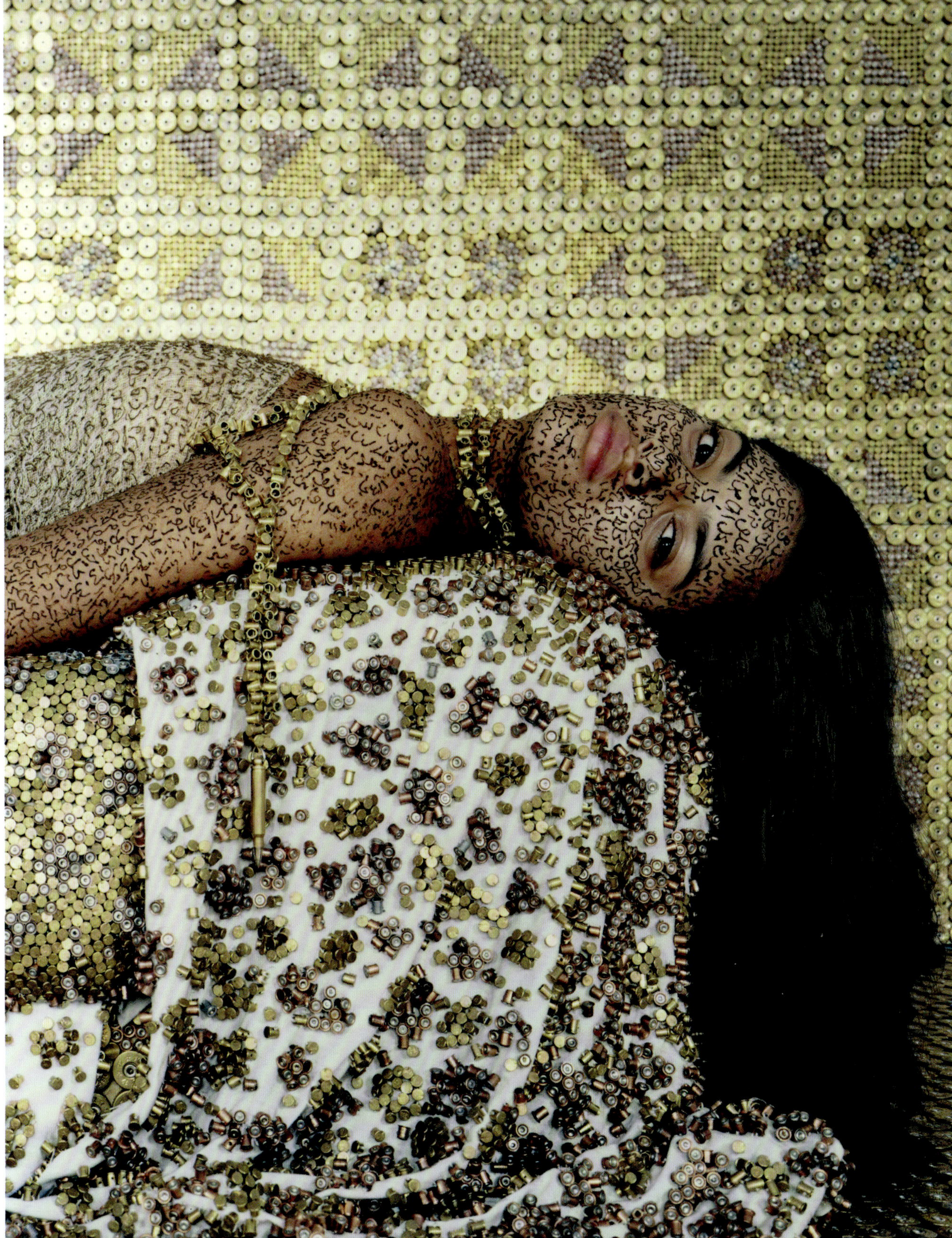

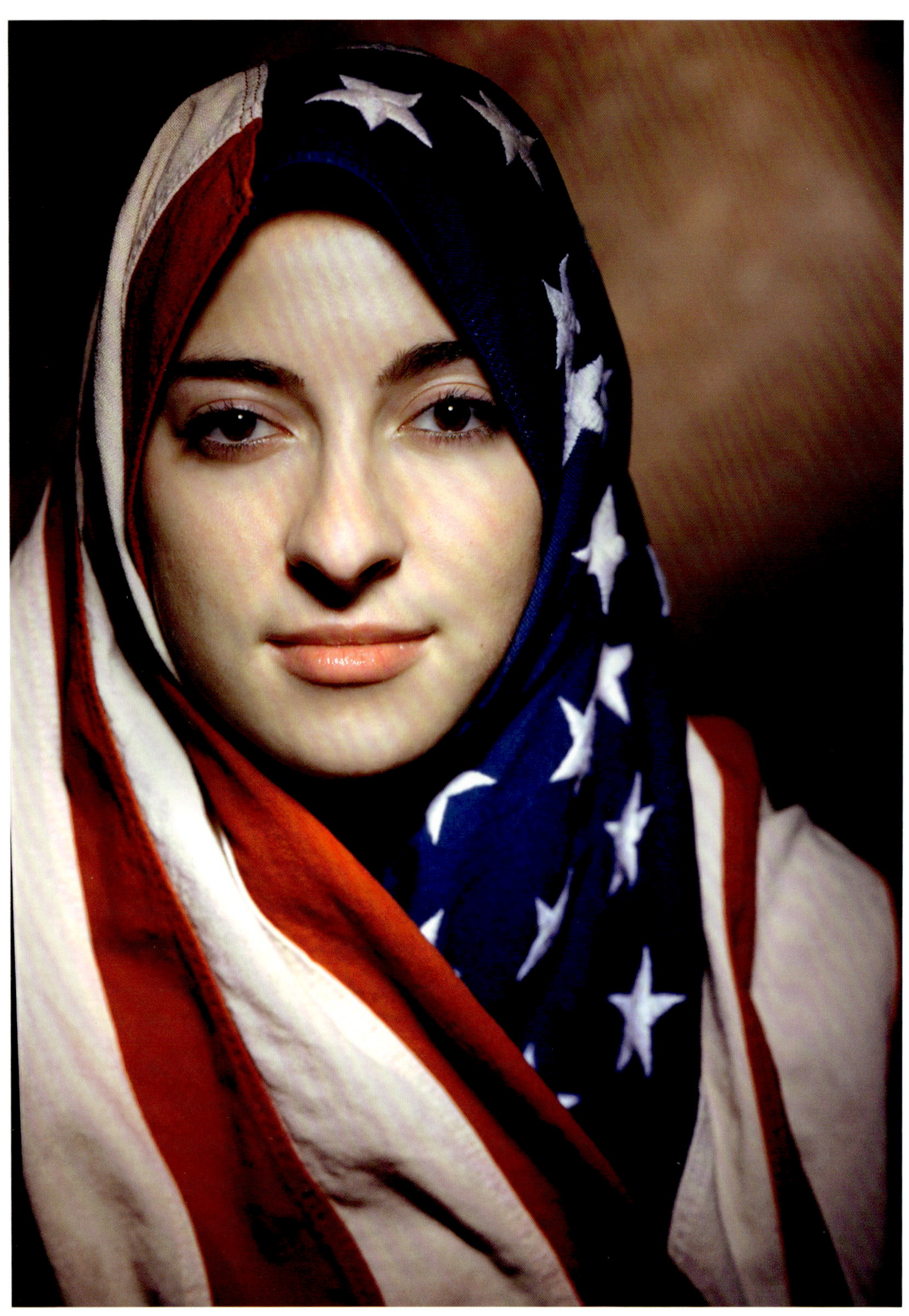

Boushra Almutawakel

Born in 1969 in Sana'a, Yemen, the pioneering Yemeni photographer Boushra Almutawakel was educated in both Yemen and in the United States. She is a founding member of Al-Halaqa, a group of artists who created an exhibition space and forum for national and international discourse in Yemen. In 1999, The Empirical Research and Women's Studies Center at Sana'a University honored Almutawakel as the first Yemeni Woman Professional Photographer. Her work has been shown to acclaim in the exhibition *Women on the Verge* (2012) at the Empty Quarter Gallery in Dubai, as well as at Art Dubai and Paris Photo 2012. Her work has also been on view at the National Museum of Sana'a.

Early in her photographic career, Almutawakel was profoundly influenced by a lecture in which the Egyptian feminist writer Nawal Elsadawi drew a parallel between women who wear the *hijab* (headscarf) or *niqab* (full Islamic veil with a slit for the eyes) and women who wear makeup. Elsadawi's argument that both practices concealed women's identities inspired Almutawakel to undertake her extended body of work *The Hijab*, which challenges the Western association of the veil with the oppression and ignorance of Middle Eastern women.

After the events of September 11, 2001, Almutawakel felt that Arabs and Muslims were, more than ever, either "demonized or romanticized" by the West. Middle Eastern women, frequently veiled, were "portrayed artistically (and/or in the media) as exotic, beautiful, mysterious, or helpless, oppressed and ugly." She wanted "to explore the many faces and facets of the veil based on [her] own personal experiences and observations: the convenience, freedom, strength, the power, liberation, limitations, danger, humor, irony, the variety, cultural, social, and religious aspects, the beauty, mystery, the *hijab*/veil as a form of self-expression, protection, the veil as not solely an Arab Middle Eastern phenomenon, the trends, the history and politics of the *hijab*/veil, as well as differing interpretations, and the fear in regards to the *hijab*/veil."[1]

The first photograph in the *Hijab* series shows a young woman veiling herself with the American flag (opposite). Created in 2001 in response to 9/11, the image questions the charged symbolism of the headscarf—particularly in Western media—as well as the implications of wearing one's national identity on one's head. Almutawakel continued to create surprising images related to the *hijab* in *What If?* (2008), a group of photographs featuring a married couple in which the husband is progressively more completely veiled. The photographer questions gender roles while alluding to the

15. Untitled, 2001
From *The Hijab* series
120 x 100 cm (47 ¼ x 39 ⅜ in.)

historical reality that traditional dress for both men and women covers most of the body. *The Hijab* series also includes *Veil-Unveil* (2008) and *Mother, Daughter, Doll* (2010).

Among the photographer's later series is *Fulla* (2010–11). Fulla is the name of a Muslim Barbie doll. In the series, headscarved dolls enact playful scenes from young women's lives. In *My Father's House* (2009–11), she takes a different direction, providing intimate views of home interiors.

Mother, Daughter, Doll (2010) is a series of nine photographs showing the artist, her eldest daughter, and the daughter's doll wearing a progression of veils. The first in the sequence portrays the mother with a light-colored headscarf that complements her plaid jacket; the heads of her daughter and the daughter's doll are uncovered. In the next image, the mother wears darker clothes with a flower-patterned headscarf, and the young girl's hair is partly covered. In the third photograph, the mother, daughter, and now doll are significantly more covered. The mother has on a black headscarf with colored embroidered patterns, and the young girl's and doll's heads are both covered. The fourth and fifth images show the three figures in two styles of all-black veils. The *niqab* is introduced in the sixth photograph, black gloves in the seventh, and a screen over each figure's eyes in the eighth. The figures disappear entirely in the final image of the series; only the pedestal remains. The progression implies criticism of the trend for extreme covering by showing the absurdity of applying it to a young girl or a doll, for whom it has no religious justification.

With symbolically charged images of veiling, Almutawakel both denounces its extremes and introduces the complexity of the subject to her viewers. She emphasizes the individuality of the women who wear the veil and the variety of color and form allowed in the covering. Her work challenges the Western perception of the *hijab*, as well as the growing trend in the Middle East for more covering. She herself wears a *hijab* in Yemen, stating: "I don't feel comfortable without it in many places in Yemen. This is a highly segregated society in which men don't have much interaction with women, though that is changing in the cities. It is advantageous and empowering in some ways as it protects and privatizes the woman's body."[2]

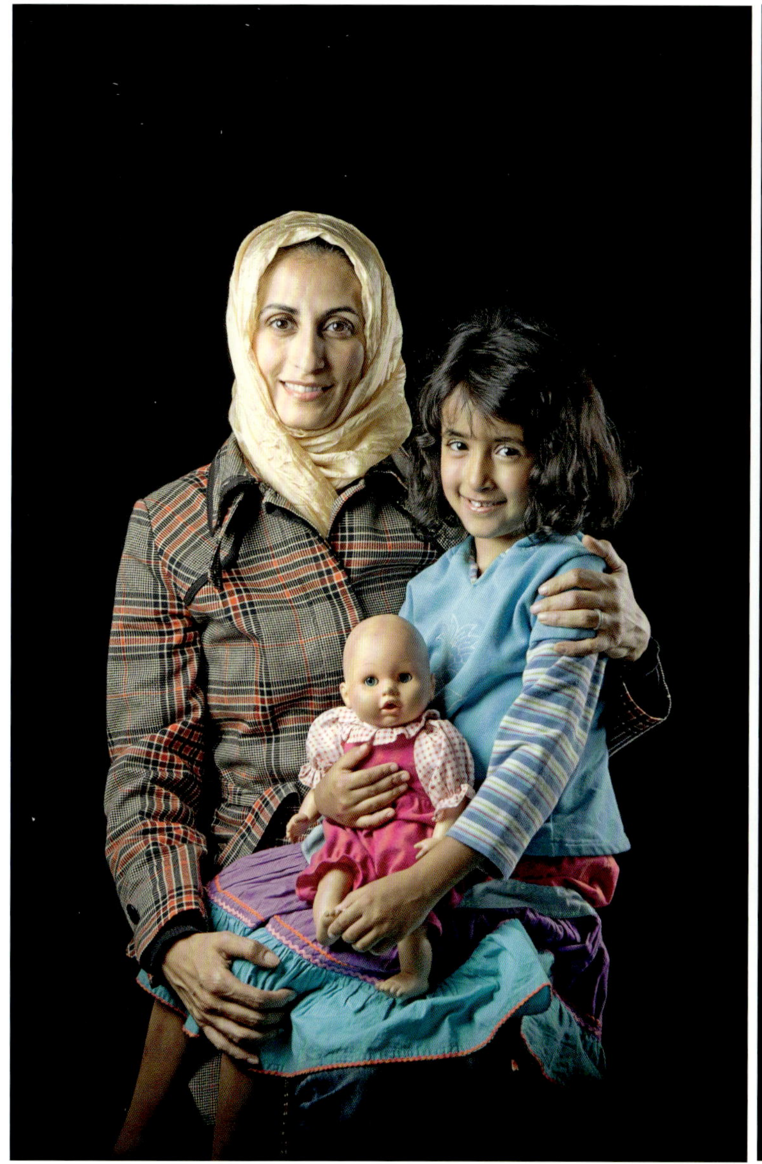

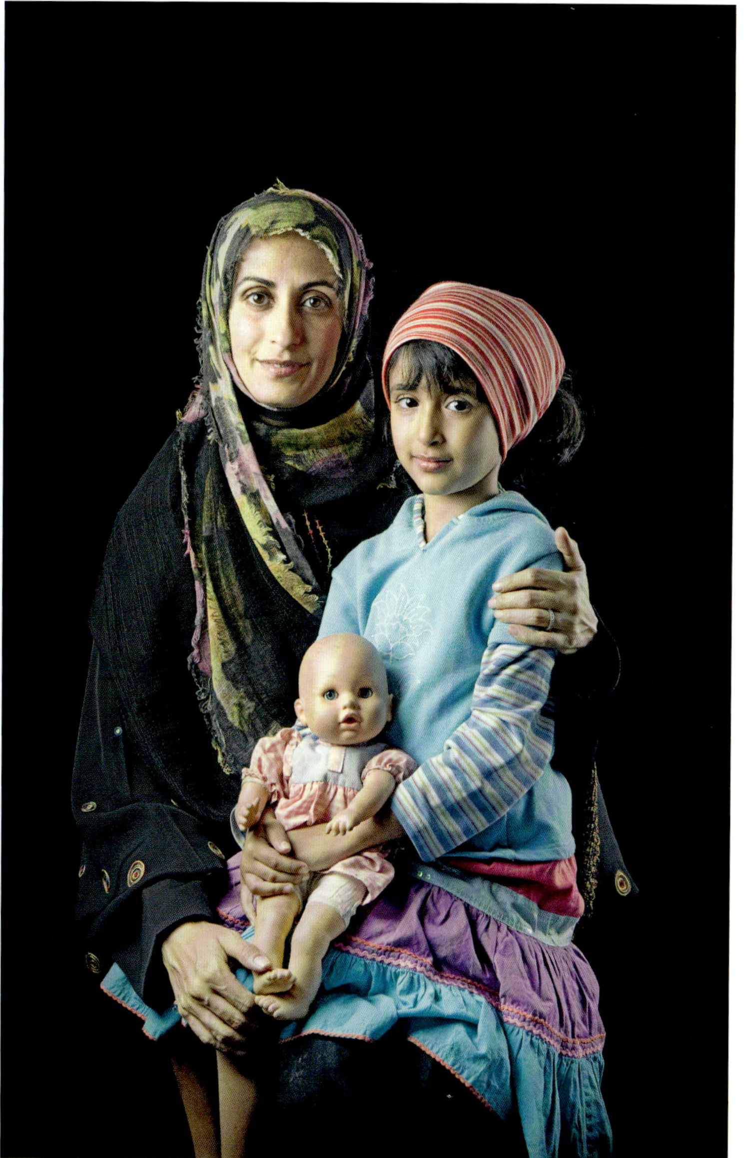

16

17

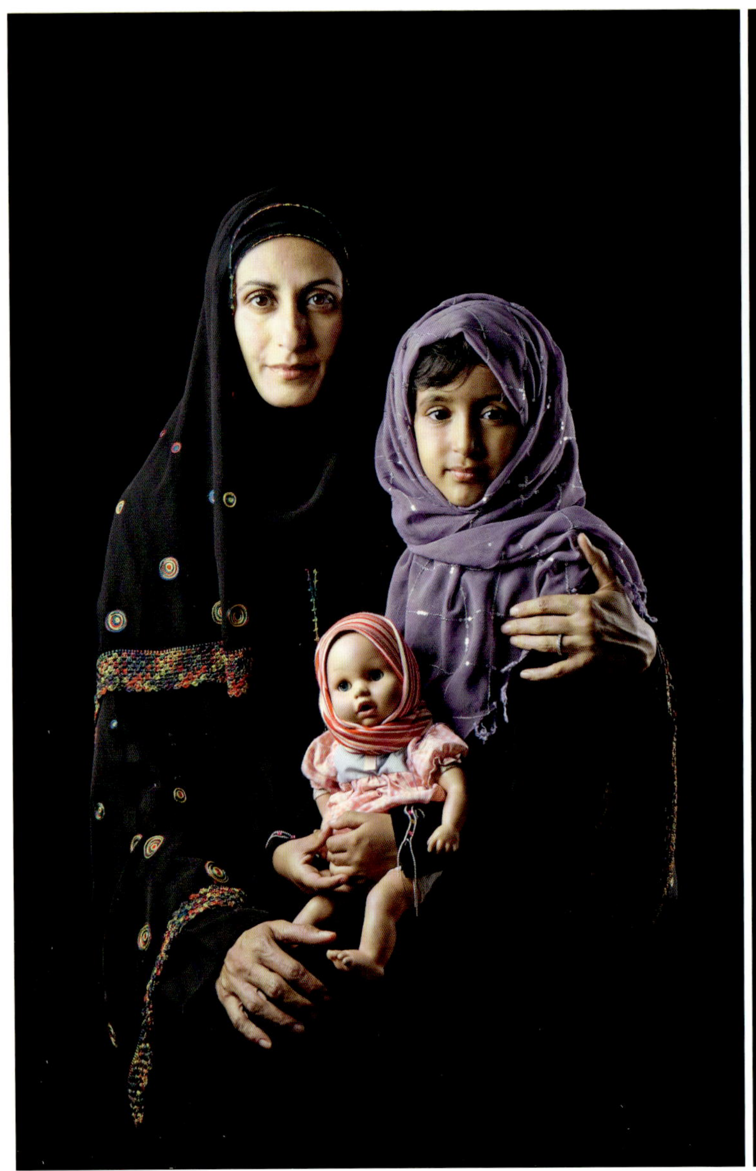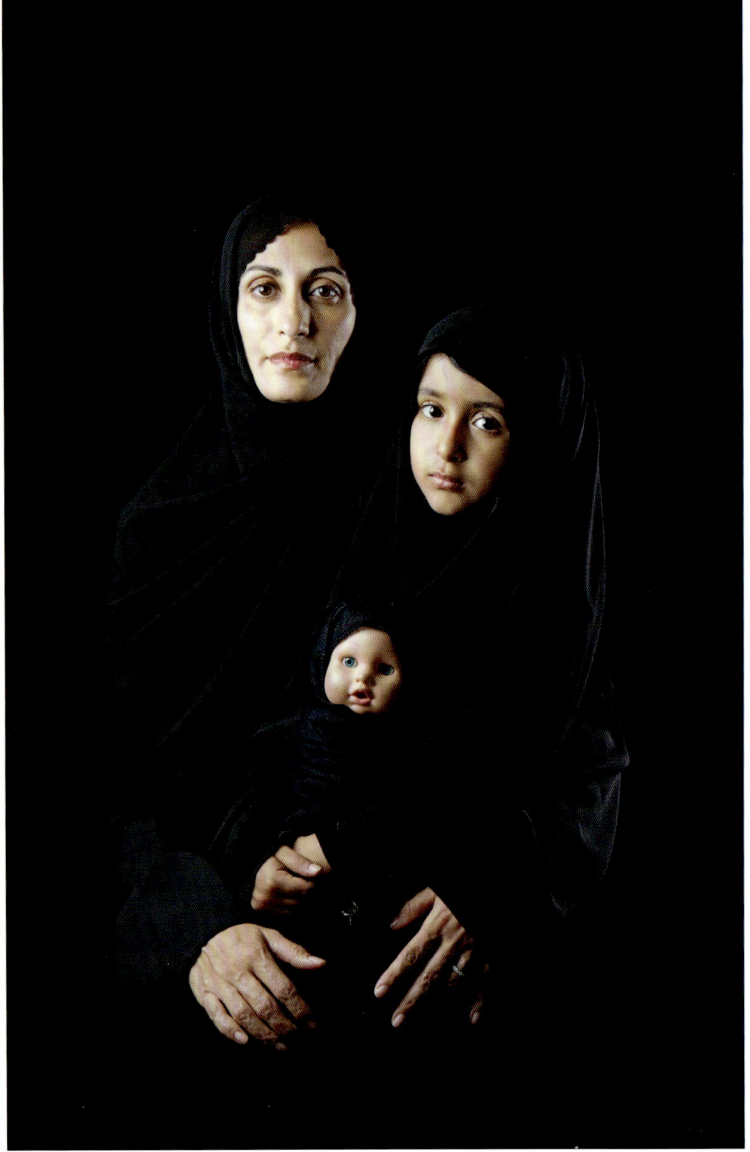

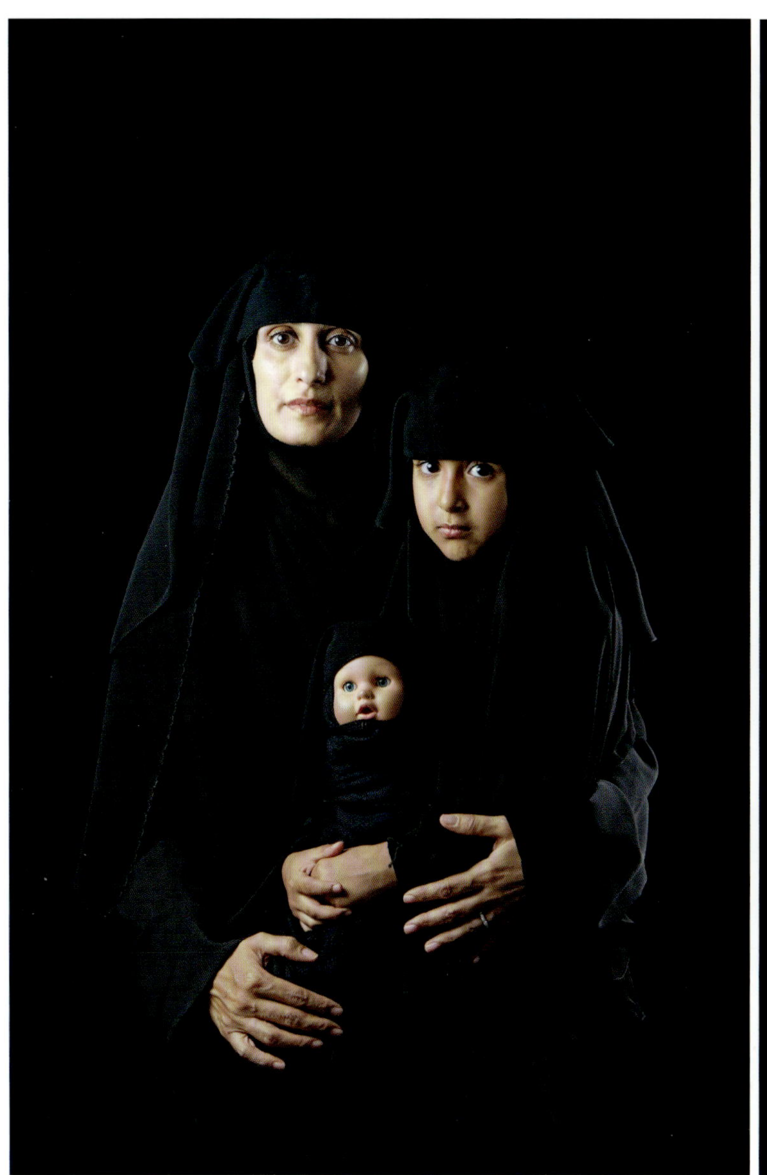

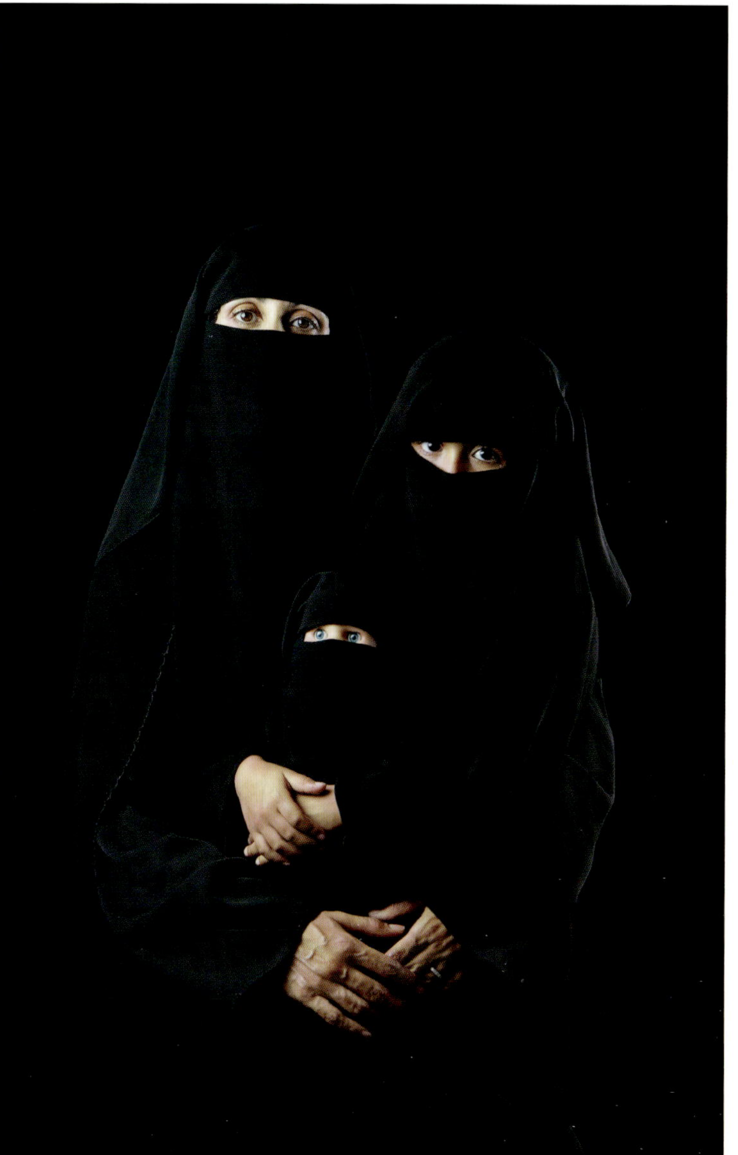

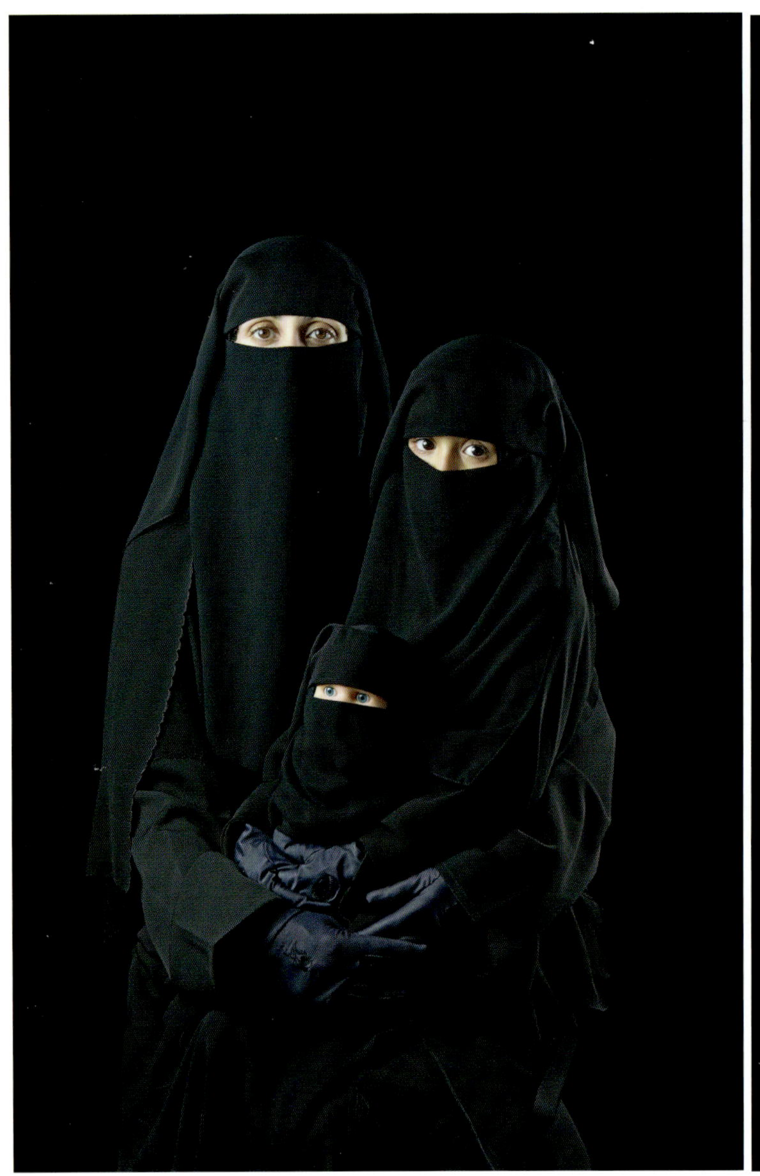

22

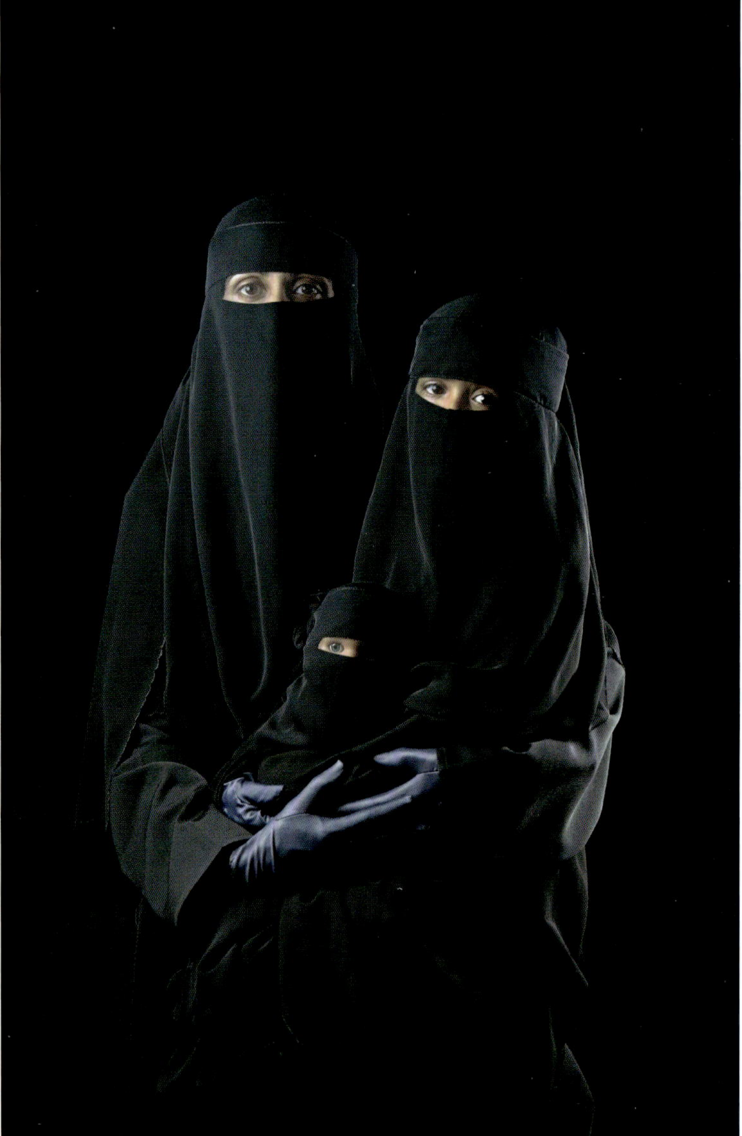

23

24

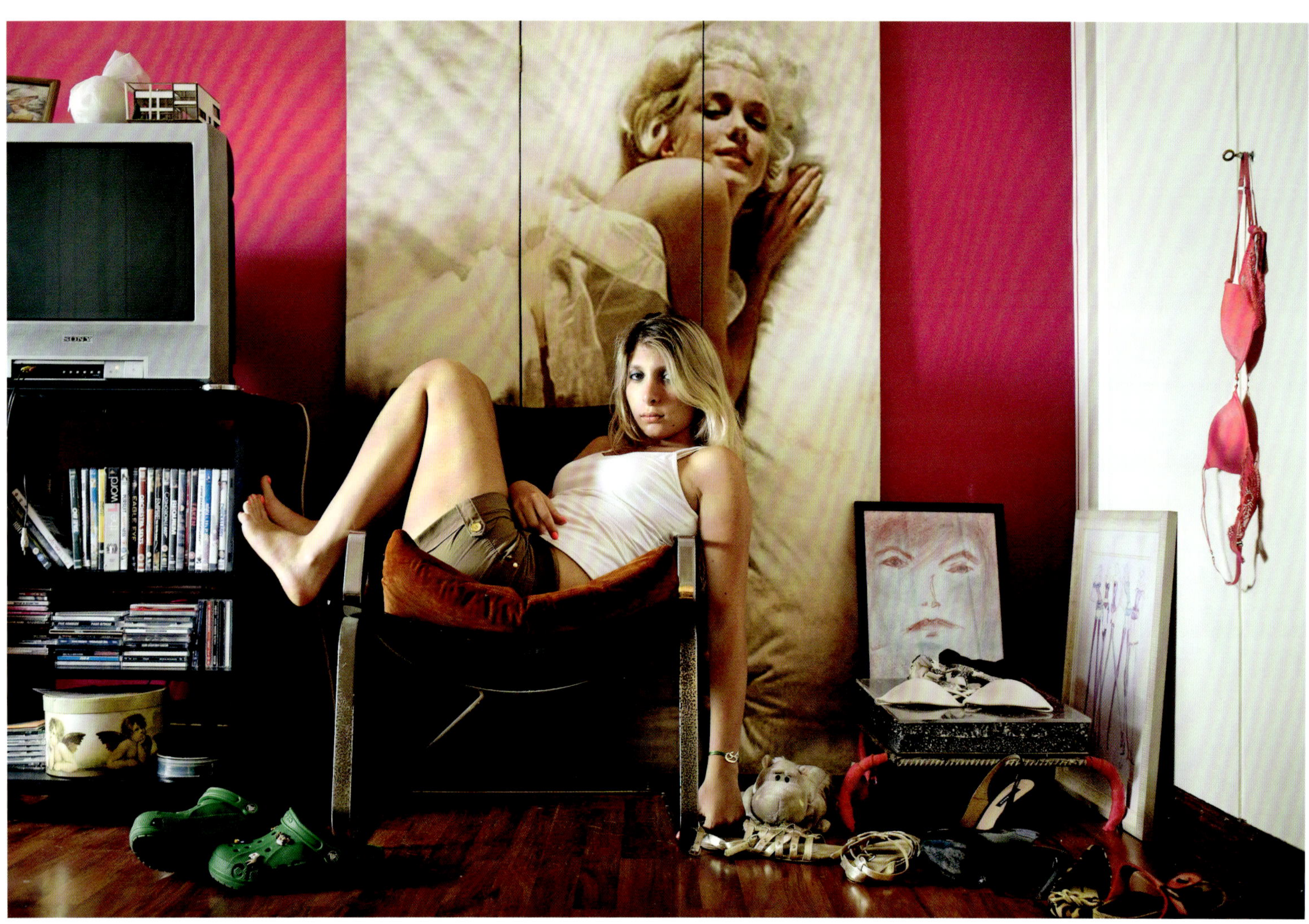

Rania Matar

Rania Matar was born in Beirut, Lebanon, in 1964 and moved to the United States at age twenty. Now based in Boston, she travels regularly to the Middle East. Trained as an architect and later as a photographer, Matar explores female identity and place in poetic documentary photographs. Her work has been exhibited widely, including shows in Greece, Singapore, Lebanon, Qatar, and the United States.

Matar's early series on the lives of women and children in the Middle East — *The Veil*, *Aftermath of War*, *Forgotten People*, and *Crossroads* — were published in 2009 in the book *Ordinary Lives*, with a foreword by the Pulitzer Prize winner Anthony Shadid, who described the subject of the photographs as "ordinary lives in times that are cursed by being anything but ordinary."[1] In the poignant *The Dead Mother* (2005), two girls in Beirut carefully style their headscarves as their late mother seems to look on from a photograph on the wall. *Juggling* (2006), made in Aita El Chaab, Lebanon, shows a girl concentrating on her juggling within the setting of a war-damaged building, with remnants of a flag hanging from a clothesline in the background.

The portraits in Matar's series *L'enfant-femme* (2011–12) convey the interactions between young adolescents and preadolescents and the camera. As Matar explains, "My aim is to portray the girl when allowed to pose herself as she wishes in front of the camera. I try to capture alternatively the angst, the self-confidence or lack thereof, the body language, the sense of selfhood and the developing sense of womanhood girls that age experience."[2]

Over time Matar's work has shifted from photographing people mainly in outdoor settings to entering their homes and bedrooms, and then to delving deeper into their psychology, leaving only a small hint of their surroundings. This trajectory from public to private space is perhaps indicative of her departure from architectural work and growing interest in the intimacy that photography allows.

In Matar's acclaimed series *A Girl and Her Room* (2009–12), she juxtaposes images of teenagers in the United States and the Middle East, revealing the universality of themes of developing identity. Fascinated by the transformation of her daughter from child to adult, Matar began photographing her and her girlfriends in their bedrooms. "This project," she explains, "is about teenage girls and young women at a transitional time of their lives, alone in the privacy of their own personal space and surroundings: their bedroom, a womb within the outside world." The photographs from this series selected for this publication are of six young women from the Middle East. *Christilla* and *Alia* show two young women in their bold pink rooms in Rabieh and Beirut, Lebanon, respectively. The dyed-blonde Christilla is curled up in a chair in front of a large blowup of Marilyn Monroe, and the pink of her wall is picked up in the accents of pink fingernail nails and a pink bra. The order of the carefully arranged DVDs coexists with the disorder of the scattered

25. *Christilla, Rabieh, Lebanon*, 2010
From *A Girl and Her Room* series
86.4 x 122 cm (34 x 48 in.)

shoes on the floor. Alia is seen reflected in a large mirror. Her oval face is echoed in the poster behind her and in the painting to the right. The neatly arranged containers of makeup along the bottom of the mirror offset the dangling laundry in the background and the lights and decorations framing the image.

Reem is depicted in a sensual pose, with her eyes closed, on her bed in her home in Doha, Lebanon. Her outfit—a sheer white top and black shorts—resembles a drawing in her sketchbook placed on the pillow beside her. *Stephanie* is a warm-toned portrait in which the subject gazes out her window in Beirut, wearing sunglasses that protect her from the outside light, and perhaps metaphorically from the world. Her carefully posed legs bask in the same light that highlights the two teddy bears on her bed.

Mariam, made at the Bourj al Shamali Palestinian Refugee Camp in Tyre, Lebanon, and *Bisan*, in Bethlehem, West Bank, represent two young Palestinian women. Mariam sits on her mattress on the floor below a prayer rug hanging from the window frame and what could be her baby photo.

Bisan sits in a chair, and on the wall above her head, there is a small circular cutout representing the Palestinian flag, an important element of her identity. These two portraits, in settings that are strikingly different from those of *Christilla* and *Alia*, are equally insightful. The same diversity of settings and sitters is found in Matar's representation of teenage girls in the United States, reflecting the shared experiences of coming of age as well as the complexities of being a young woman in a particular historical and cultural place.

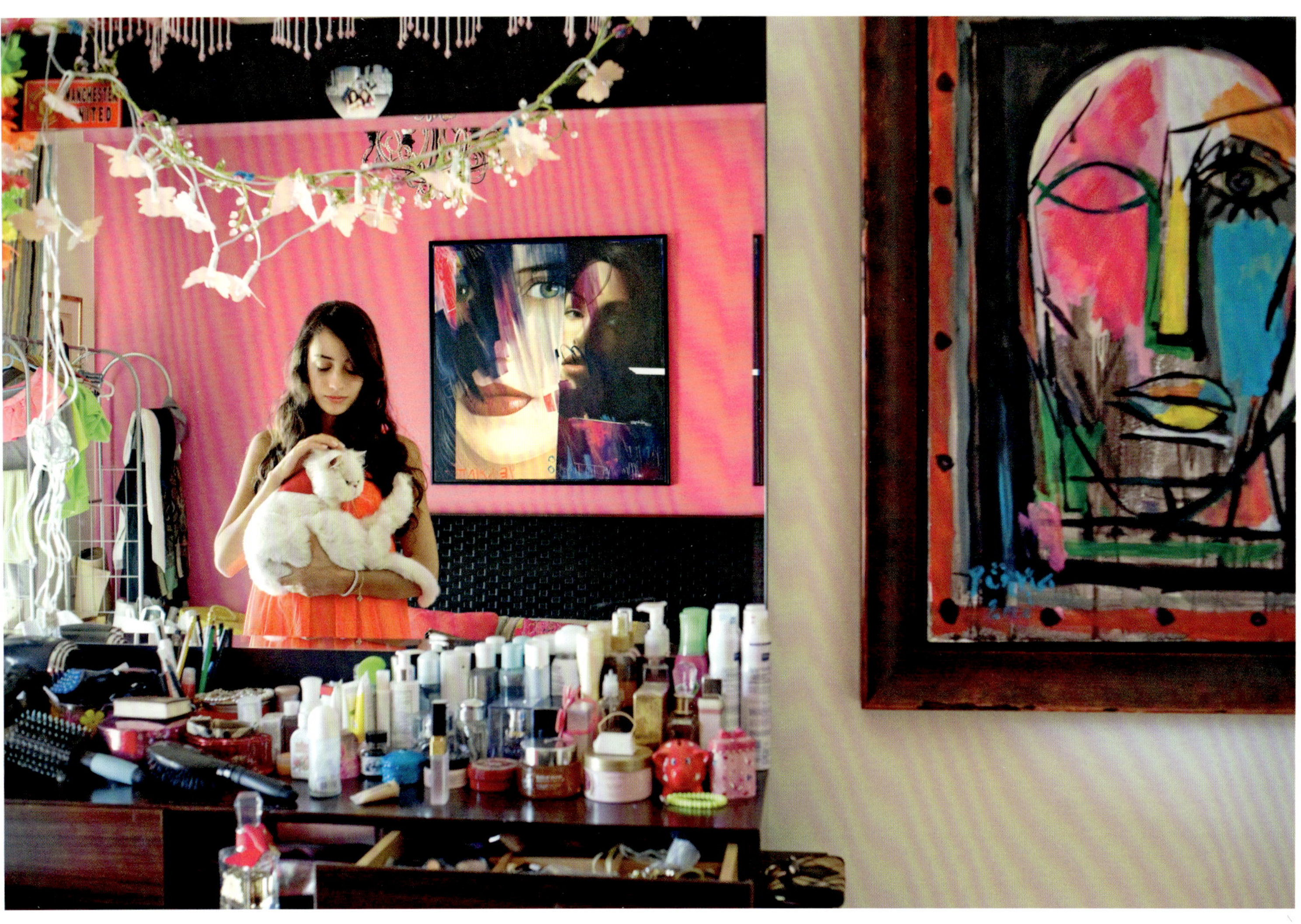

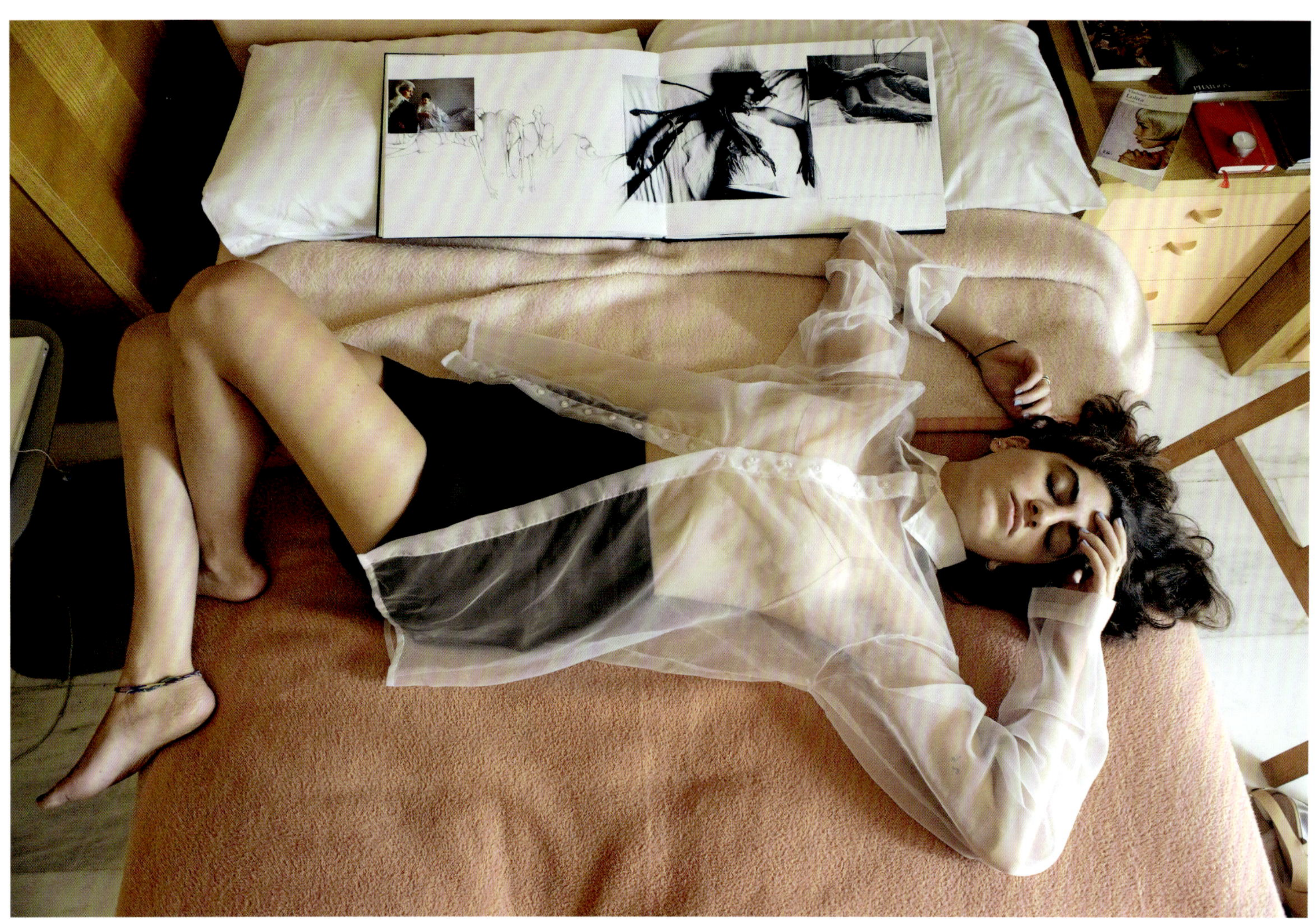

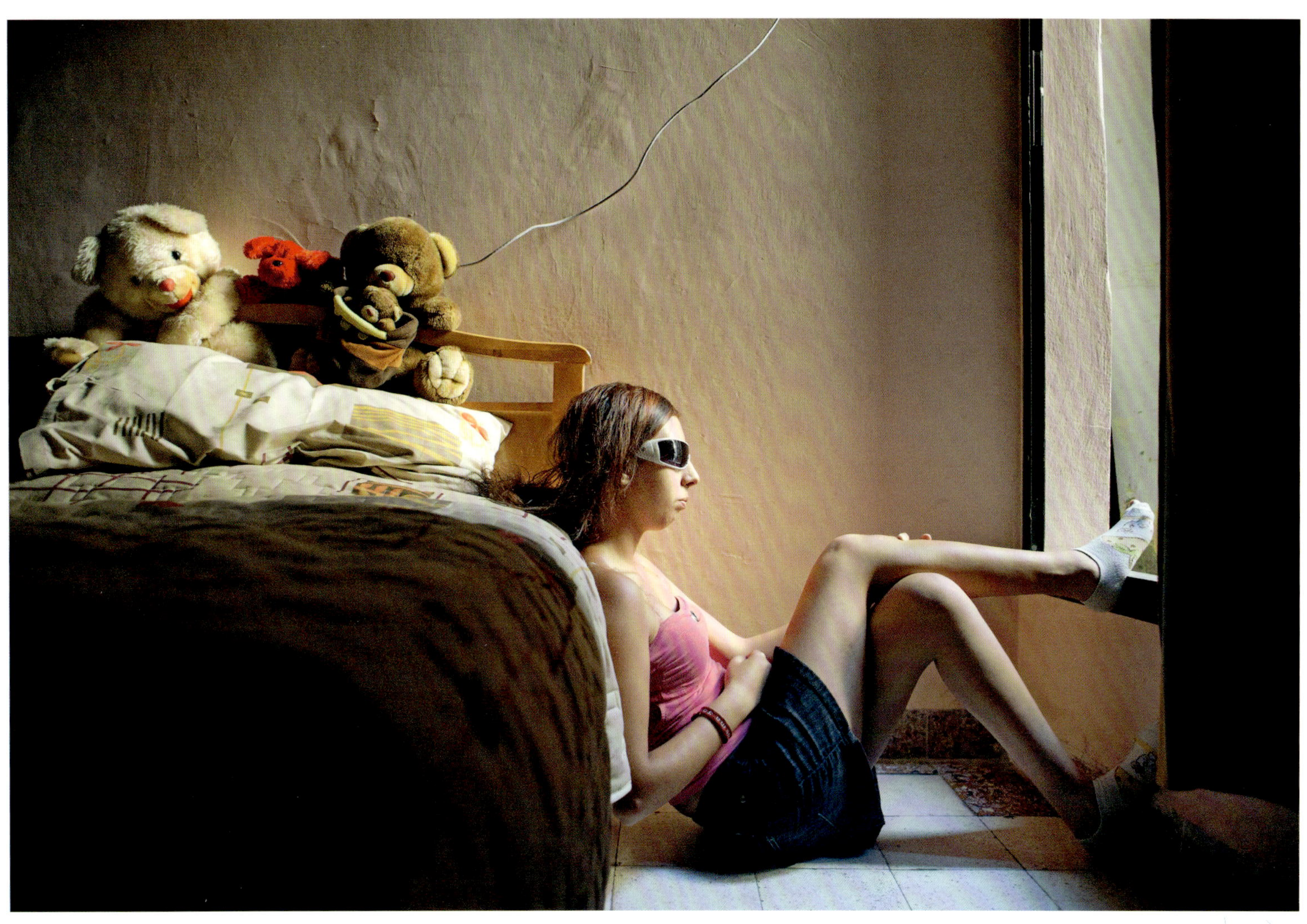

27. *Reem, Doha, Lebanon*, 2010
From *A Girl and Her Room* series
86.4 x 122 cm (34 x 48 in.)

28. *Stephanie, Beirut, Lebanon*, 2010
From *A Girl and Her Room* series
86.4 x 122 cm (34 x 48 in.)

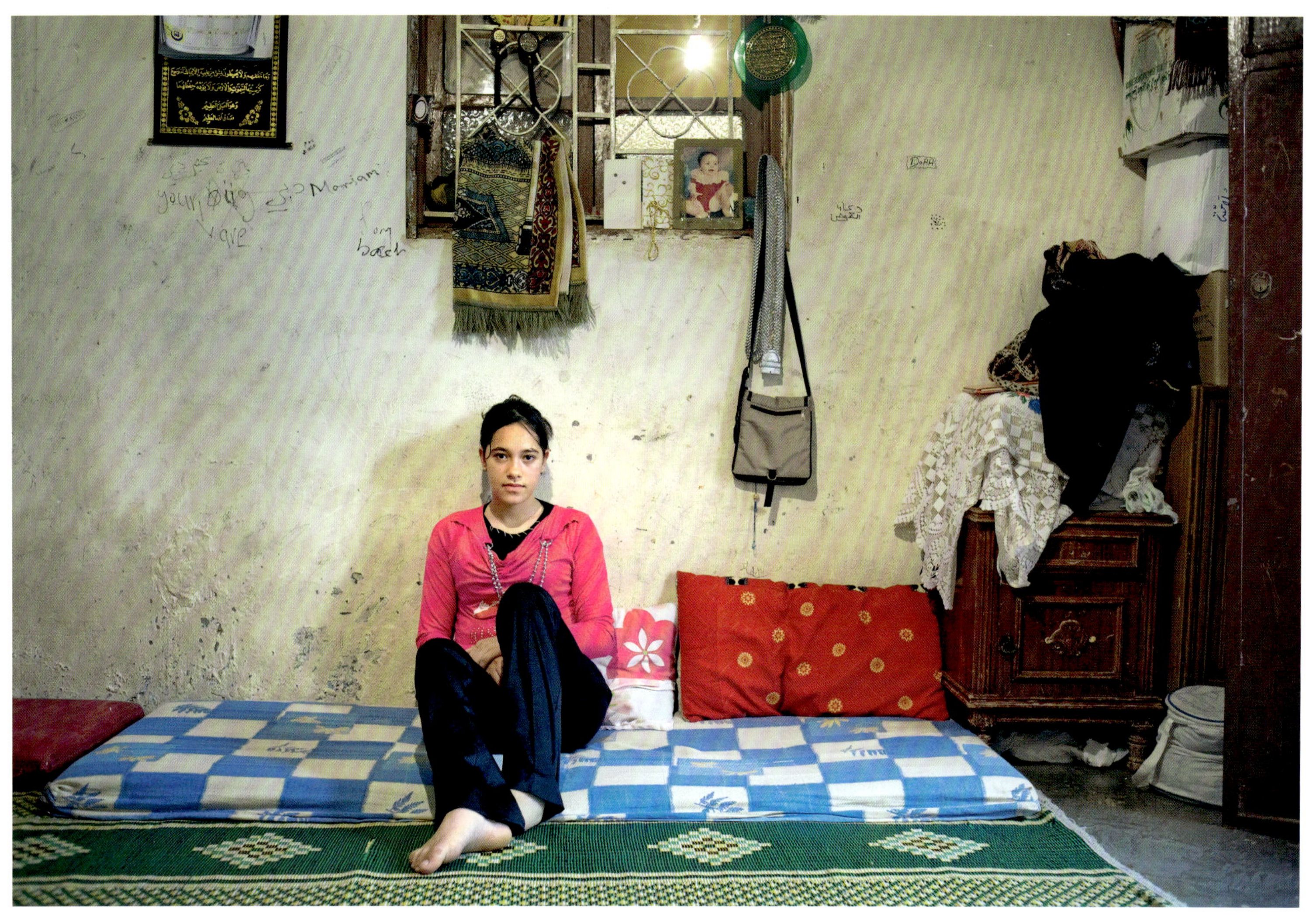

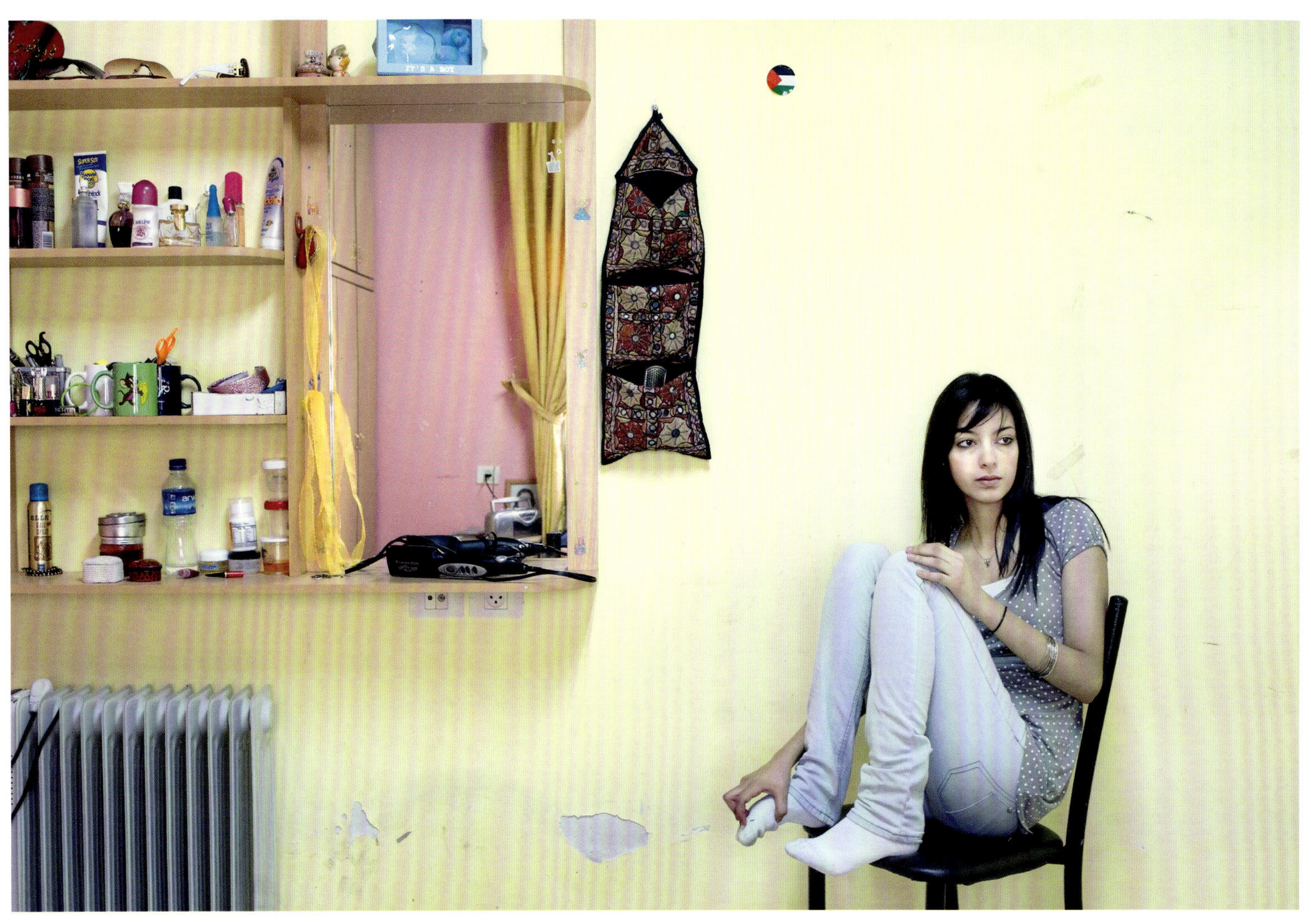

29. *Mariam, Bourj al Shamali Palestinian Refugee Camp, Tyre, Lebanon*, 2009
From *A Girl and Her Room* series
86.4 x 122 cm (34 x 48 in.)

30. *Bisan, Bethlehem, West Bank*, 2009
From *A Girl and Her Room* series
86.4 x 122 cm (34 x 48 in.)

Shirin Neshat

Born in 1957 in Qazvin, Iran, Shirin Neshat moved to the United States during the time of the Iranian Revolution and later studied fine arts. In 1990, while living in New York City, she returned to her homeland to find a radically changed country. This visit resulted in her best-known photographic series, *Women of Allah* (1993–97). In her own words, Neshat sought in this series to transform "the feminine body into that of a warrior, determined and even heroic."[1] On the surface of the photographs and frequently over the face and hands of the women, she wrote in pen in Farsi, primarily the words of contemporary Iranian women writers (see plates 1, 5, 10, 11).

Neshat went on to produce numerous videos and films, including *Turbulent*, for which she won the Lion d'Or at the Venice Biennale in 1999 (see plate 12). Like her photographs, Neshat's videos address the duality between her native culture and her exilic identity while questioning social, cultural, and religious codes and taboos. Poetic language, both visual and textual, and politics are combined in her powerful film stills and videos such as *Fervor*, *Soliloquy*, *Passage*, and *Tooba*. Neshat has received international critical acclaim for the feature film *Women Without Men* (2009), composed of five independent video works created between 2004 and 2008 — *Mahdokht*, *Zarin*, *Munis*, *Faezeh*, and *Farokh Legha* — whose heroines search for identity and individuality. Neshat's work has been exhibited widely and was the subject of a major retrospective at the Detroit Institute of Arts (2013).

The series *Book of Kings* (2012) marks a return to black-and-white photography. It is composed of portraits of groups Neshat calls the Masses, the Patriots, and the Villains. For the first two categories, she inscribes contemporary poetry and verses from the *Shahnameh* (Book of Kings), an epic Persian poem central to Iranian culture, which was written a thousand years ago by the poet Ferdowsi. The *Shahnameh* narrates the deeds of legendary and historical kings of Iran, stories rife with heroism, violence, rebellion, and betrayal. Neshat uses this text to create a lyrical homage to past and present Iranian history that also responds to contemporary politics in the Middle East, in particular the Iranian Green Movement of 2009 and the Arab Spring of 2011. The figures in this series stand for the thousands that have taken to the streets in protest across the Middle East.

The Masses are represented by forty-five headshots of Arab and Iranian men and women whose faces are subtly ornamented with calligraphy, except for their eyes and mouths. These portraits are intended to be exhibited side by side in a group, to simulate the power of the people.

31. *Roja*, 2012
From *Book of Kings* series (Patriots)
152.4 x 114.3 cm (60 x 45 in.)

The selections from the Masses presented here illustrate the presence of both men and women and the age range of the figures. The Patriots consist of six large waist-length portraits of four men and two women, holding their hands in front of their hearts in a universal gesture of feeling and conviction. The size of written characters across the print gets progressively smaller from the top to the bottom of the portrait. The verses are broken into columns, and the spaces between the columns create two parallel vertical lines on the figures' faces; their eyes, free of calligraphy, confront the viewer. *Roja* is a striking example of the Patriots. The intensity of the subject's eyes and the subtlety and delicacy of the calligraphy across her face and body contribute to the portrait's majesty. Her gesture also reflects larger questions of identity, coupled with ideas of patriotism and nationalism. The Villains are generally men, their images overlaid with black-and-red reproductions of epic scenes from the *Shahnameh*. The same technique covers the disembodied legs of *Divine Rebellion* in visual renderings of heroic stories, accented with a bold red detail on the lower right of the calf.

The *Book of Kings* reflects Neshat's artistic development and evolution since her *Women of Allah* series. In this series, which is devoid of religious symbolism, she continues to pursue visible paradoxes of past and present, and power and submission, through a poetic choreography of portraiture and history.

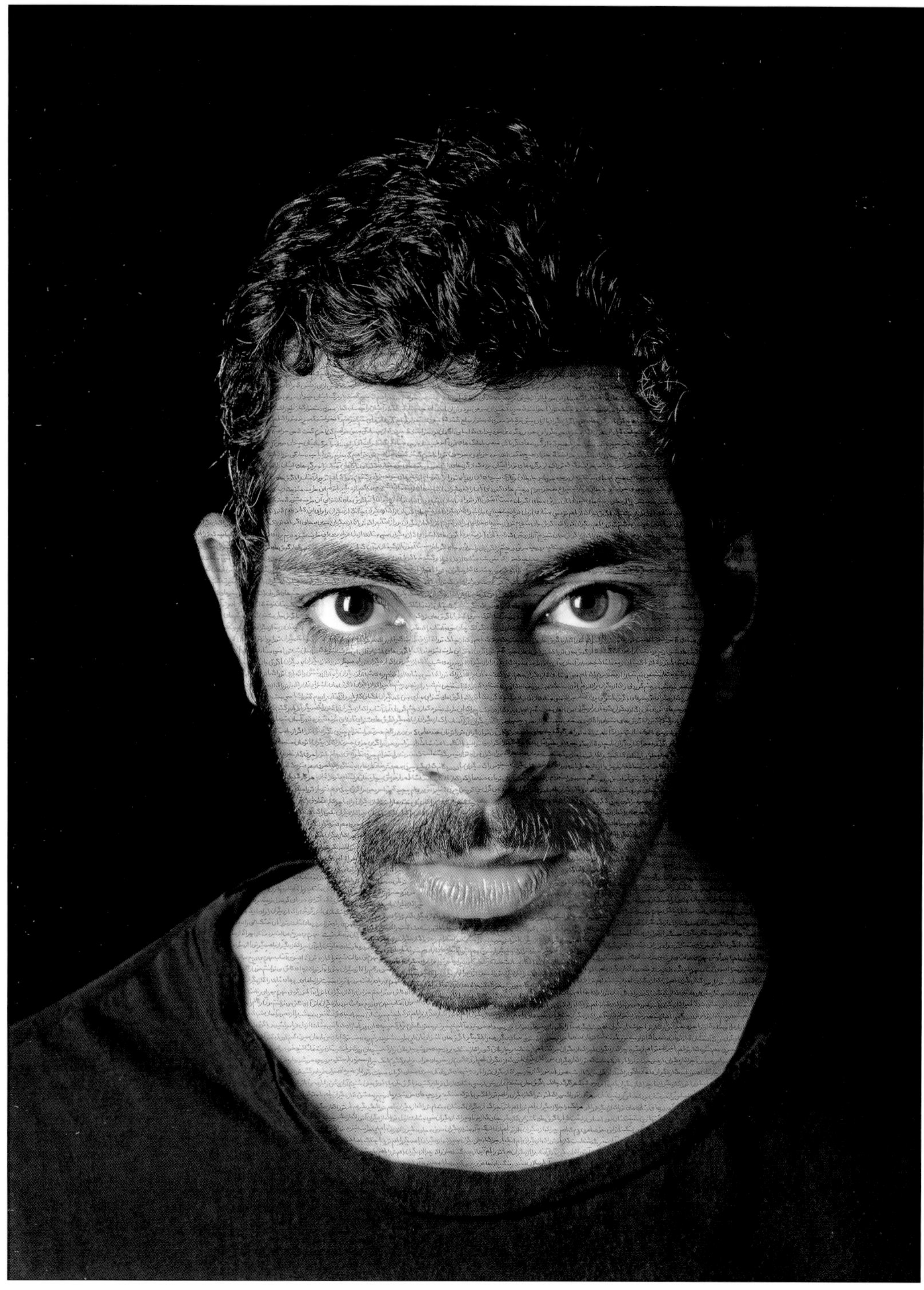

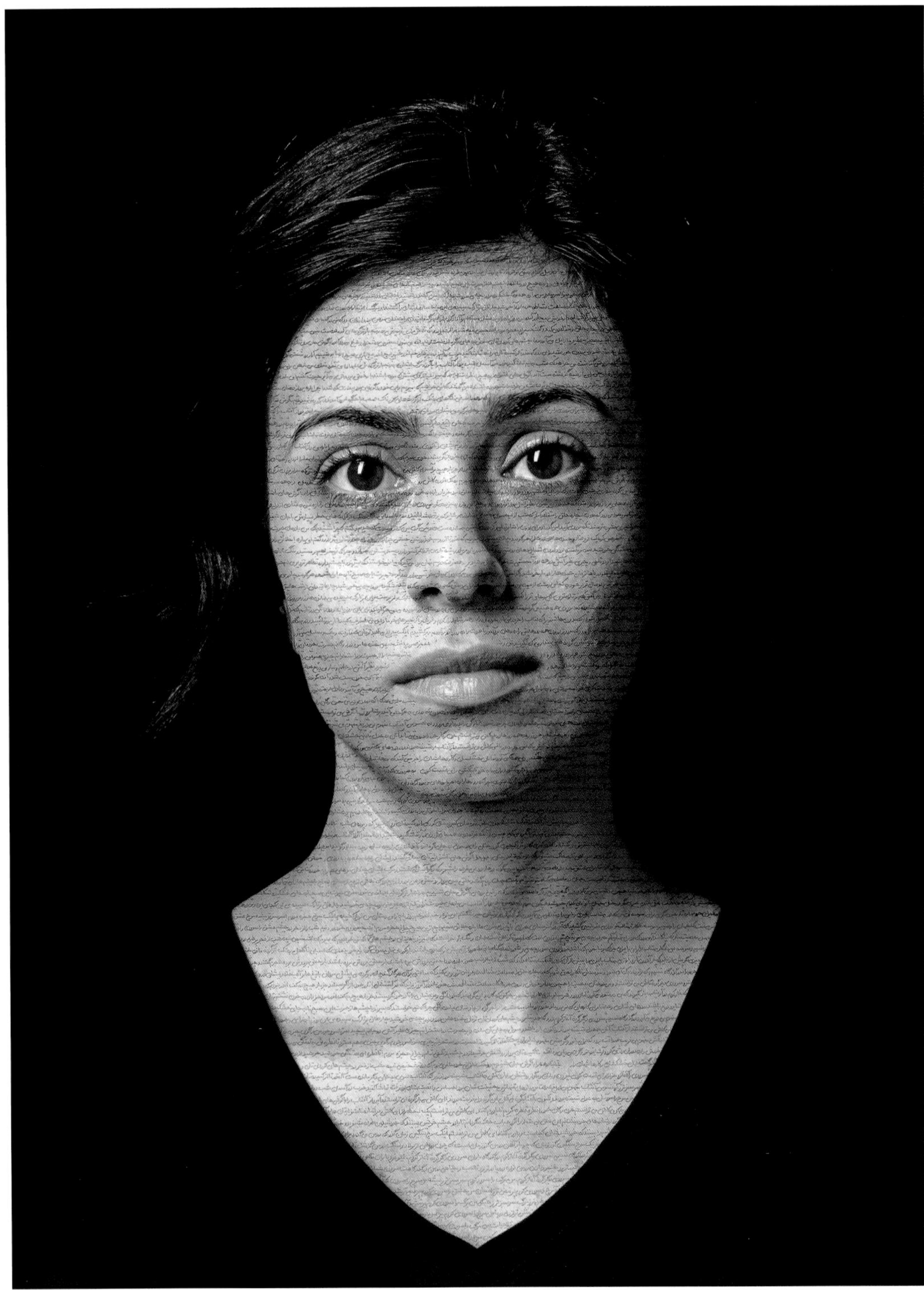

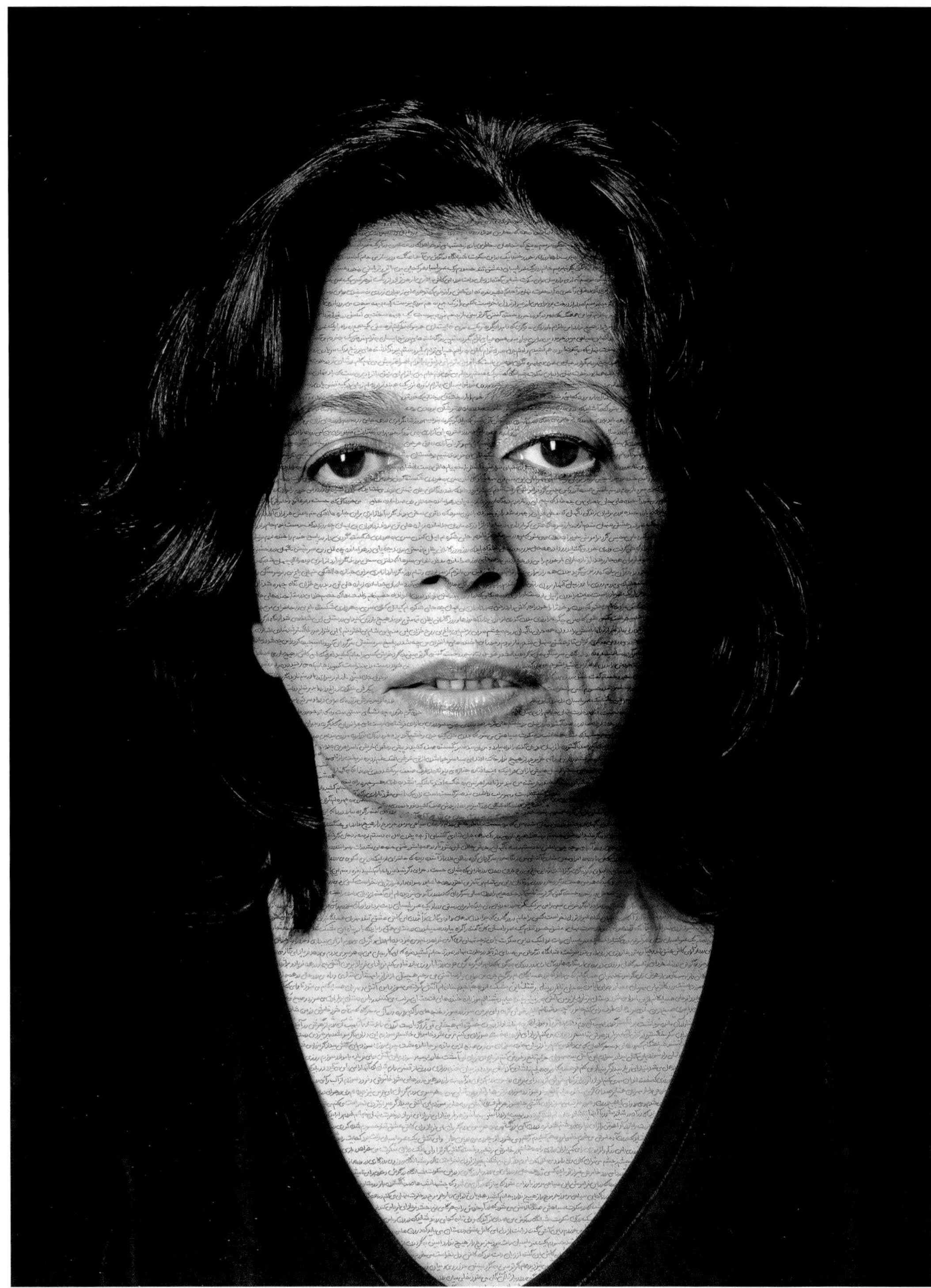

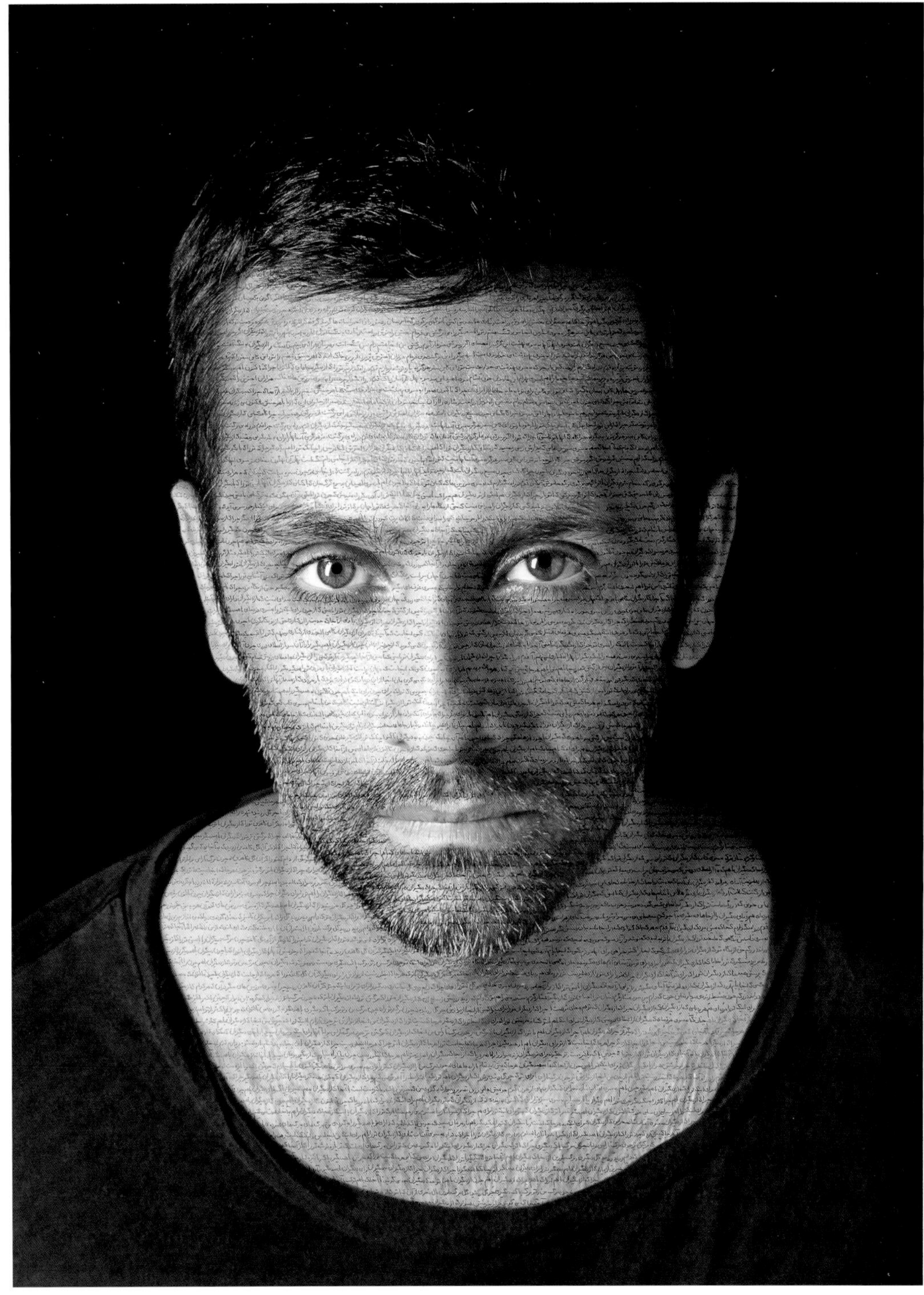

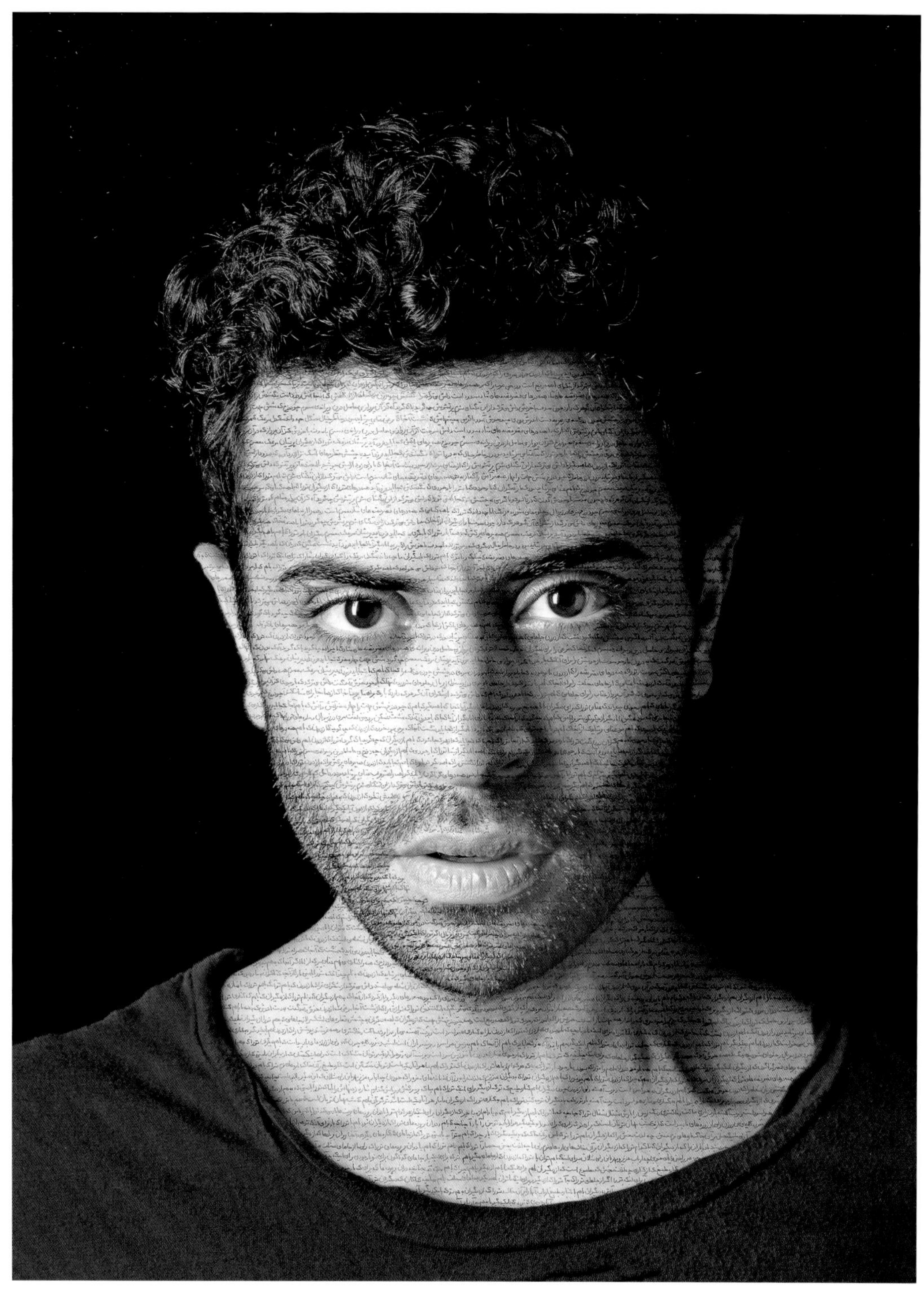

35. *Kouross*, 2012
From *Book of Kings* series (Masses)
101.6 x 76.2 cm (40 x 30 in.)

36. *Mosaeb*, 2012
From *Book of Kings* series (Masses)
101.6 x 76.2 cm (40 x 30 in.)

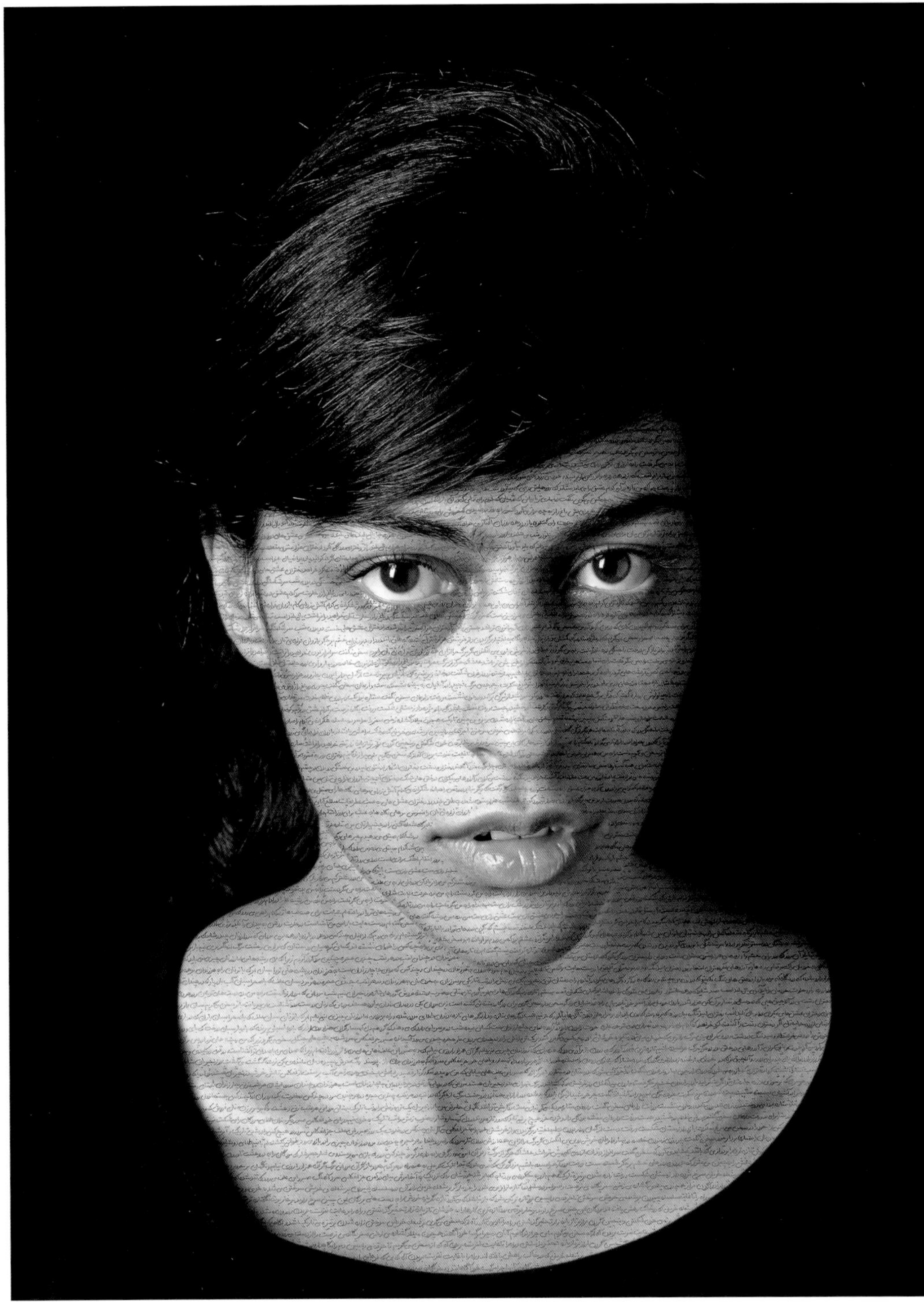

37. *Ava*, 2012
From *Book of Kings* series (Masses)
101.6 x 76.2 cm (40 x 30 in.)

38. *Divine Rebellion*, 2012
From *Book of Kings* series
157.5 x 124.5 cm (62 x 49 in.)

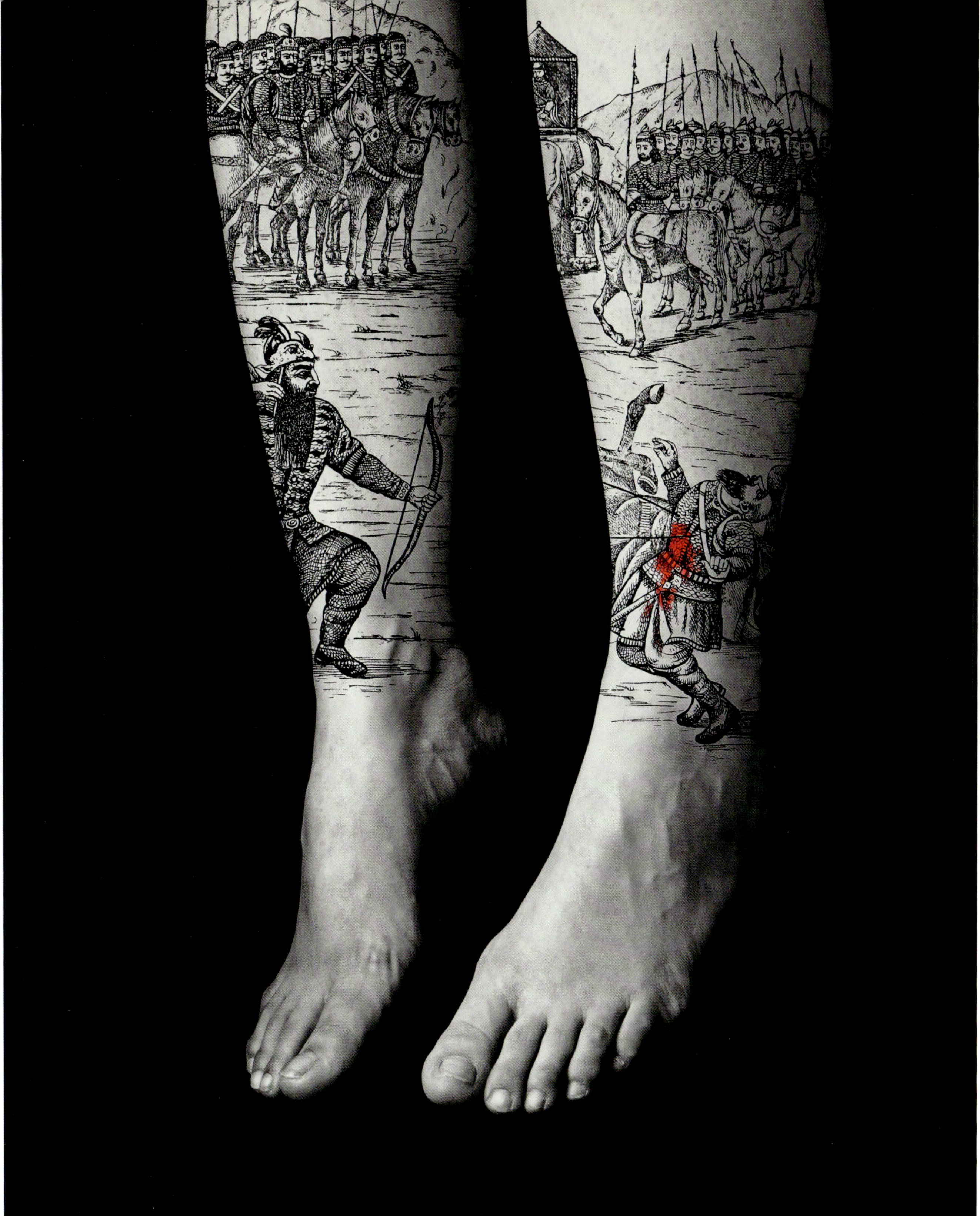

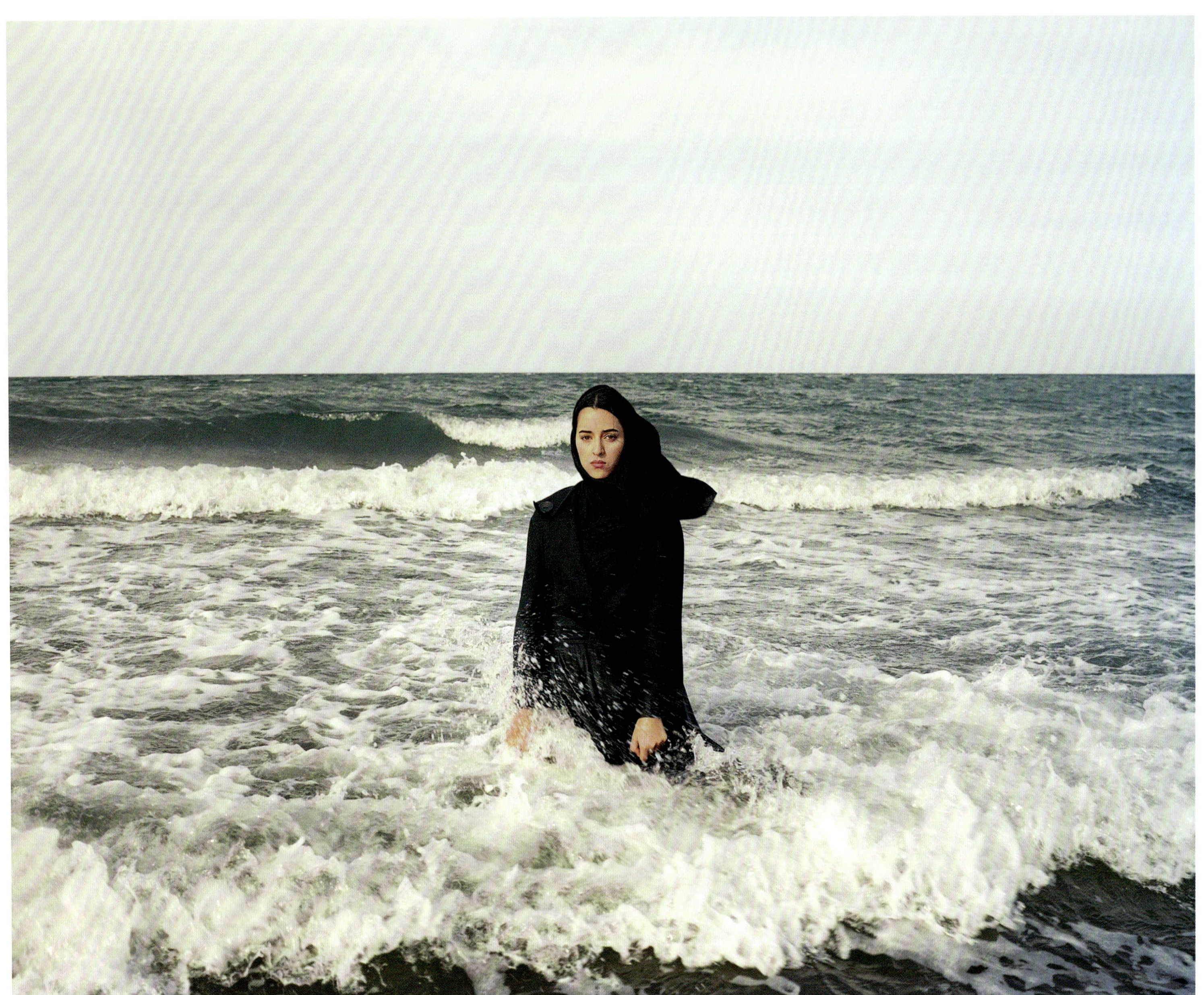

Newsha Tavakolian

Newsha Tavakolian was born in 1981 in Tehran, Iran, where she currently lives and works. A self-taught photographer, Tavakolian has gained an international reputation with images that innovatively combine documentary photography, fine art, and video.

Tavakolian began her career as a photojournalist for the Iranian press, after teaching herself to use her family's camera at age sixteen. She started at the national women's daily newspaper *Zan-e Rooz*, and later worked for nine reformist publications that have all subsequently been banned. By her early twenties, Tavakolian had become one of the few women among Iran's top photojournalists. In 2002 she began to work for foreign press agencies, and her photography has since appeared regularly in publications including *The New York Times*, *Time*, *Newsweek*, *Stern*, *Der Spiegel*, and *Le Monde*. Tavakolian was a founding member of the women photographer's collective Rawiya. Her creative work has been exhibited in Tehran, London, New York, and Berlin. She received the National Geographic Society All Roads Film project prize in 2006 and was a finalist for the Magnum Pictures Inge Morath Award in 2007 and the Magic of Persia Contemporary Art Prize in London in 2009.

The photographs that Tavakolian makes alongside her journalistic assignments confront Western stereotypes about the daily lives of women in Iranian society. Her 2006 series *Iran: Women in the Axis of Evil* depicts young Iranian women in headscarves socializing and smoking cigarettes. Her *Mothers of Martyrs* (also 2006) assembles six portraits of Iranian women holding framed photographs of their young sons who lost their lives in the Iran-Iraq war of the 1980s; the power of the images lies in the mothers' expressions, years after their sons' death. Tavakolian's ability to connect sensitively with her subjects also informs her series *The Day I Became a Woman* (2011), which documents a celebration and prayer ceremony called Jashne Taklif ("celebration of responsibility") in the Islamic Shia tradition. The ceremony is held at school during the year that girls turn nine years old; it marks the first time they wear the *chador*, and when they begin to pray daily in school. In 2008, Tavakolian documented pilgrims at the Hajj pilgrimage to Mecca, one of the five pillars of Islam. In her intimate photographs of men and women, Tavakolian's work offers insight into the role and presence of women in the traditionally masculine ritual.[1]

In the period leading up to the 2009 Iranian elections, restrictions on photojournalists had made her work increasingly difficult. Political tensions following protests against the elections eventually prevented Tavakolian from photographing freely within the country. Stripped of her Iranian press card—and her privileged position as a female photojournalist—Tavakolian transitioned into fine-art photography. She likens her situation to the proverbial "when they keep you from breathing through your nose, you open your mouth to breathe."

In Tavakolian's series *Listen* (2010) she creates a new visual language for the expression of social concerns, particularly about women, outside the

39. Untitled, 2010
From *Listen* series
100 x 120 cm (39 ⅜ x 47 ¼ in.)

realm of press photography. An introductory text accompanies the series:

Imaging a dream.

Eyes closed, mouths open, as if in a dream. Standing facing us with their backs to the darkness, they sing, soundless; they have been standing here, singing for themselves for a long time, imagining us, hearing. Standing, facing the days of tedium, facing a world that has adorned them with a false crown.

Standing, waiting.

Listen consists of six large-format portraits of Iranian singers, six images of covers for imaginary CDs, and a video. The subjects of this two-and-a-half-year-long project are Maral Afsharian, Mahsa Vahdat, Azita Akhavan, Ghazal Shakari, Sayeh Sodaifi, and Sahar Lotfi, singers who are forbidden, as women, by Islamic tenets to perform by themselves in public or to produce recordings. Some of the women portrayed in *Listen* sing background vocals, two have sung at women's parties, and one has performed outside Iran. For *Listen*, they sang in Tavakolian's studio in front of sequined curtains, a different color for each woman. This glamorous stage for the private, otherwise forbidden performances recalls the sets of prerevolutionary Iranian television shows.

In still images in the series, the women's eyes are closed and their mouths open as they sing. Tavakolian not only provides them with a photographic stage but also captures the depth of their emotion. In silent video clips of the performances, the women can be seen but not heard, paralleling their professional situation.

After photographing the singers, Tavakolian created covers for imaginary albums by each of them; the CD cases are left empty as a statement about the restrictions they face. The covers, made by the artist unbeknownst to the singers, feature a young woman (the artist's sister) dressed in black posed in a variety of settings, with poetic titles inspired by feminist Persian slogans.

The album cover entitled *When I Was Twenty Years Old* depicts the young woman wearing red boxing gloves in front of the cityscape of Tehran, evoking ideas of youth, protest, and empowerment. *I Am Eve* is a beautifully lit image in which she represents the crowned mother of all human beings. *This Is Not in the Dream of Eastern Women* shows her carrying two dead chickens. *Glass Ceilings* is a surrealistic image in which her head is surrounded by a cube; Tavakolian is very conscious of obstacles in her own life, "various glass ceilings and invisible barriers" that she and other women, such as the singers, in Iran confront. *Again, I Stayed Behind, in the Empty Cold* depicts the model in front of a seemingly abandoned car and trash bags, in a moment of emptiness and solitude under an ominous-looking sky. In *Don't Forget This Is Not You* she stands still in a vast, wavy ocean, the album title underscoring the limitations on her freedom.

Listen brings to the forefront the unheard and untold stories of these passionate professional singers. Tavakolian's photojournalist past and social consciousness push her to interrogate her society as she watches it become progressively more conservative and more restrictive of citizens' rights. Her first audience is always her native Iran.

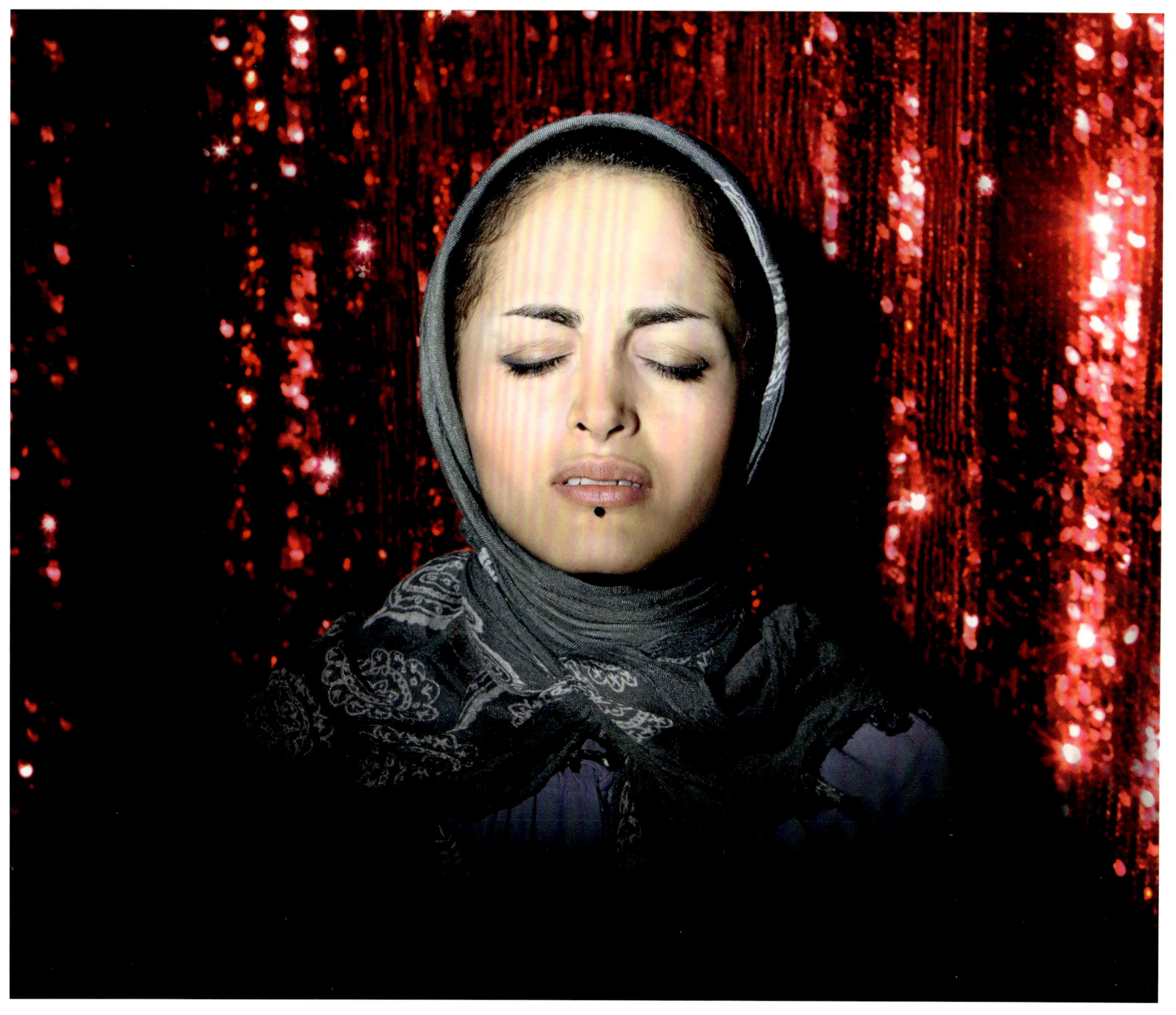

40. *Maral Afsharian*, 2010
From *Listen* series
60 x 80 cm (23 ⅝ x 31 ½ in.)

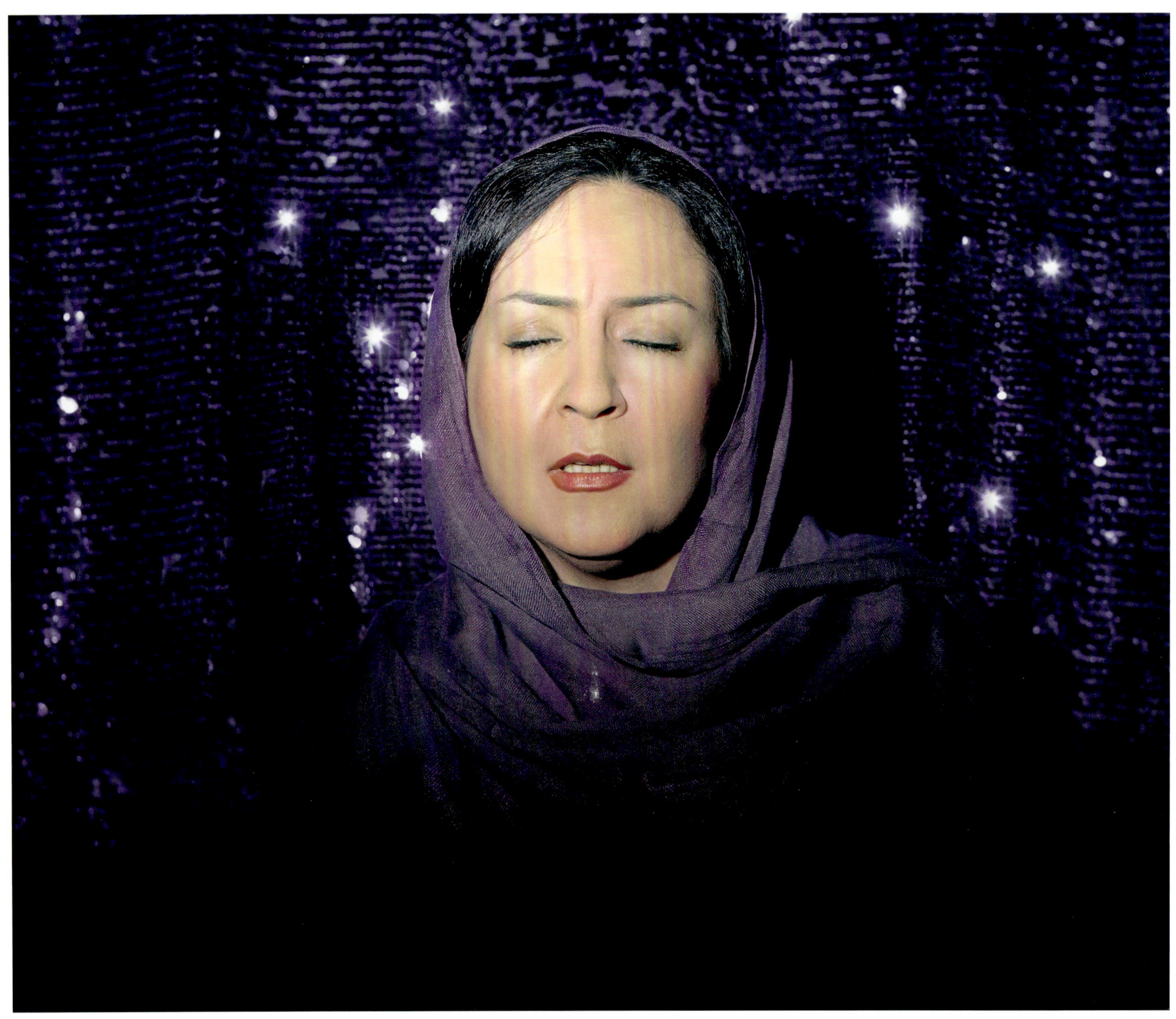

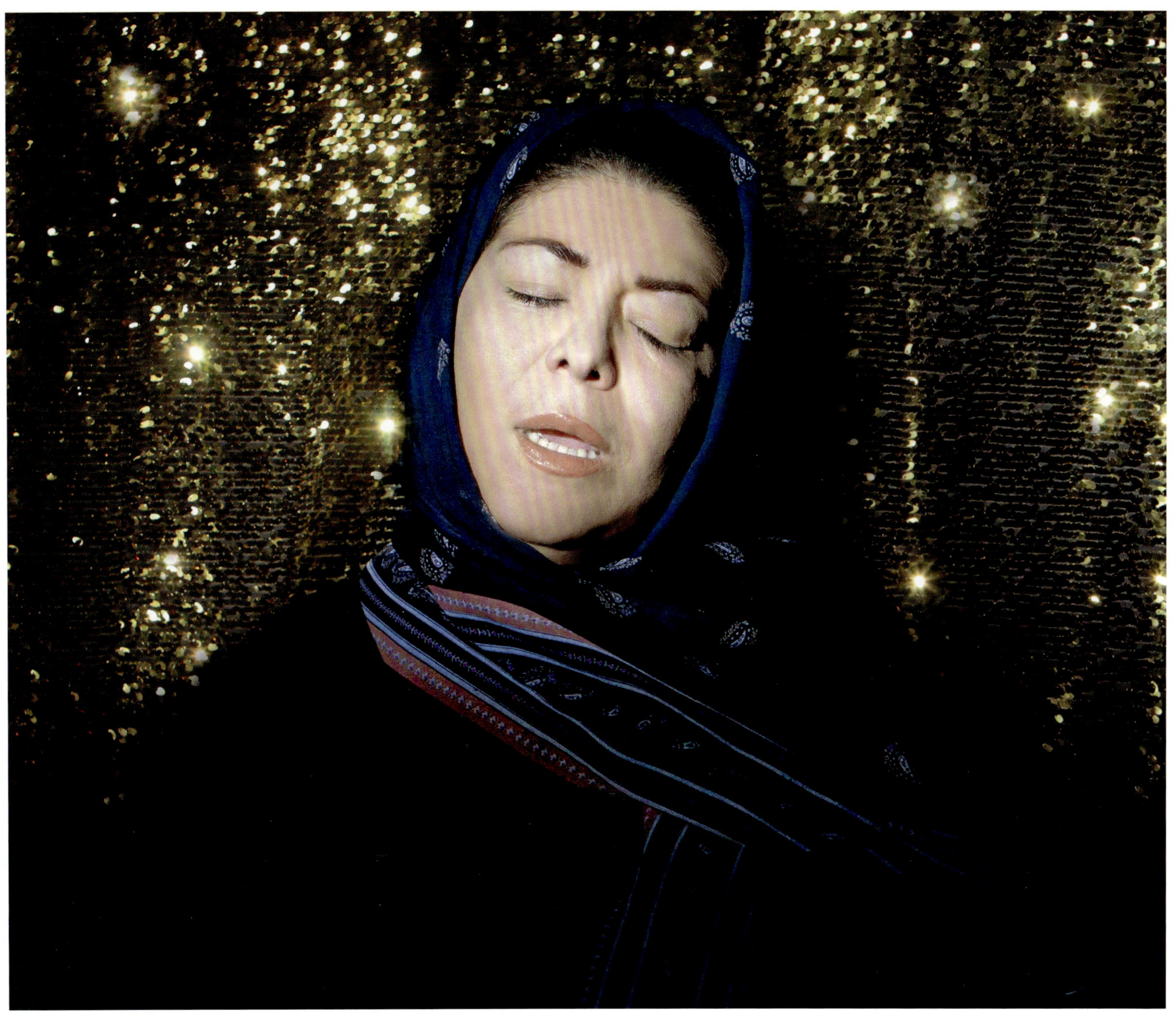

41. *Mahsa Vahdat*, 2010
From *Listen* series
60 x 80 cm (23 ⅝ x 31 ½ in.)

42. *Azita Akhavan*, 2010
From *Listen* series
60 x 80 cm (23 ⅝ x 31 ½ in.)

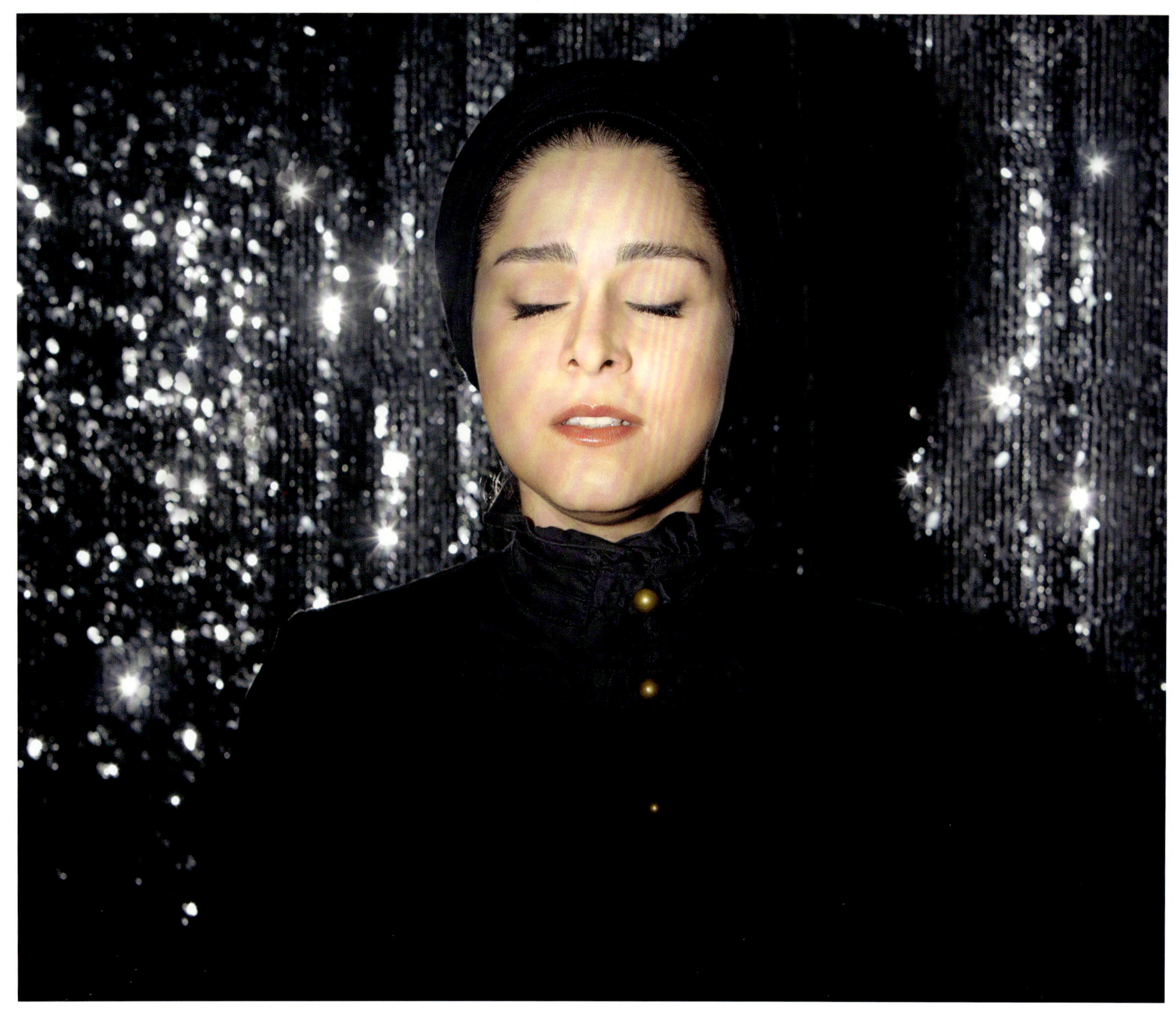

43. *Ghazal Shakari*, 2010
From *Listen* series
60 x 80 cm (23 ⅝ x 31 ½ in.)

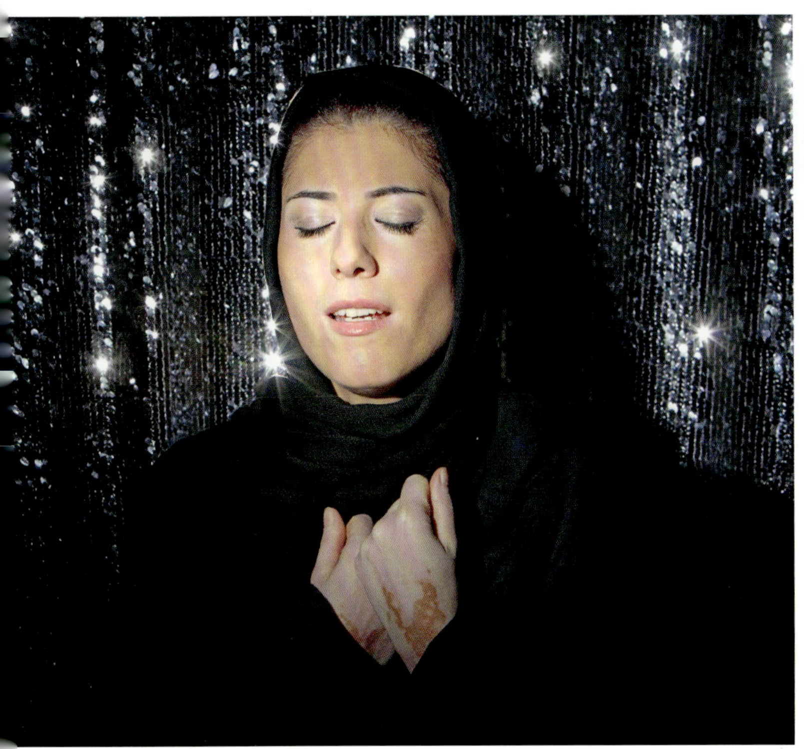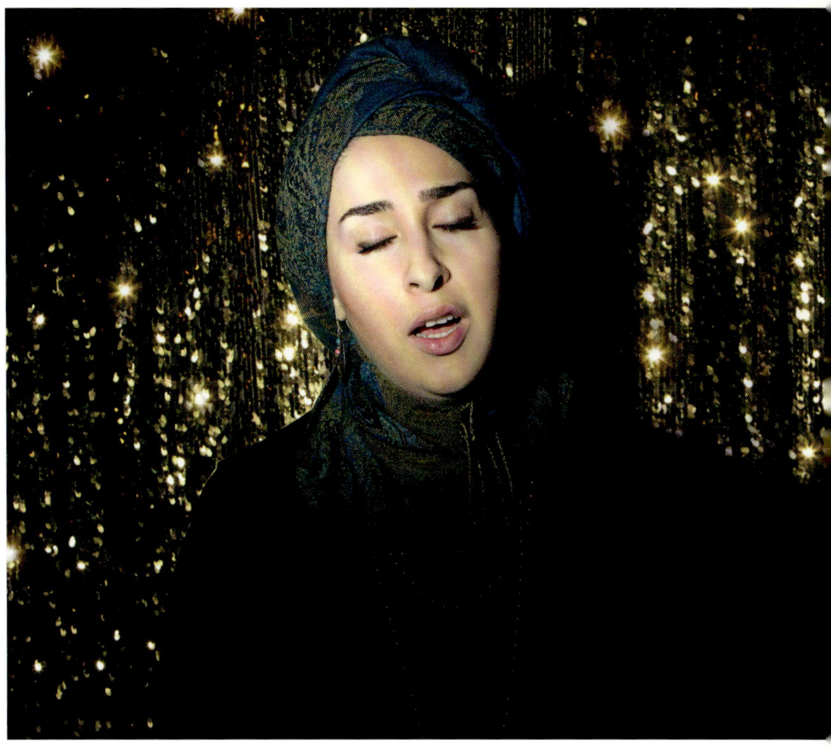

44. *Sayeh Sodaifi*, 2010
From *Listen* series
60 x 80 cm (23 ⅝ x 31 ½ in.)

45. *Sahar Lotfi*, 2010
From *Listen* series
60 x 80 cm (23 ⅝ x 31 ½ in.)

46. Installation photography
of *Listen*, 2010
Video from *Listen* series

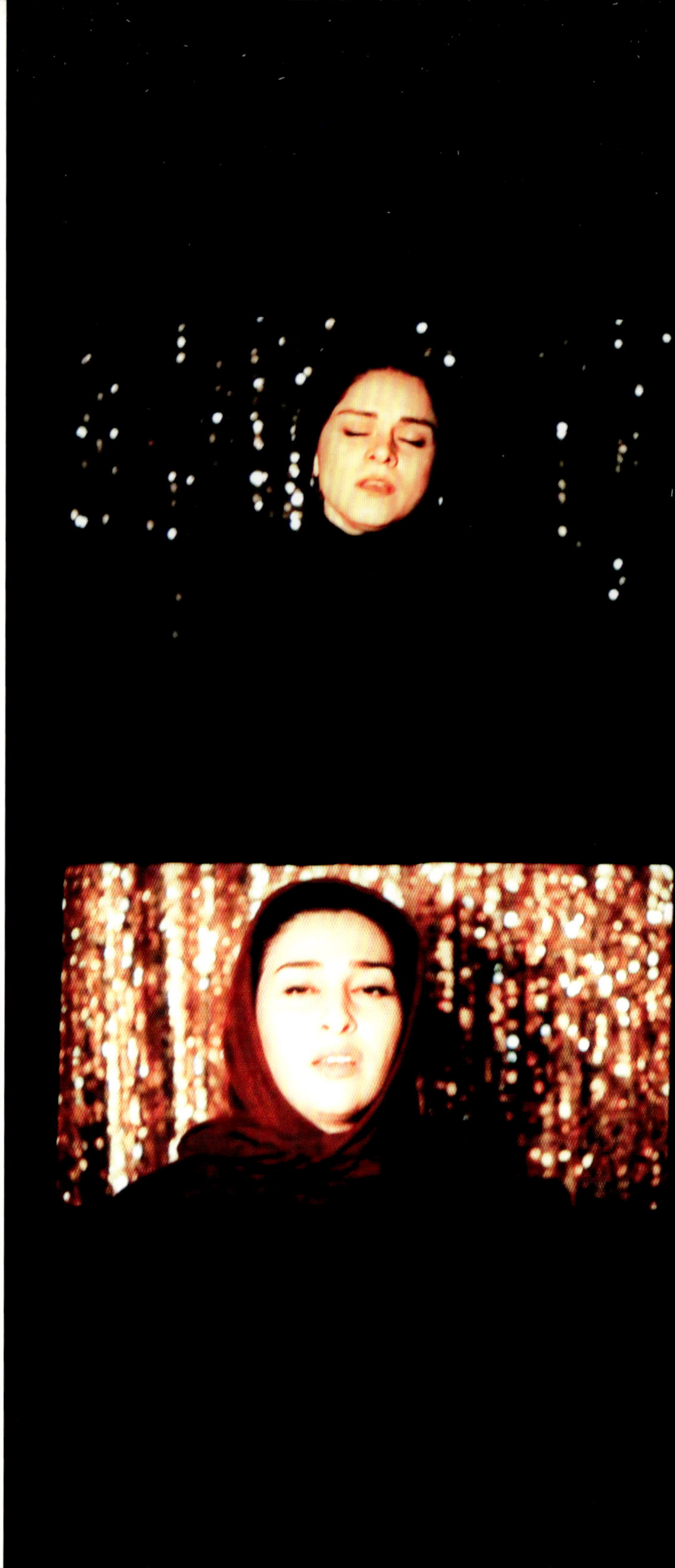

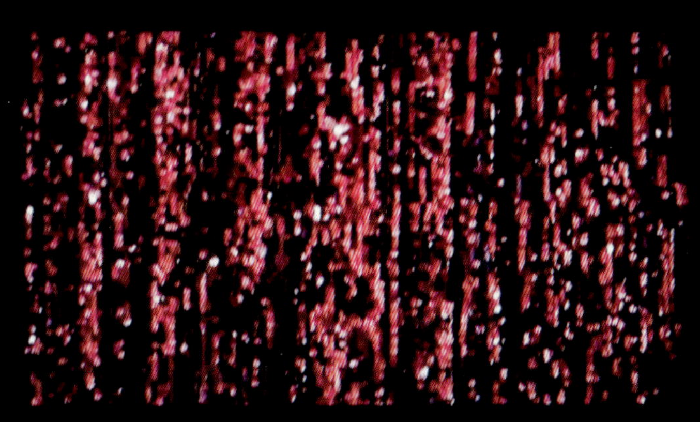
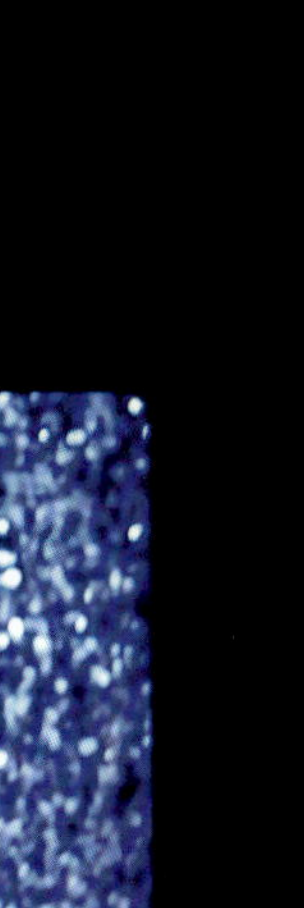
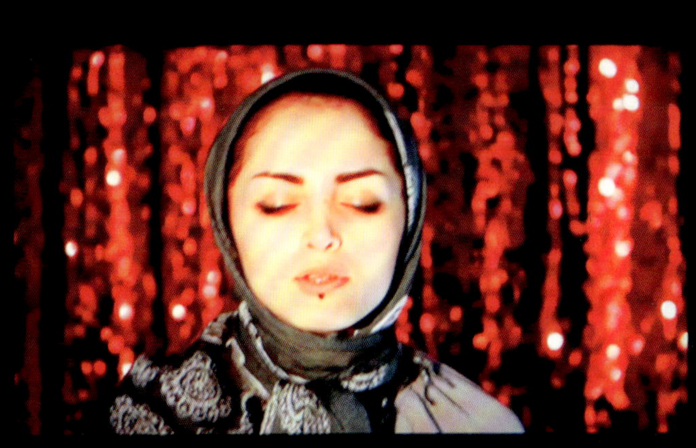

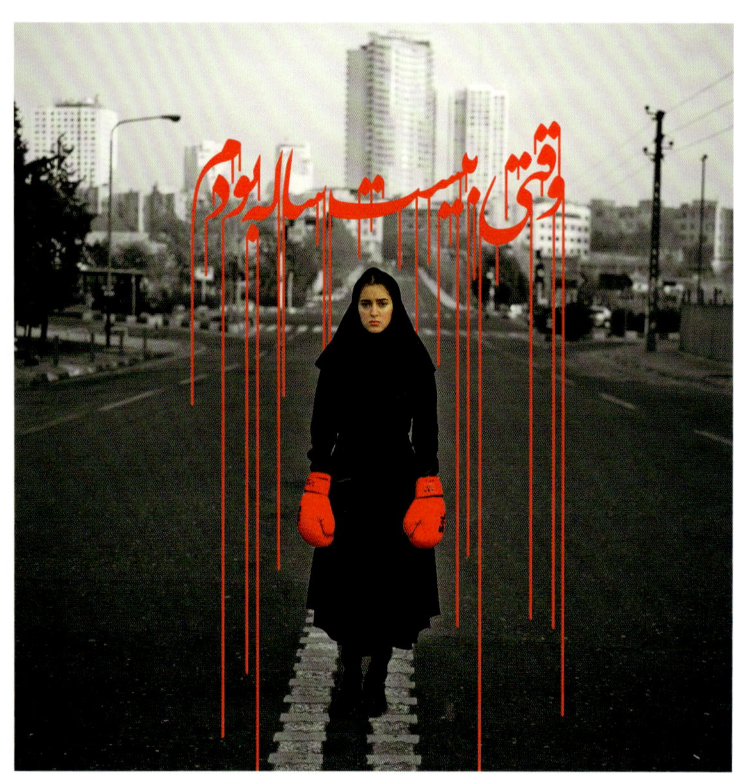

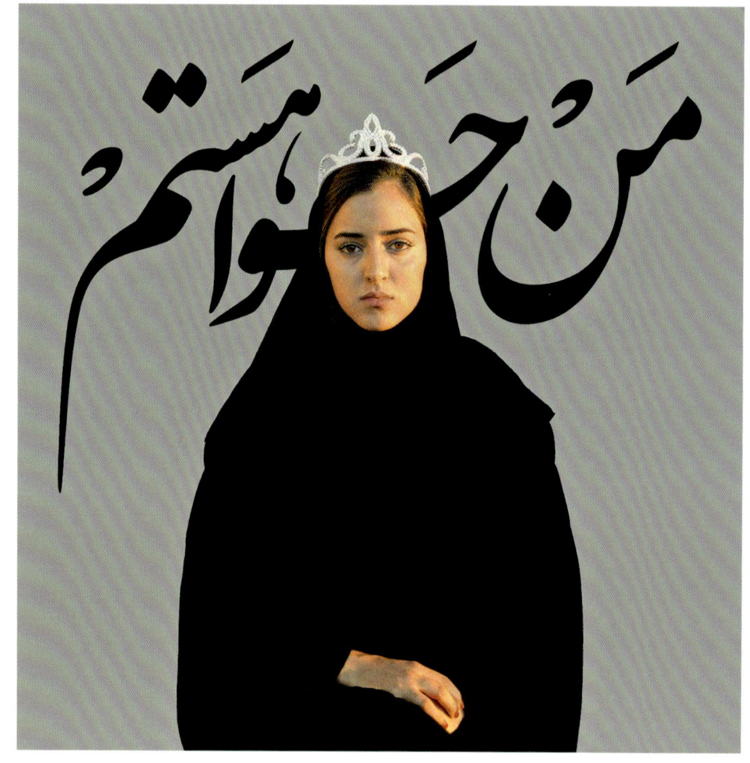

47. *When I Was Twenty Years Old*
(for Maral Afsharian), 2010
From *Listen* series
31 x 31 cm (12 ¼ x 12 ¼ in.)

48. *I Am Eve* (for Mahsa
Vahdat), 2010
From *Listen* series
31 x 31 cm (12 ¼ x 12 ¼ in.)

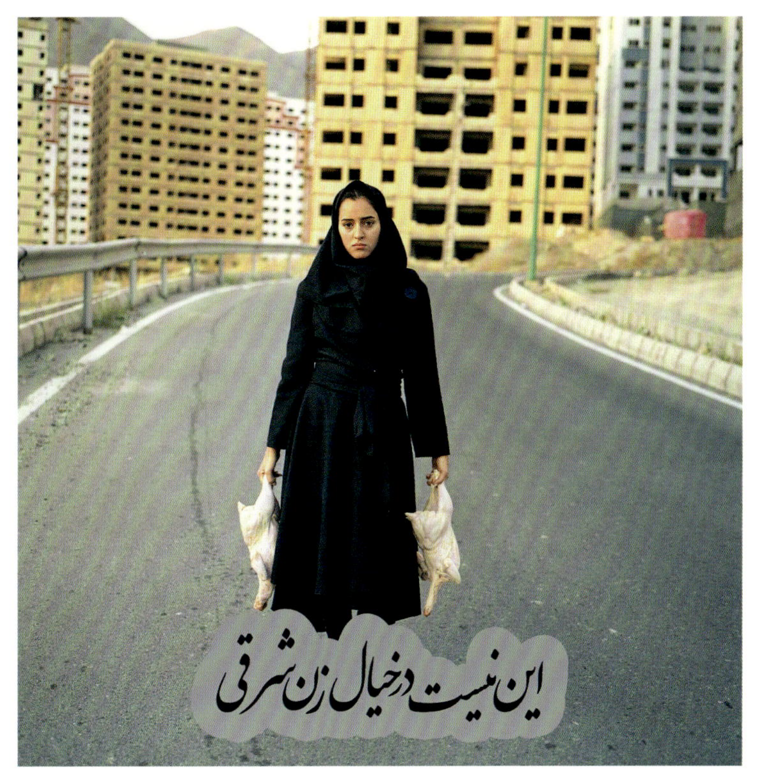

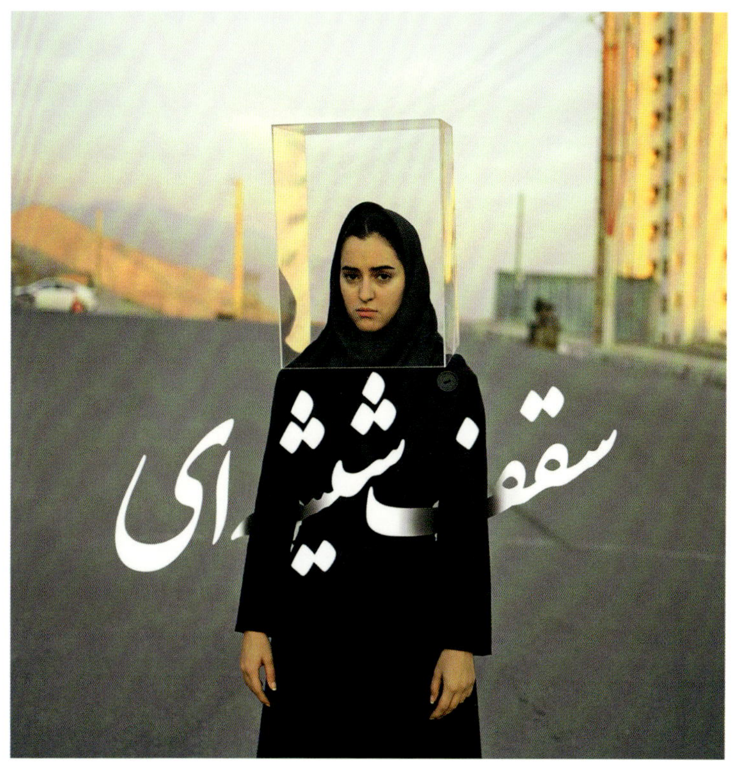

49. *This Is Not in the Dream of Eastern Women* (for Azita Akhavan), 2010
From *Listen* series
31 x 31 cm (12 ¼ x 12 ¼ in.)

50. *Glass Ceilings* (for Ghazal Shakari), 2010
From *Listen* series
31 x 31 cm (12 ¼ x 12 ¼ in.)

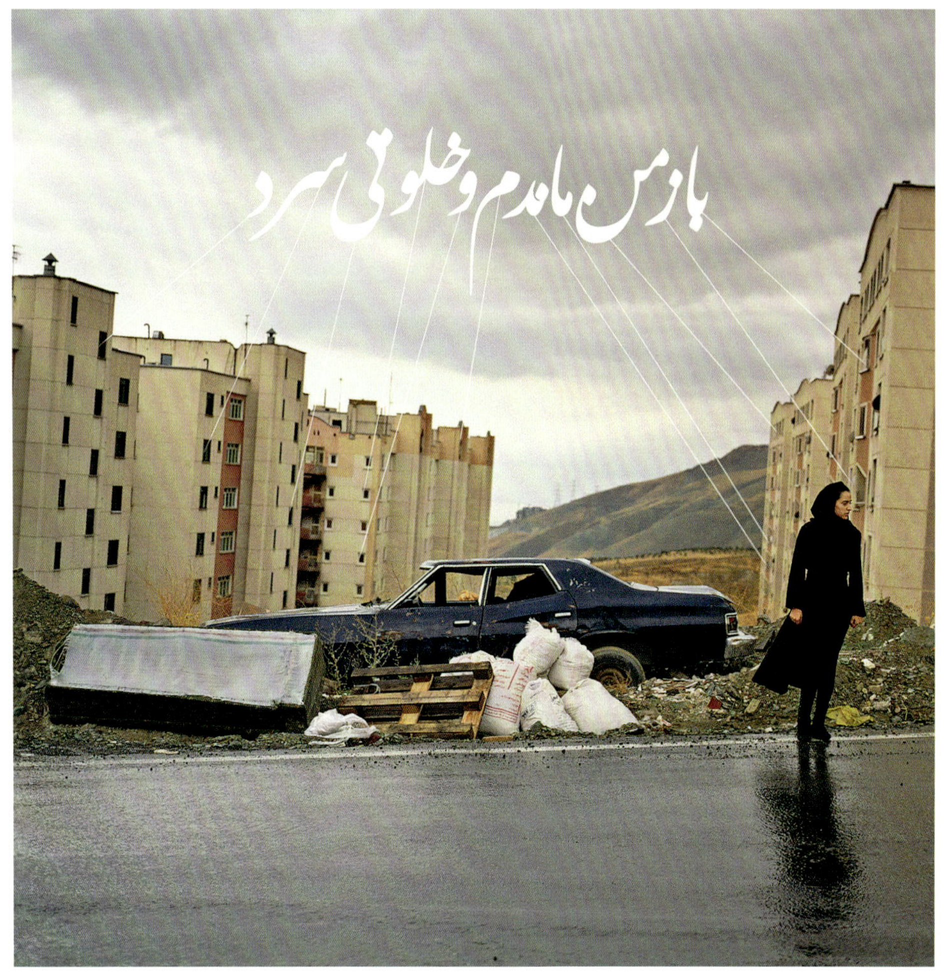
باز من ماندم و خلوتی سرد

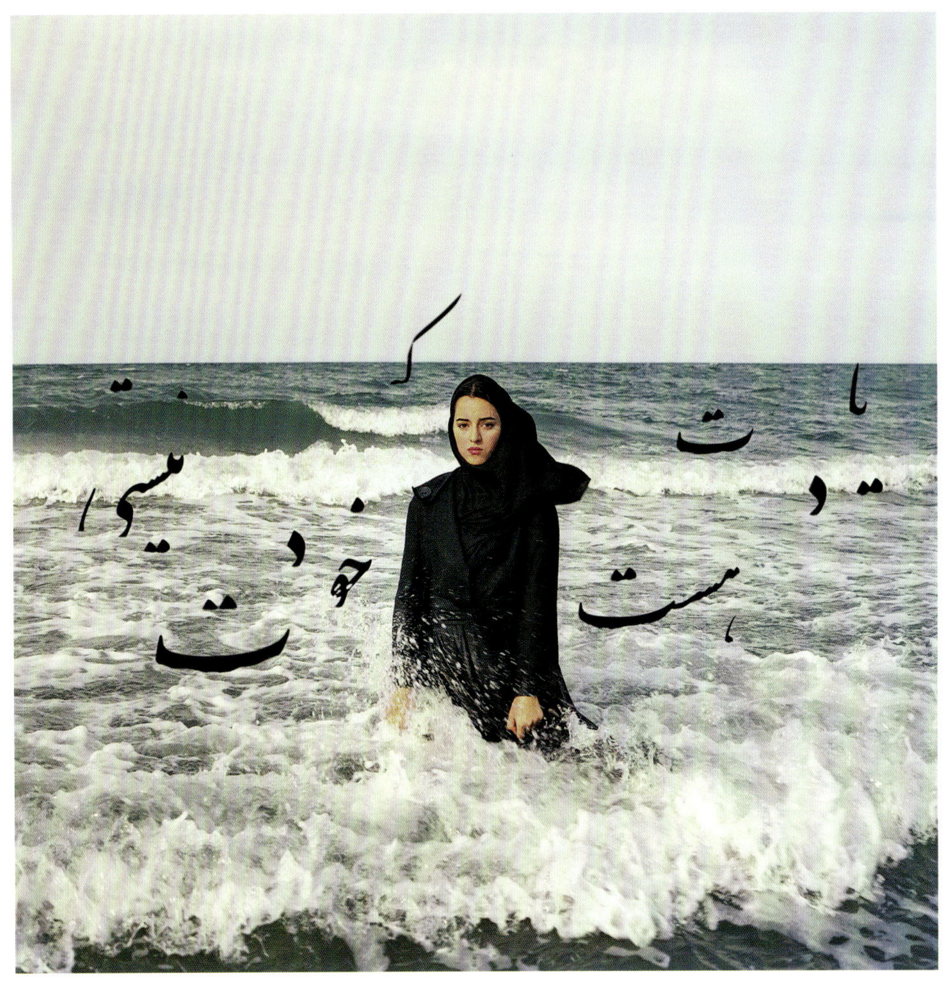

51. *Again, I Stayed Behind, in the Empty Cold* (for Sayeh Sodaifi), 2010
From *Listen* series
31 x 31 cm (12 ¼ x 12 ¼ in.)

52. *Don't Forget This Is Not You* (for Sahar Lotfi), 2010
From *Listen* series
31 x 31 cm (12 ¼ x 12 ¼ in.)

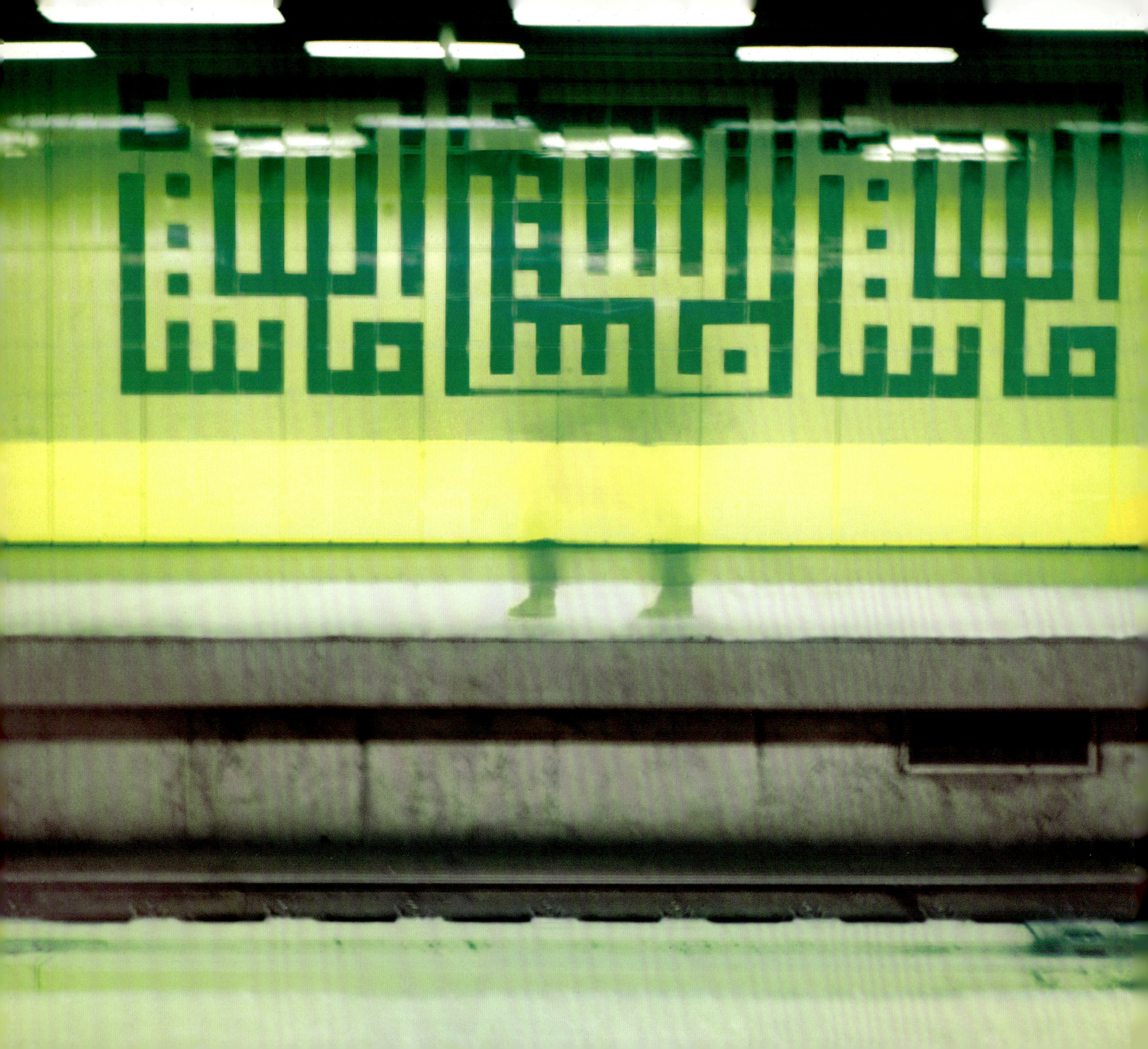

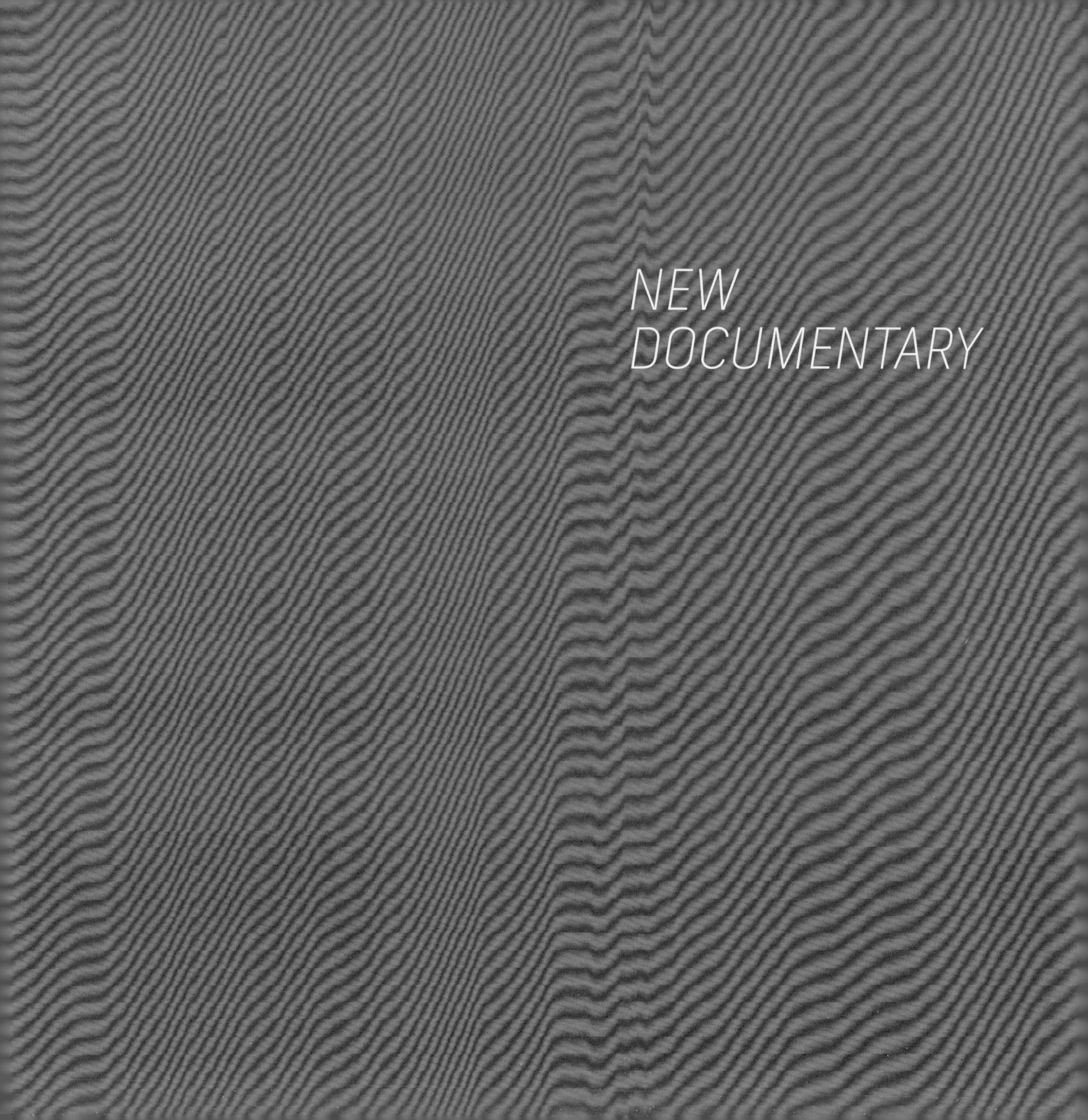
NEW
DOCUMENTARY

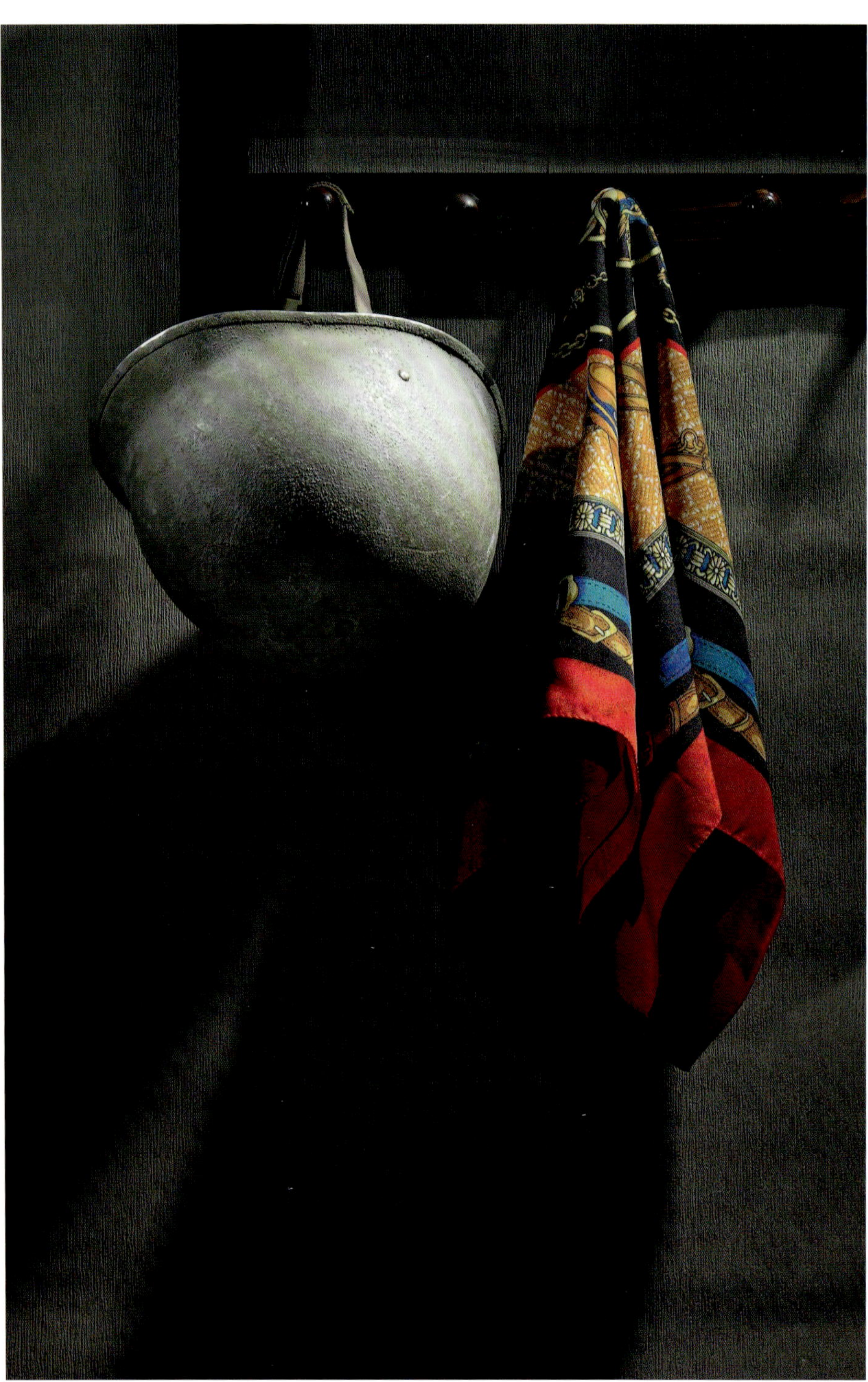

Shadi Ghadirian

One of Iran's leading contemporary photographers, Shadi Ghadirian was born in 1974 in Tehran, Iran, where she lives and works today. A student of the renowned photographer and photography historian Bahman Jalali, Ghadirian was among the first to graduate in photography from Azad University in Tehran. Her photography explores contemporary life in postrevolutionary Iranian society, with a focus on the role of women of her generation. Ghadirian is a cofounder of the association Fanoos Photo, a platform for contemporary photography in Iran. Her work has appeared in several solo exhibitions, such as those at the Los Angeles County Museum of Art (2008 and 2011), as well as in Mumbai, Jerusalem, and Paris, among other cities. Her work has also been featured prominently in several major exhibitions of contemporary Middle Eastern art, such as *Light from the Middle East: New Photography* at the Victoria and Albert Museum in London (2012).

Ghadirian's early series *Qajar* (1998; see plates 4, 6–9) shows thirty-three female subjects posed in front of a painted backdrop, most often one used for studio portraits in Iran in the nineteenth century, toward the end of the Qajar era (1786–1925). The women are each shown with an anachronistic modern object that in 1998 was either "forbidden" or restricted, ranging from a Pepsi can to a boom box, and including bicycles, musical instruments, books, and makeup. One image from the series portrays a young woman with the newspaper *Hamshahri*, a repeatedly banned publication that Ghadirian and her husband, the novelist and photographer Peyman Houshmandzadeh, once worked for (see plate 8). While working at the National Museum of Photography in Tehran, Ghadirian had archived nineteenth-century portraits that include seemingly incongruous props. In these historical prints, the props are not intended to add an ironic twist as in Ghadirian's photographs, but reflect a more open society, just as the clothes the sitters wear are more revealing than what is acceptable for Iranian women to wear in public today.

Ghadirian's series are frequently autobiographical, including *Like Every Day* (2001–2), made shortly after the artist married. In these photographs, controversial within Iran, the faces of women in *chador*s are obscured by domestic objects. Ghadirian's depiction of women as machines who perform the banal tasks of domesticity comments on the expectations for married women.

Ghadirian raises questions of censorship in the series *West by East* (2003–4) by blacking out parts of the bodies and clothes of subjects she photographed. For the series *Be Colorful* (2004–5), she photographed women behind glass that was covered with a translucent layer of gray paint that creates a veil or screen between the viewer and the subject. Bits of color and fashion showing through create a metaphor for the distinction between the public and private lives of women, required by law to dress a particular way in public.

Ghadirian's series *White Square* (2009) is focused on objects that people save after wars have ended. *Miss Butterfly* (2011), based on an old

53. *Nil, Nil #4*, 2008
110 x 75 cm (about 45 x 30 in.)

Iranian story about a butterfly caught in a spider web, could reflect the difficulty of being a photographer in Iran after the 2009 elections.

In the eighteen photographs that constitute the series *Nil, Nil* (2008–9), named after a short story of the same title about war by Ghadirian's husband, military objects are juxtaposed with feminine elements to form domestic still lifes. As in the *Qajar* series, Ghadirian subtly introduces incongruous objects into everyday tableaux.

The war helmet and colored headscarf hanging on a somber grey wall in *#4* refer to the diverging paths of men and women. The helmet protects the man on the battlefield and the headscarf is the woman's outside "protection." *Nil, Nil #1* juxtaposes shiny red high heels and army boots with a small bloodstain on the toe. One of the high heels faces the open door, ready to go out, while the army boots face away from the door, one leaning up against the wall. The frozen dance expresses the female desire to be free, as it confronts the male preparedness for warfare and injury. In *#14* an army uniform and a deep purple velour coat that looks hand-embroidered hang in a closet beside everyday clothes, again evoking the male and female spheres in wartime. In *#8*, white bed linens and soft, warm-toned blanket startlingly frame a 40mm Famas rifle grenade on a bed, suggesting wars both inside and outside the home. *Nil, Nil #11* shows a woman's small beaded purse filled with accessories and makeup, both metallic—gold and silver—and brightly colored. Gold-colored bullets are also stuffed into this vessel of artifice and luxury. *Nil, Nil #10* presents a hand grenade in the middle of a fruit bowl; the objects in the bowl, associated with warfare and nourishment, are equated by size.

All these objects, in anonymous yet intimate settings, evoke the complexities of male and female public personas and private desires, bringing out the female experience of war: "I wanted to talk about the woman and the man both inside the house. And show also the war, there is a war. The man is in the war. The woman is inside the house. She is waiting for him."

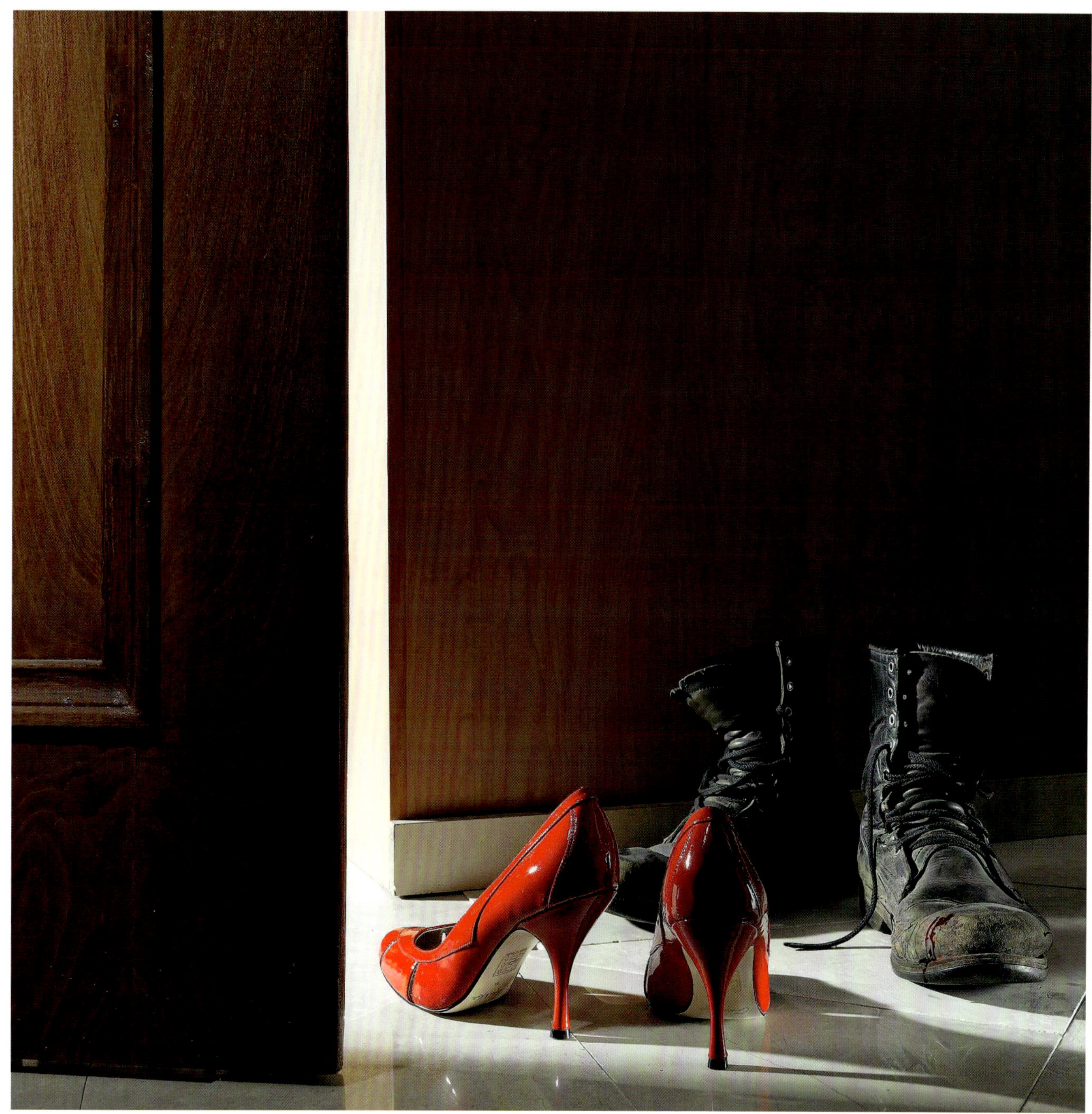

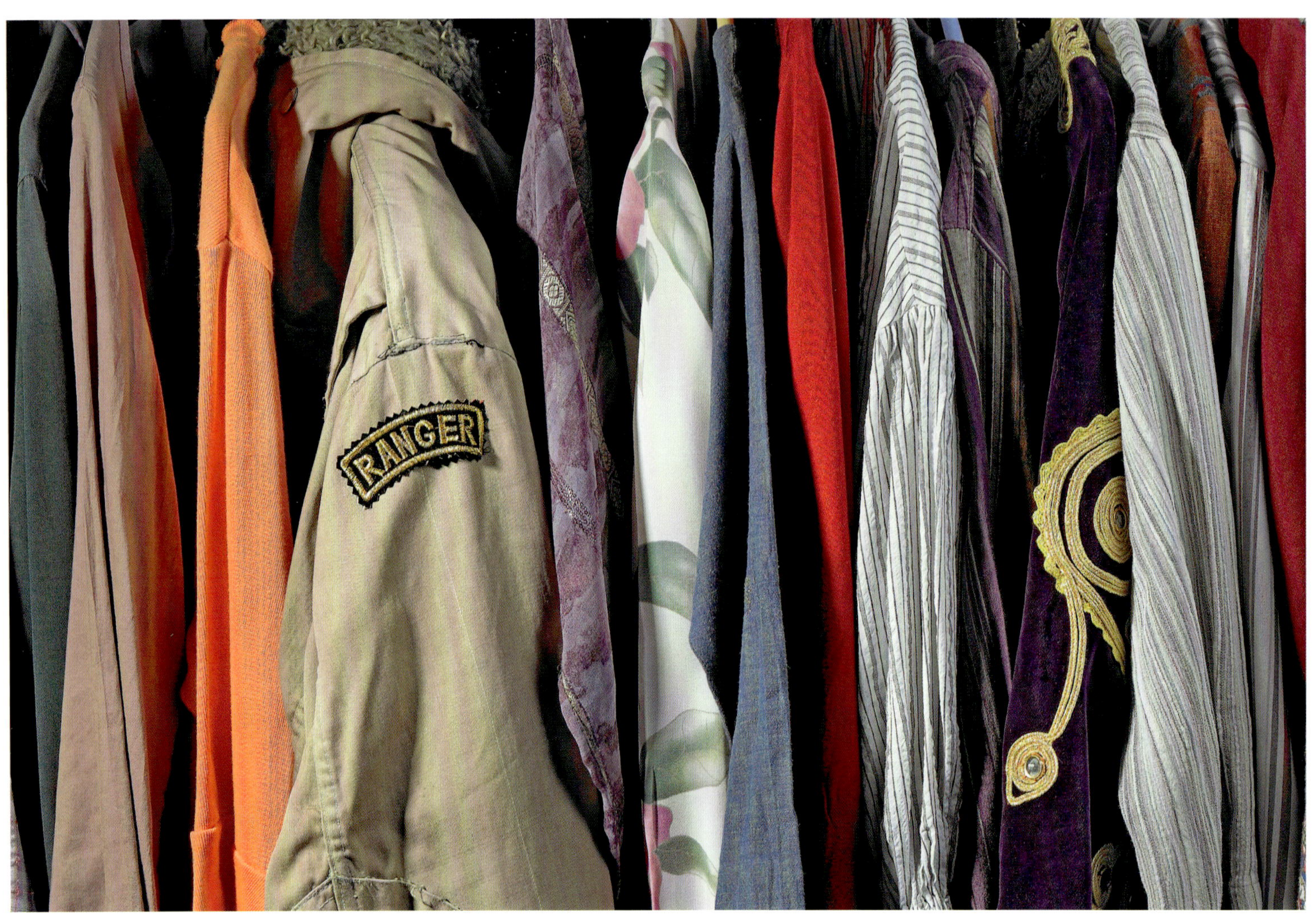

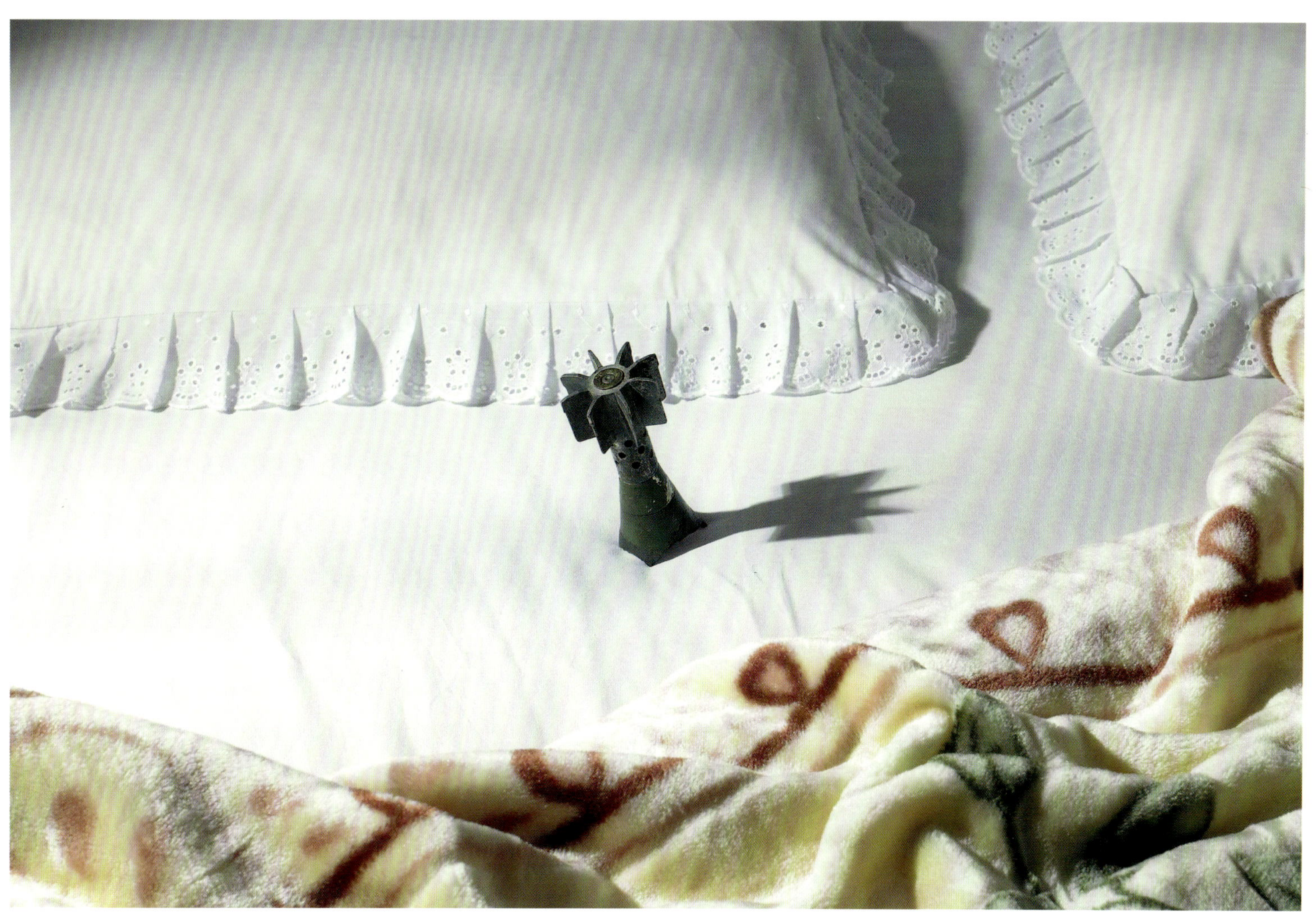

55. *Nil, Nil #14*, 2008
75 x 110 cm (about 30 x 45 in.)

56. *Nil, Nil #8*, 2008
75 x 110 cm (about 30 x 45 in.)

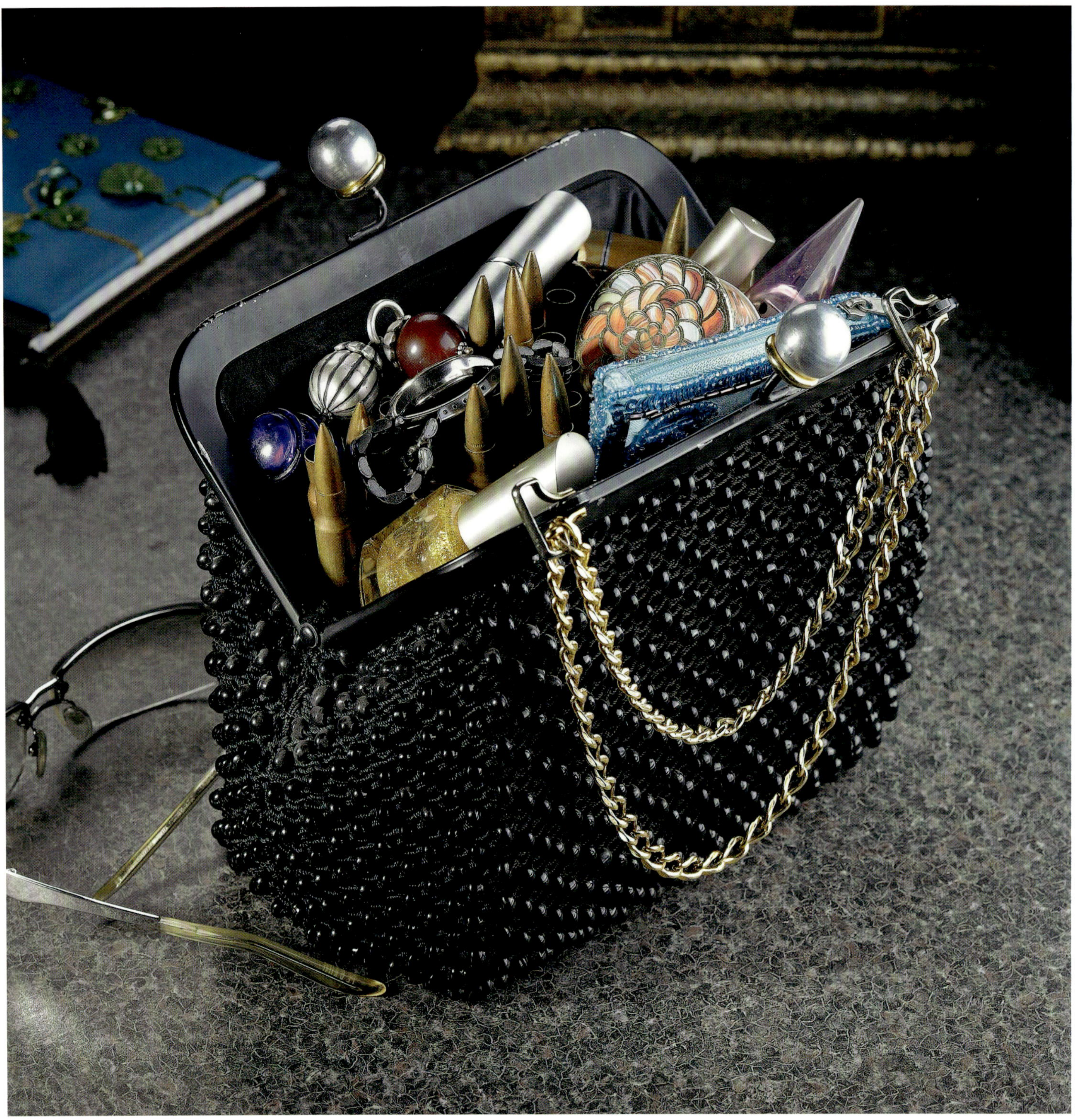

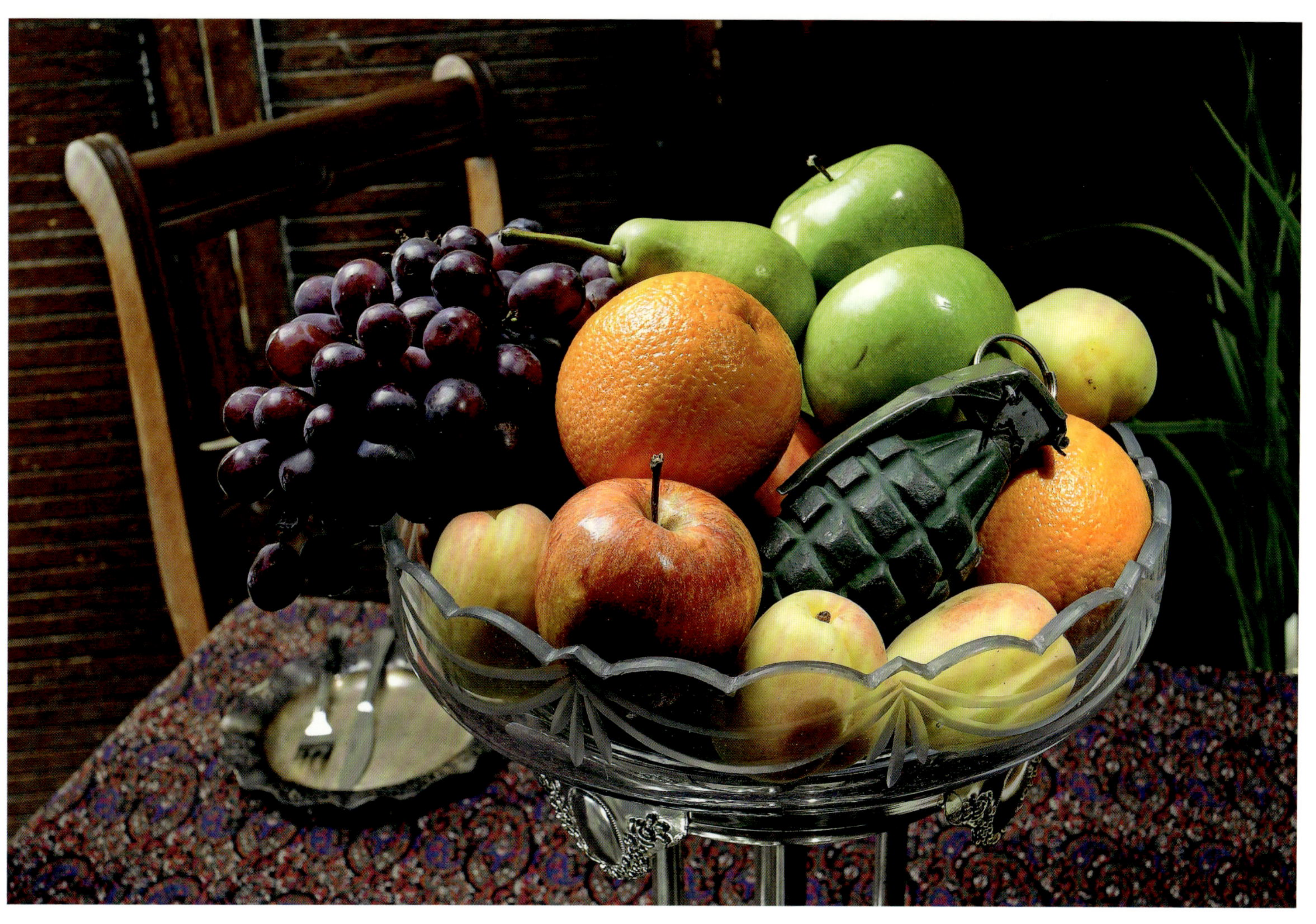

57. *Nil, Nil #11*, 2008
75 x 75 cm (about 30 x 30 in.)

58. *Nil, Nil #10*, 2008
75 x 110 cm (about 30 x 45 in.)

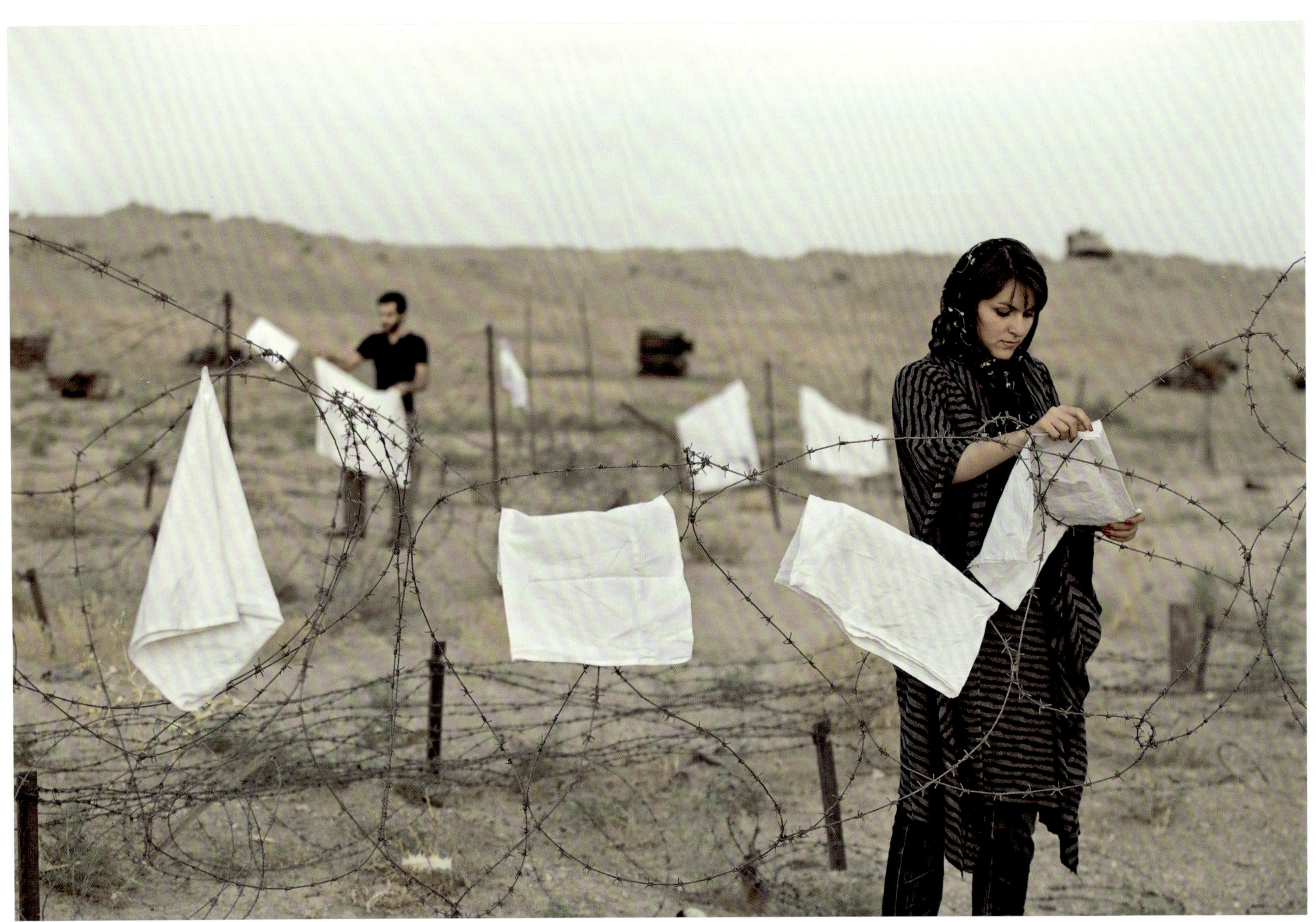

Gohar Dashti

Gohar Dashti was born in 1980 in Ahwaz, Iran, and has a Master of Fine Arts degree in photography from the University of Tehran. Living and working in Tehran since 1999, she has established an international reputation through photographs that address questions of identity and social concerns in postrevolutionary Iranian society. Dashti's work has been featured in many exhibitions, festivals, and biennales internationally including Printemps de Toulouse 2012 and Photoquai 2009 in Paris. She has had solo shows in Tehran and Brest and has participated in group exhibitions in Tokyo, Berlin, Toronto, and Zurich.

For the early *Family Albums* (2006), Dashti created a photographic work without a camera, juxtaposing photographs from old albums with writing found on the back of the images. Discovering untold stories from the past encouraged her to find and tell her own story within photography that later led to an impressive career behind a camera.

Me, She, and the Others (2009) is a series of triptychs featuring women born after the 1979 Iranian Revolution, from a variety of professions. Each triptych consists of three portraits that depict the woman dressed for the workplace, for home, and for going out in the street. In describing the series, Dashti points to women's lack of freedom to choose what they wear in public or in the workplace. Changing their clothes as they move from one setting to another has become a daily ritual for young Iranian women since the Islamic revolution.

While Dashti's series *Today's Life and War* (2008) evokes courage and tenacity amid the scenery of war, *Slow Decay* (2010) is a more somber group of eight staged narratives, each photograph with a trace of blood in it. The photographer explains that the blood symbolizes "the collective memory of a people who have suffered silently for generations and tolerated so much torment. . . . The agony, little by little, has wrapped around their souls, much like a disease that, bit by bit, attacks the body."[1] Dashti describes the series as being about internalized pain; the models gaze intensely at the viewer, almost devoid of emotion.

The ten staged narratives in *Today's Life and War* relate to Dashti's experiences as a child born after the Iranian Revolution who lived through the Iran-Iraq war (1980–88), in a city very close to the border between the two countries. The carefully composed scenes juxtapose a couple in moments of daily life with both discreet and overt signs of military presence, ranging from tanks to bunkers to smaller objects. Dashti says that the series explores "how the violence [of war] symbolically influences the emotional life of [her] generation [and] permeates all aspects of contemporary society." She explains that while the man and woman do not visibly express emotion, "they nevertheless have a power of perseverance, determination, and survival."

In an image of the couple hanging laundry on a long strand of tangled barbed wire, the simplicity of the flag-like white cloths suggests peace and innocence, while the barbed wire is a harsh reminder of war frontiers (opposite). In

59–64. *Untitled #2, 1, 4, 5, 7,* and *8*
From *Today's Life and War* series, 2008
Each: 70 x 105 cm (about 30 x 40 in.)

another photograph, the couple watches television, enclosed in a space with a wall of sandbags
(plate 60). A reflection on the television screen of
red, white, and green corrugated metal on the wall
behind the couple evokes the postrevolutionary
Iranian flag. The national colors also appear in
the woman's clothing. A breakfast scene includes
a military tank whose gun is aimed alarmingly at
the young man perched over his teacup (plate 61).
The couple begins their day over a typically Iranian
meal, as the young woman speaks on her cell
phone. Army greens, blues, and browns dominate
the image while the pink edging of the woman's
headscarf and the delicate patterns of the table-
cloth create tension with the looming presence
of the tank.

Three photographs depict celebrations. The
couple appears as newlyweds in the shell of a
burned out and abandoned car decorated with
bright pink ribbons and bows, an uncertain vehicle
for embarking on a new life (plate 62). In another
image, the couple appears determined to celebrate
Nowruz, the Persian New Year, having laid out
each of the symbolic objects that are part of the
ritual—mirror, apple, candles, *golab* (rosewater),
sabzeh (wheat or barley sprouts), painted eggs, and
a goldfish in a bowl—on a makeshift table on the
ground (plate 63). The distant circles of light on the
horizon attempt to counteract the military helmets
scattered around the festivity. In the third image of
celebration, the man and woman sit behind a wall

of sandbags, as if on a puppet stage, with festive
colored garlands hung around them; the one in
front is strung from the remnants of a missile shell
(plate 64). The shiny decorations contrast with the
muted colors of the scene. Between the couple,
balanced precariously atop a sandbag, is a yellow
cake with a large sparkler on top—perhaps a reference to "yellowcake," a chemical used in nuclear
reactors.

Dashti's staged photographs offer powerful visual metaphors about the experience of
war and collective cultural memories. The small
hints of bright colors that appear against muted
backgrounds may indicate small glimmers of
hope in the midst of conflict and war. When asked
about the narrative of *Today's Life and War*, Dashti
remarks, "I think it's my life. . . . You ask, What's the
story? I think it's my story."

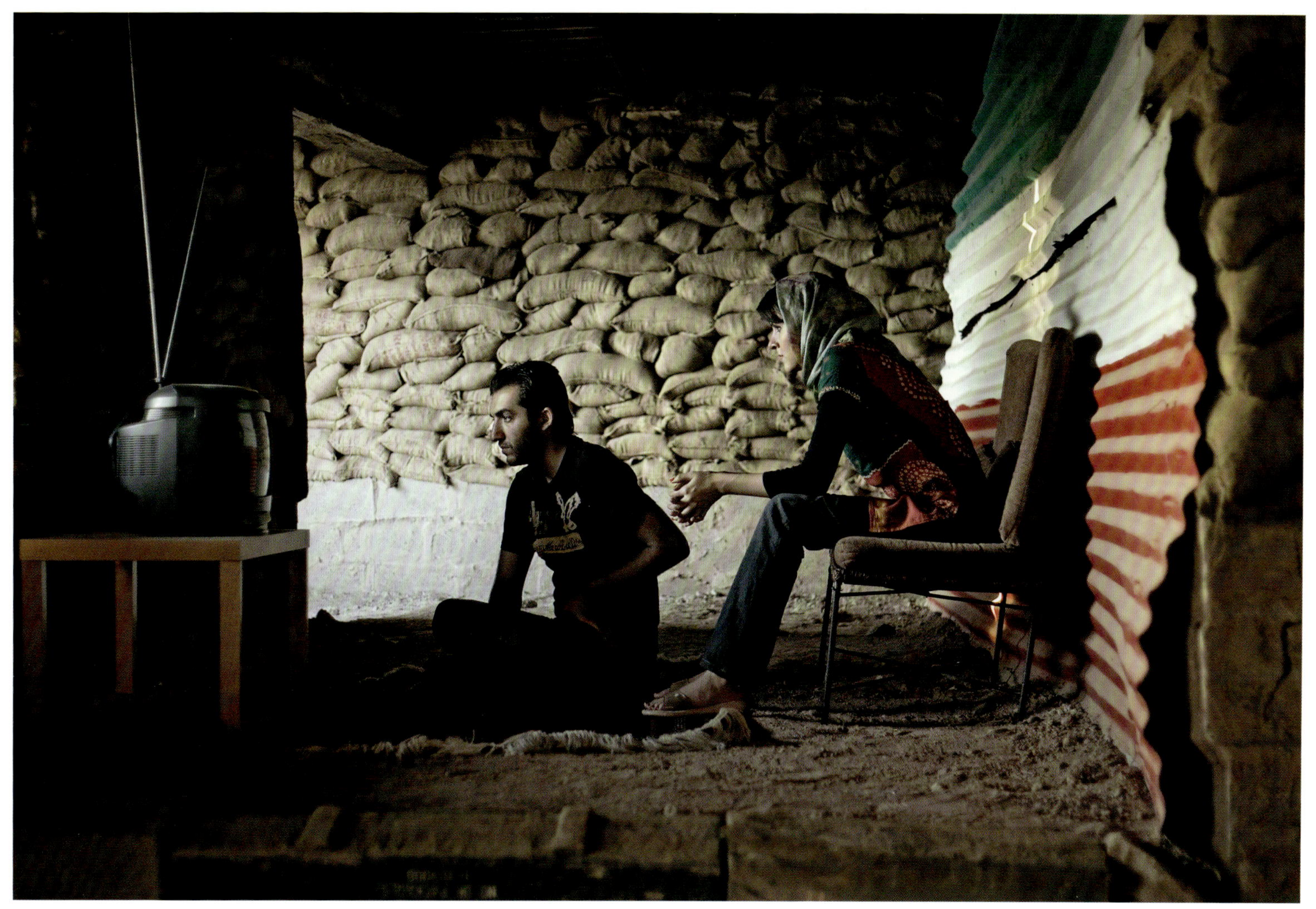

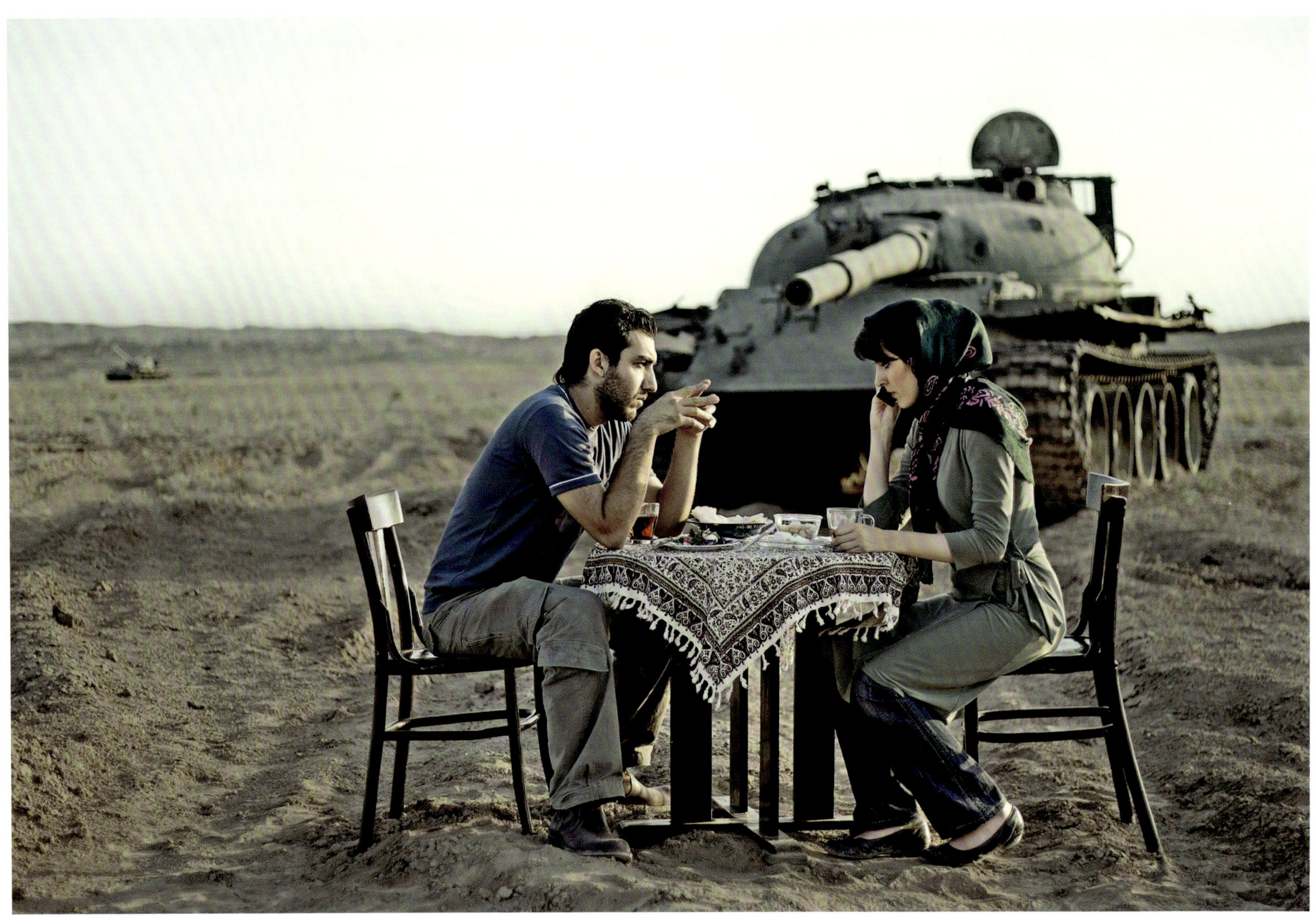

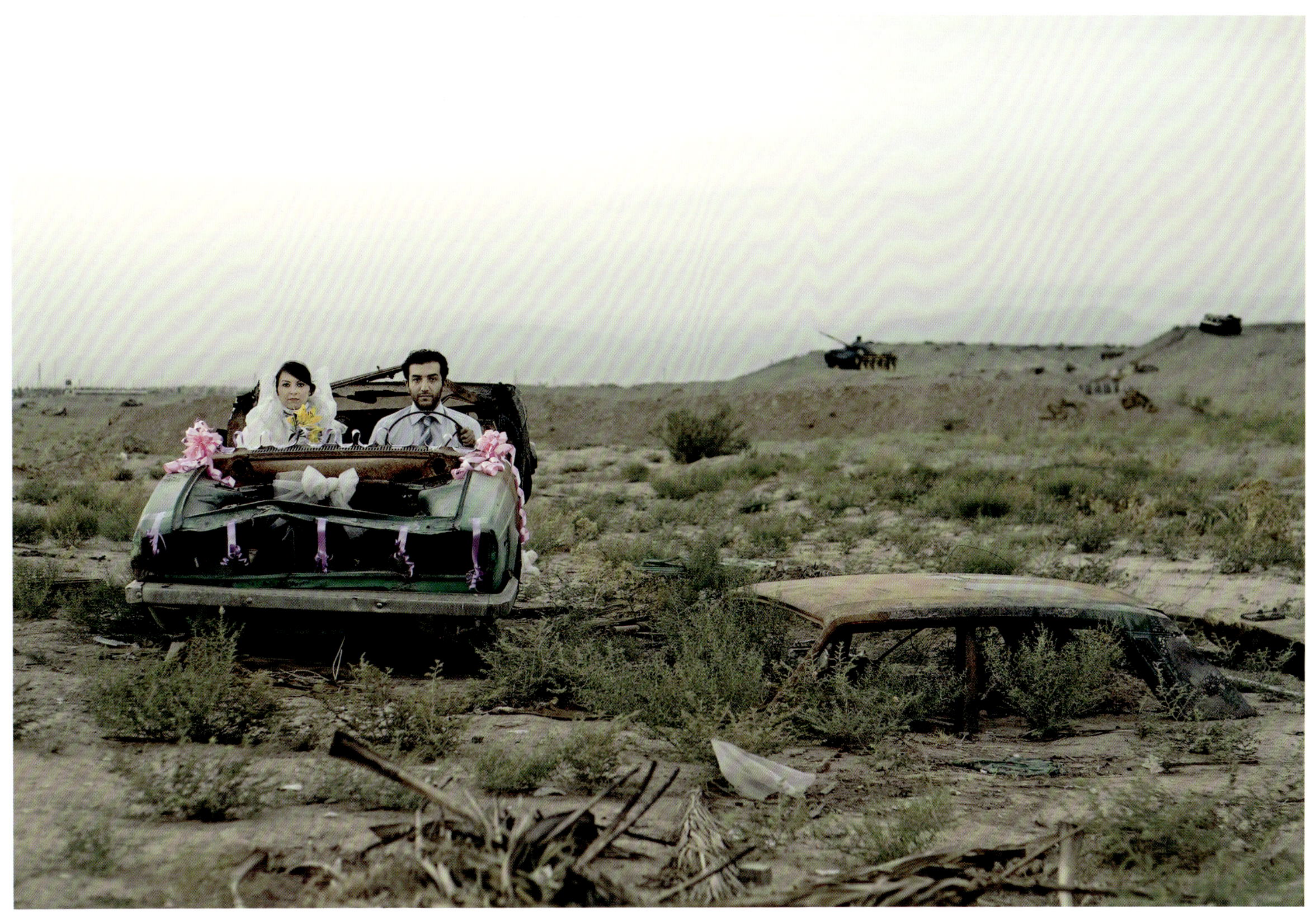

62

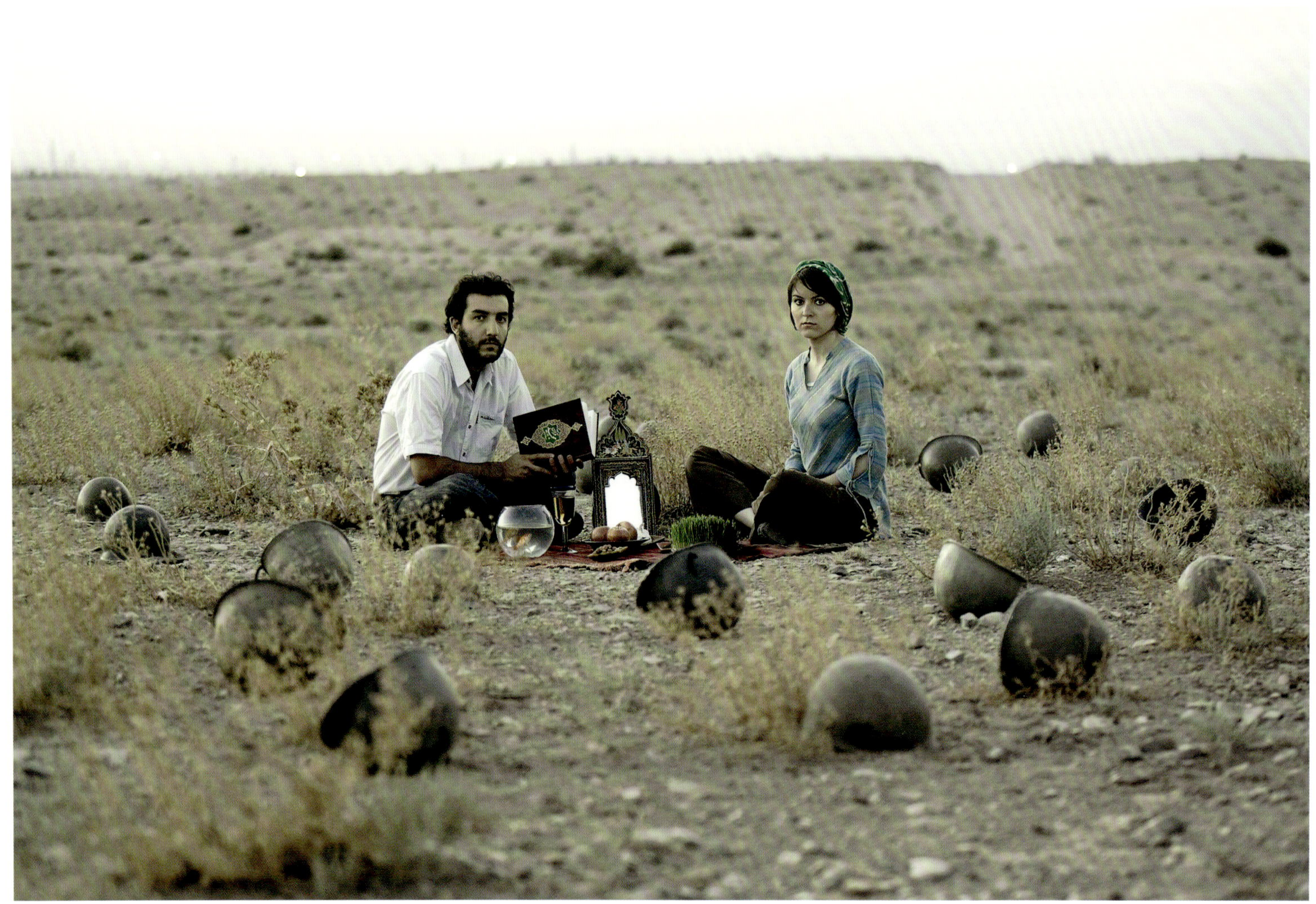

63

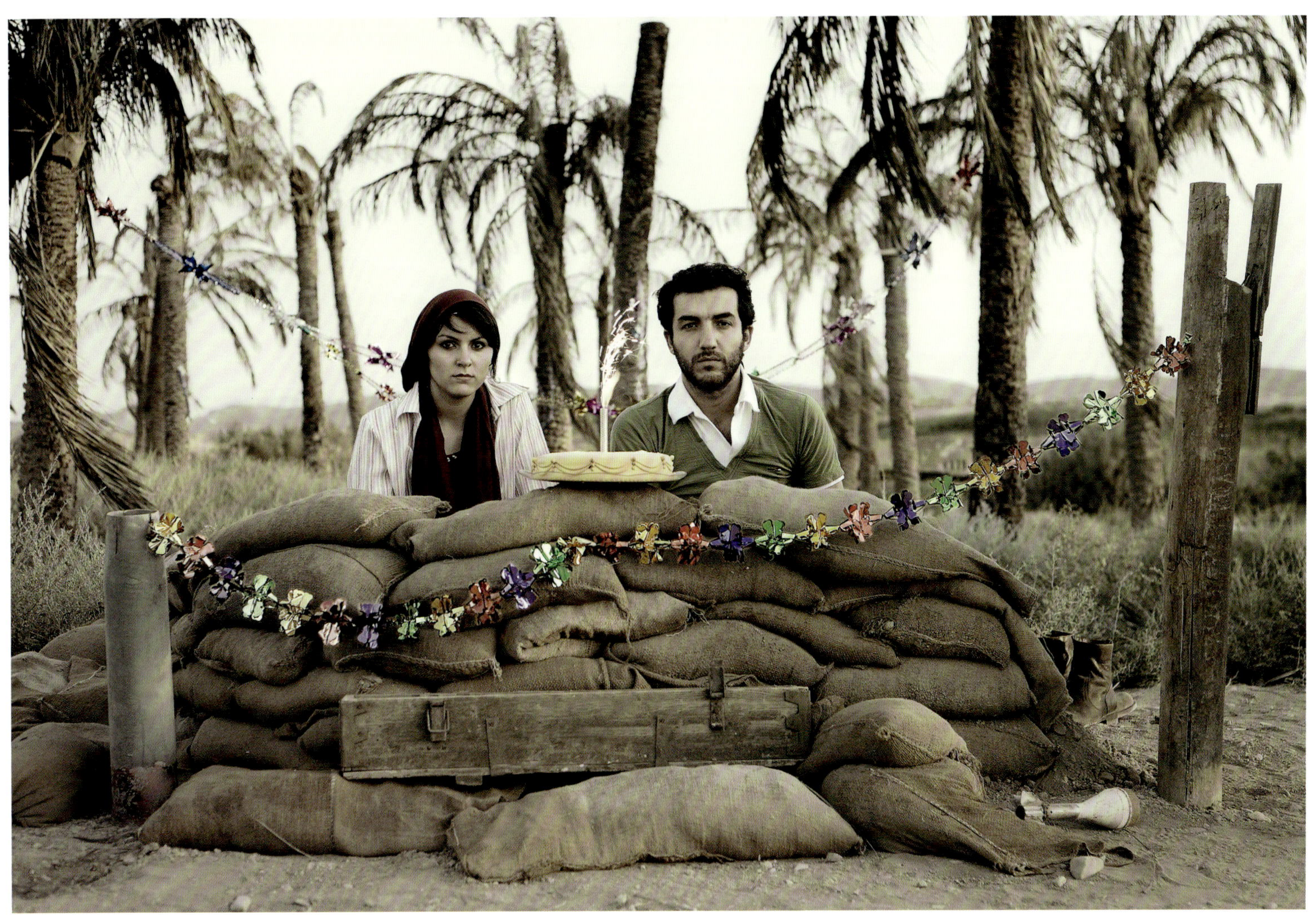

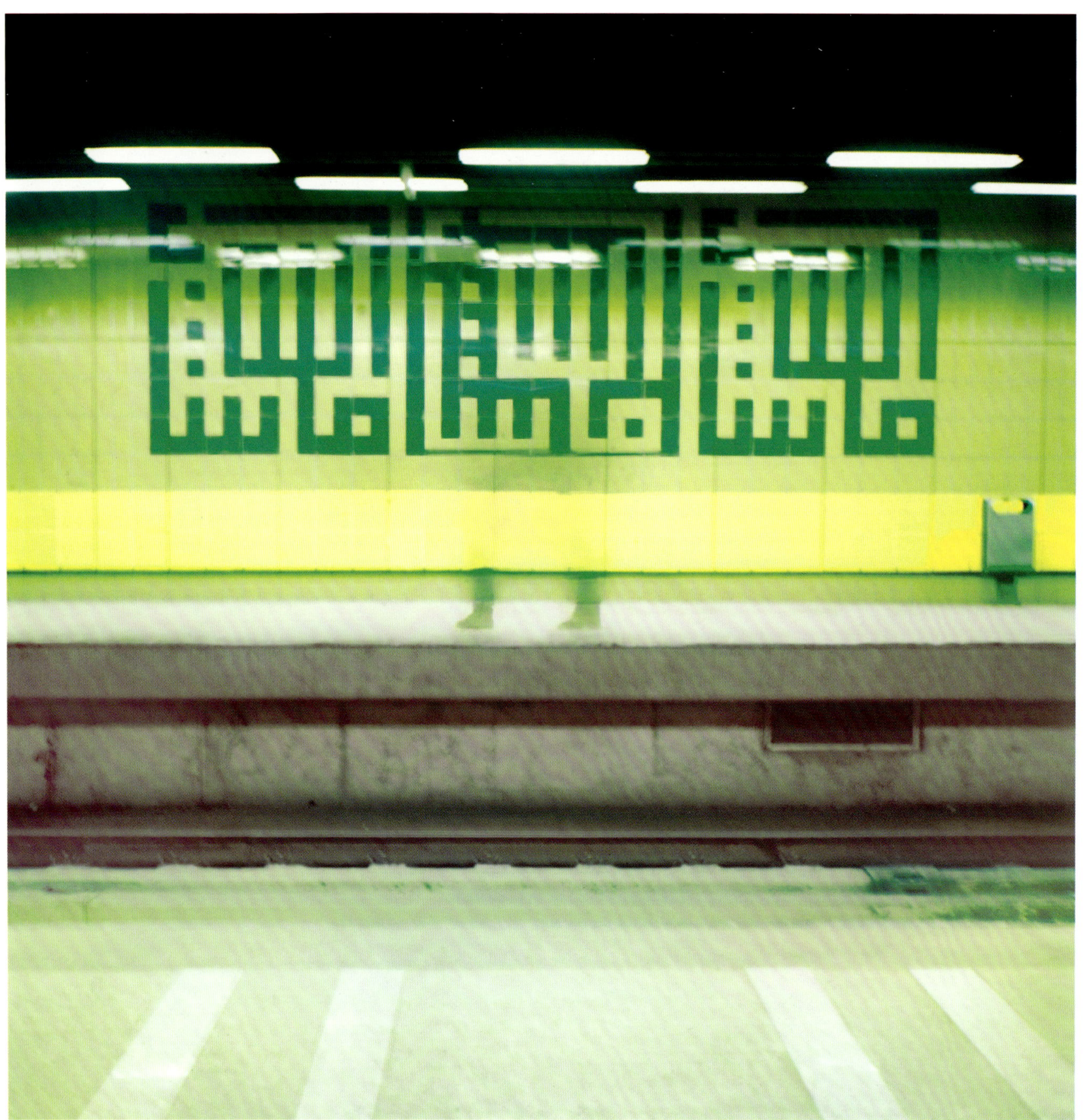
ما شاء الله ما شاء الله ما شاء الله

Rana El Nemr

The Egyptian artist Rana El Nemr was born in
1974 in Germany, and lives and works in Cairo.
She studied photojournalism, advertising, and
arts at the American University in Cairo. She was
a founding member of the Contemporary Image
Collective (CIC) in Cairo, a platform for contemporary Egyptian art and media, with a particular
interest in the social role of the photographic
image. El Nemr's photography has been exhibited widely outside Egypt in countries including
Lebanon, Switzerland, Germany, Japan, Finland,
and the United States. Her work has also been
featured in international festivals and biennales
such as PhotoCairo3 and Photoquai 2007. Her
series *The Metro* (2003) won the Grand Prix at the
Photography Biennale in Bamako, Mali, in 2005.
El Nemr was nominated for the Paul Huf Young
Photographer of the Year Award in 2007 and 2009
and the Prix Pictet in 2010. *Giza Threads* (2012)
was the subject of a solo show at the Townhouse
Gallery in Cairo in 2012.

The series *Balconies* (2003–8) documents the
brightly painted and tiled balconies of otherwise
nondescript concrete buildings in Cairo's ghettos.
El Nemr captures the ways that city dwellers make
these common architectural features of housing
complexes into a private haven. *The Olympic Garden*
(2008–10) is a provocative multimedia project
concerning the creation of a wall between the
Egyptian Olympic Center in the upper-middle-class
neighborhood of New Maadi and the poorer Arab
Al-Basateen area. She combines spoken accounts
by residents, radio recordings, and her own photographs to emphasize tensions between local
authorities and residents resulting from changes

imposed in the use of public space. The projection
of photographs is set to a cacophonous soundtrack
that captures the many conflicting voices.

The poetic series *Giza Threads* (2012) brings
together work from the first decade of this century.
These photographs present details, or "threads,"
of life in the open spaces — public and private — of
Giza, a sprawling suburb of Cairo that is home
to the Pyramids. About these "threads," El Nemr
explains, "I see long streams, which are strong,
dark, constant. . . . I find them abstract, incompre-
hensible, and flowing recklessly most of the time. I
call them *currents*. And I see finer streams, shorter
in length, and momentary in nature, but they come
in greater numbers. They carry music, warmth,
and color. I find myself collecting evidence of the
threads' existence, and of their occasional displacement and replacement."

El Nemr's series of photographs taken in
the Cairo subway, *The Metro*, records the rapid
changes being experienced by middle-class
urban Egyptians. She describes how the strang-
ers united in this public space are "vulnerable to
cycles of depression, indifference, and religious
intolerance — illnesses that are both caused by,
and transmitted to, the rest of Egyptian and Arab
society and the world." About her process — whose
subjects are unaware that they are being photographed — she says, "I try to capture the riders'
response to the urban underground, the train, the

station, and its vibrant ceramic designs. Riders become figures defined by form, line, and color in the midst of a congested modernity in which they no longer have a sense of place."

Selected here are images of women featured in the series, which represents both genders. *Metro #22* introduces the bright yellow and green palette of the Cairene metro. In the center of the image, the ghostly trace of two figures on the far platform combined with reflected light evokes the train's recent and transitory presence. In another photograph (#16), a woman in a blue skirt walks along the wall, her figure breaking up the repeating geometric patterns that cover the architectural surfaces. In front of the woman is an advertisement, which recurs in other works in the series, that shows a woman singing into her telephone. A sticker has been placed over her mouth, leaving her voiceless. The woman walking on the seemingly empty subway platform conveys the solitude of the underground, while the poster, surrounded by a windowlike frame, evokes the outside world.

The first car of the Cairene subway is reserved for women and children, though they are free to travel in the other cars if they wish. El Nemr's subjects in this car all seem to be traveling alone. In one image, natural light illuminates the cheek of a young woman who clutches her bag, with a carefully tied package on the other side of her (plate 67). In another, the mouth of a woman wearing lipstick is echoed by a red shape on her headscarf, which also resembles a heart shape created by a reflection in the window (plate 68).

Two other photographs in the series each juxtapose two travelers. In one, a woman wearing a dark headscarf and red sweater sits in a subway seat and appears to look intensely in the same direction as a woman reflected in the window to her right, who also wears a red sweater, but no headscarf (plate 69). The color consonance is picked up in a rectangular element of the sign on the wall of the subway car above and between the figures. In another low-angle shot, one woman wearing a white *abaya* is contrasted with another wearing a leather jacket and no headscarf (plate 70). The two women face in opposite directions, each in her own world—one looking inward with her face buried in her hand, and the other looking out at something beyond the frame of the photograph. The subway windows and door create another form of tension between inside and out.

A view of the blue-and-white exterior of the women's car shows two subway riders within, seen from the back (plate 71). The pairing of their black-and-white *abayas*, each framed by a window of the closed subway doors, demonstrates El Nemr's eye for graceful, asymmetrically balanced compositions.

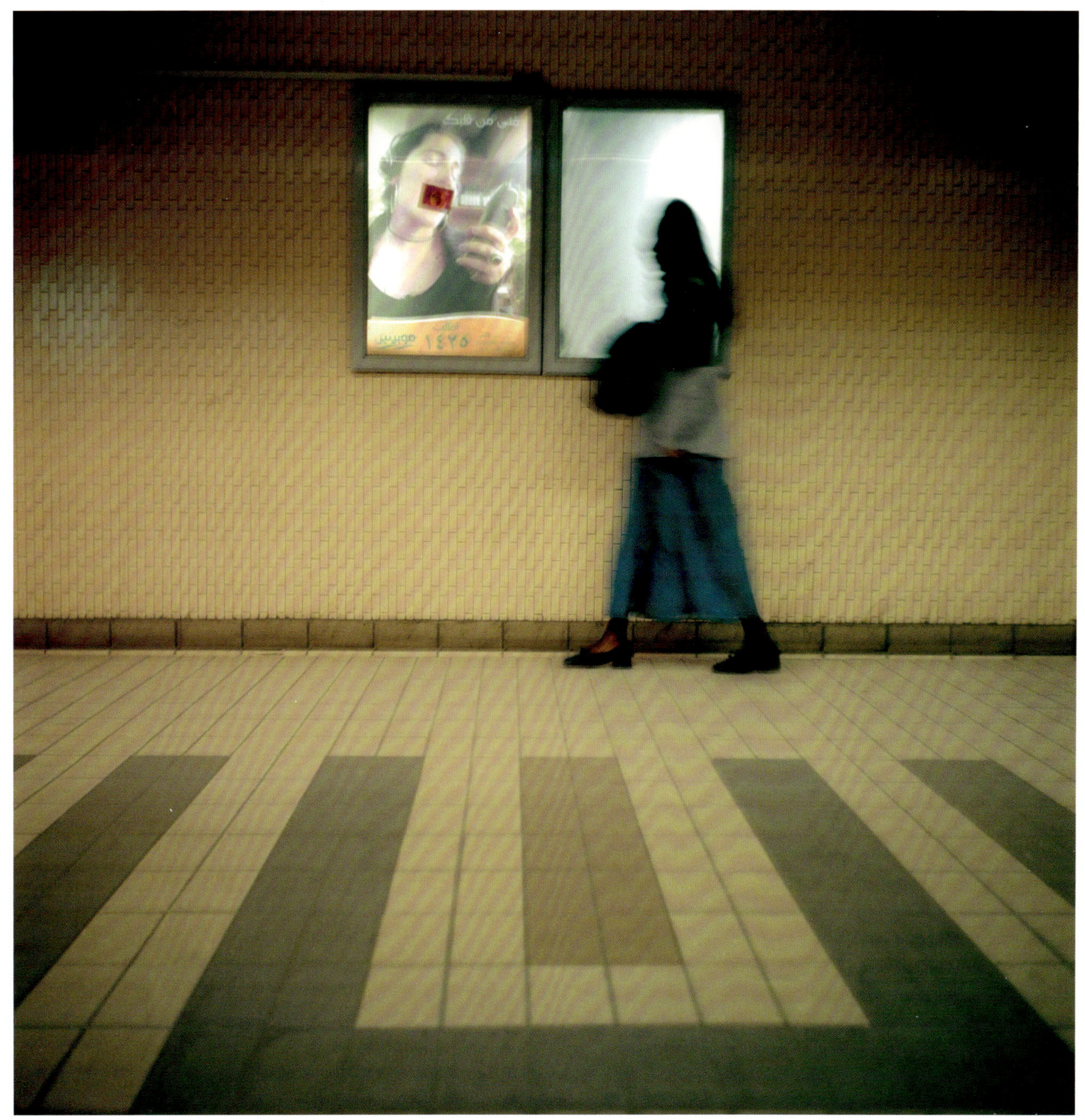

66

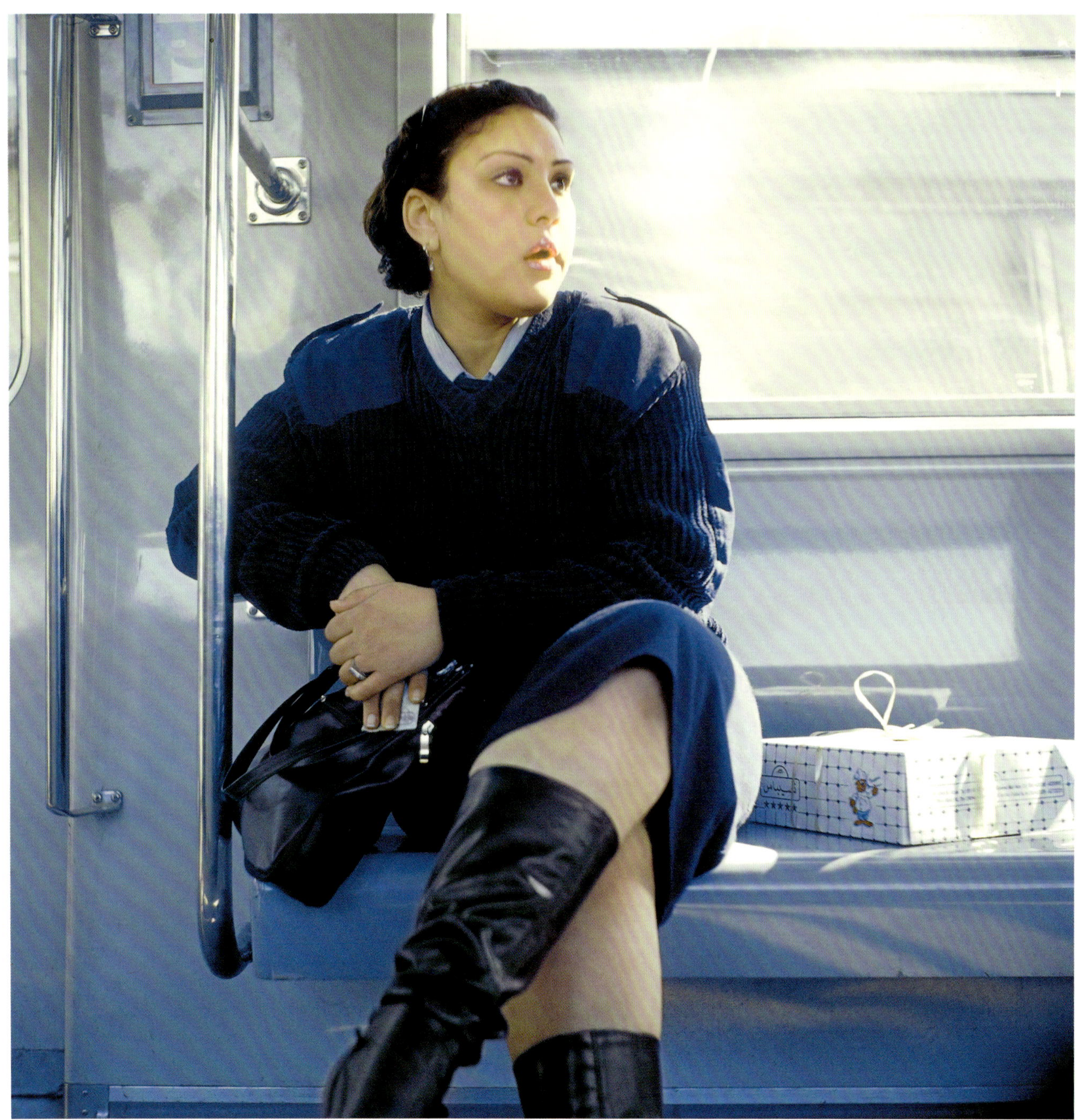

لبـاس

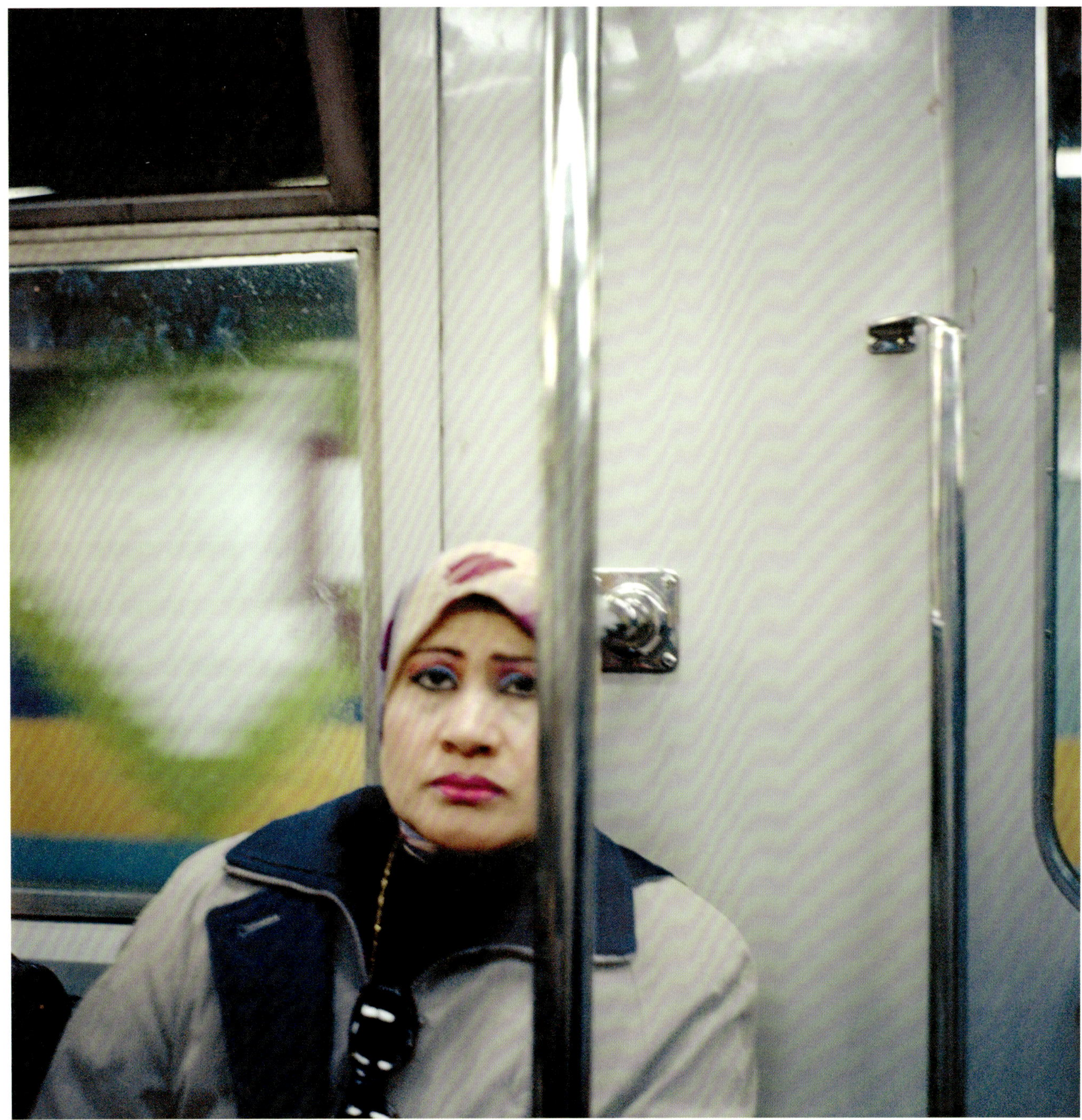
68

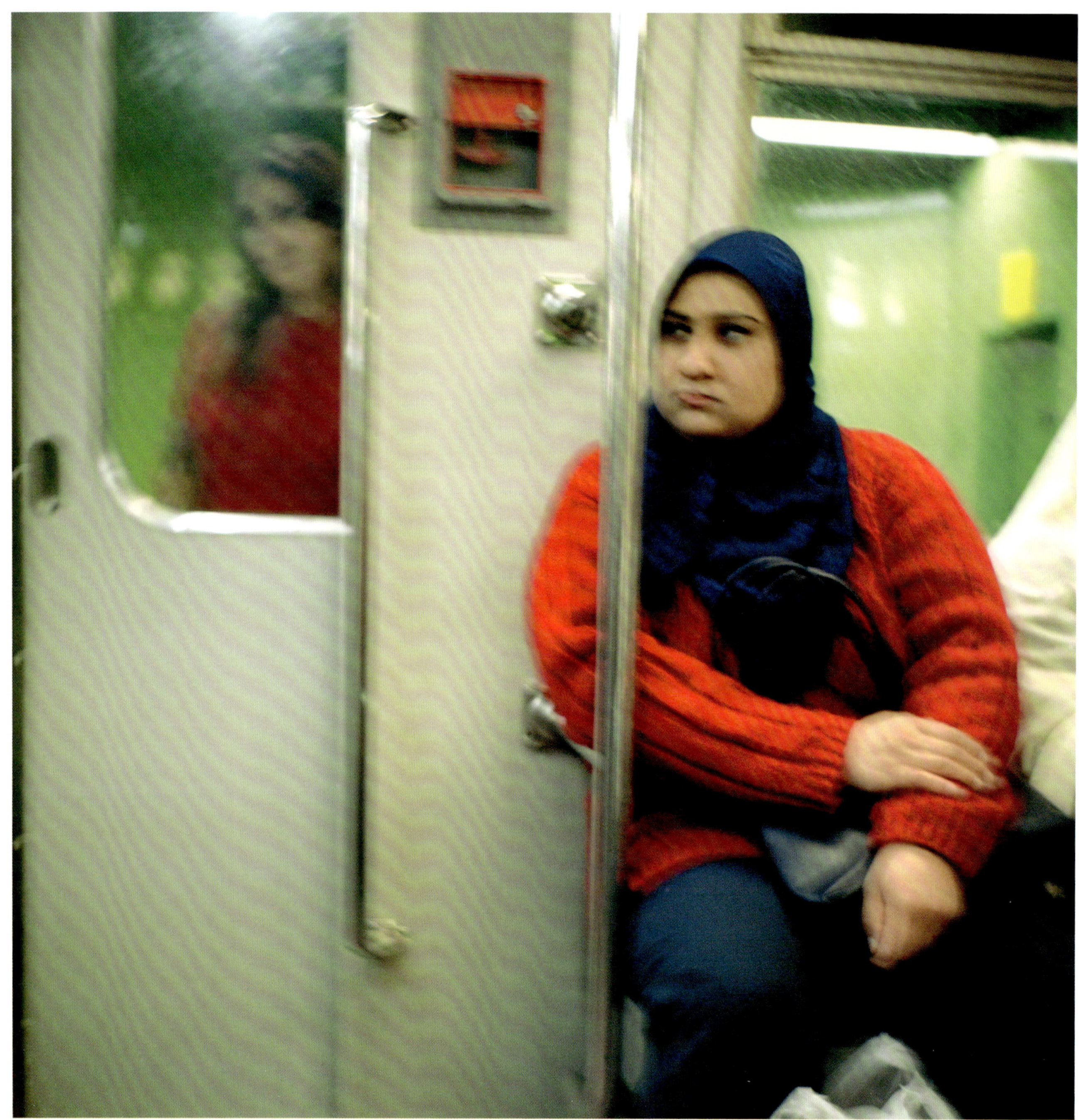

69

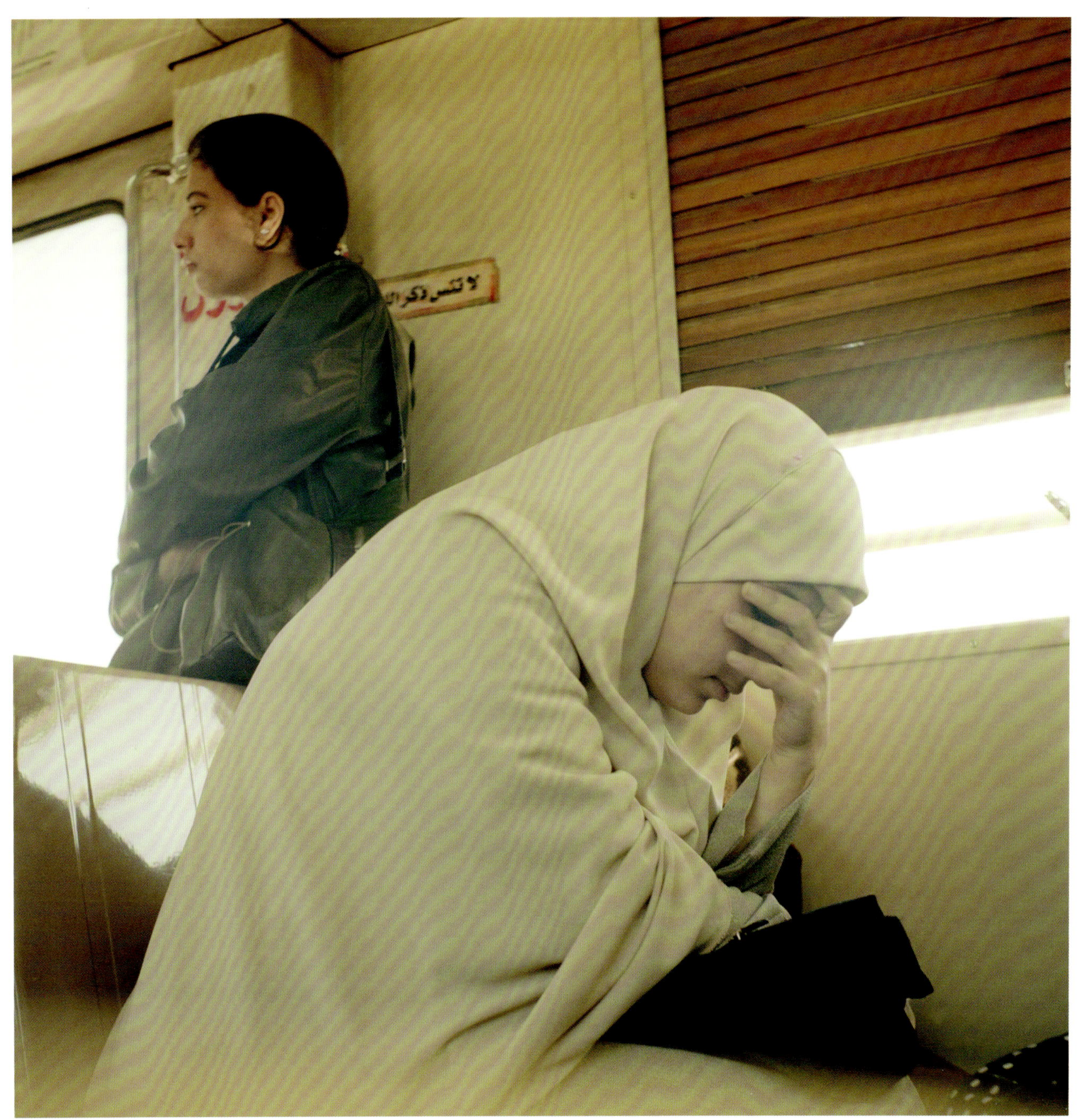

70

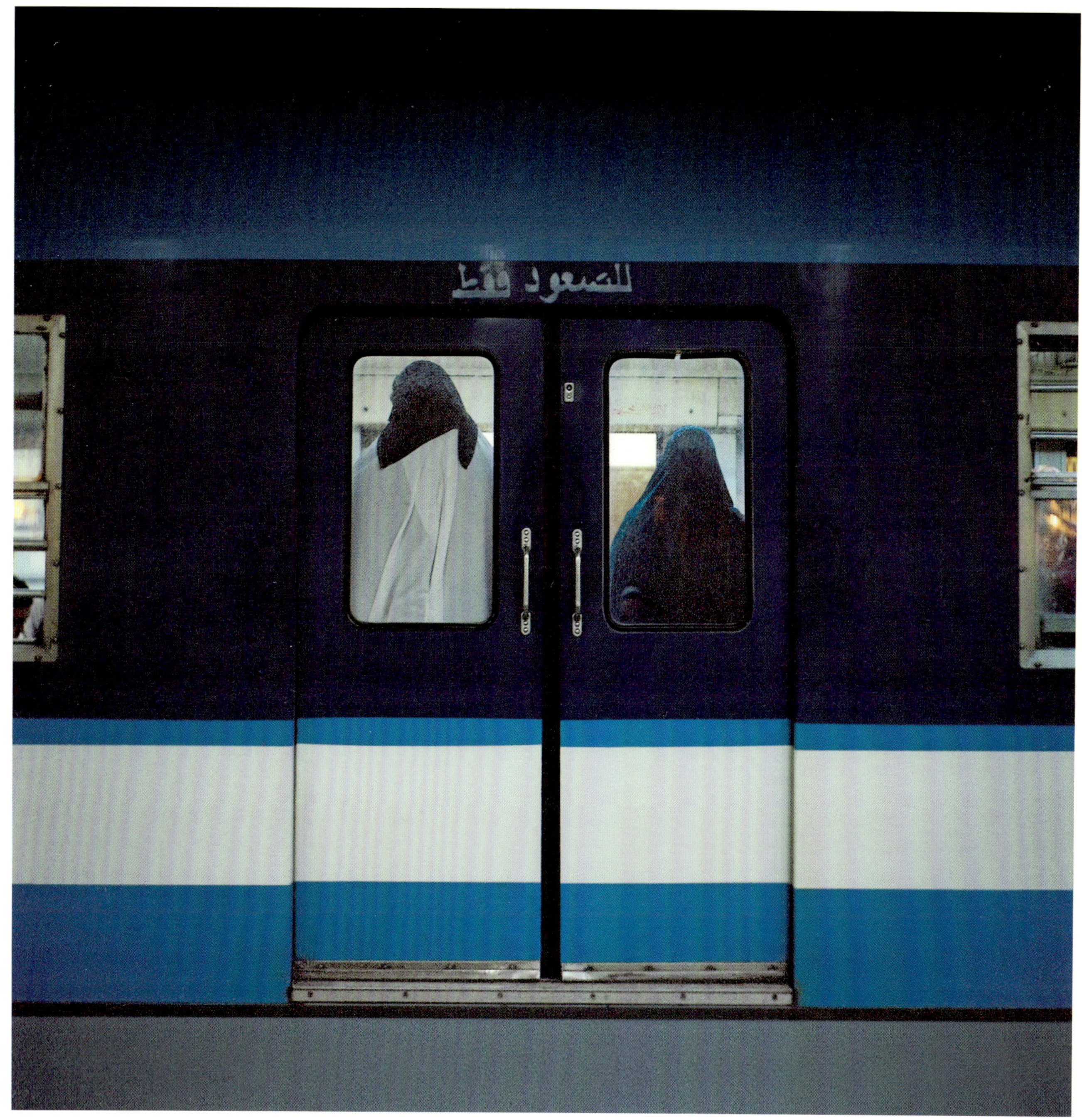

71

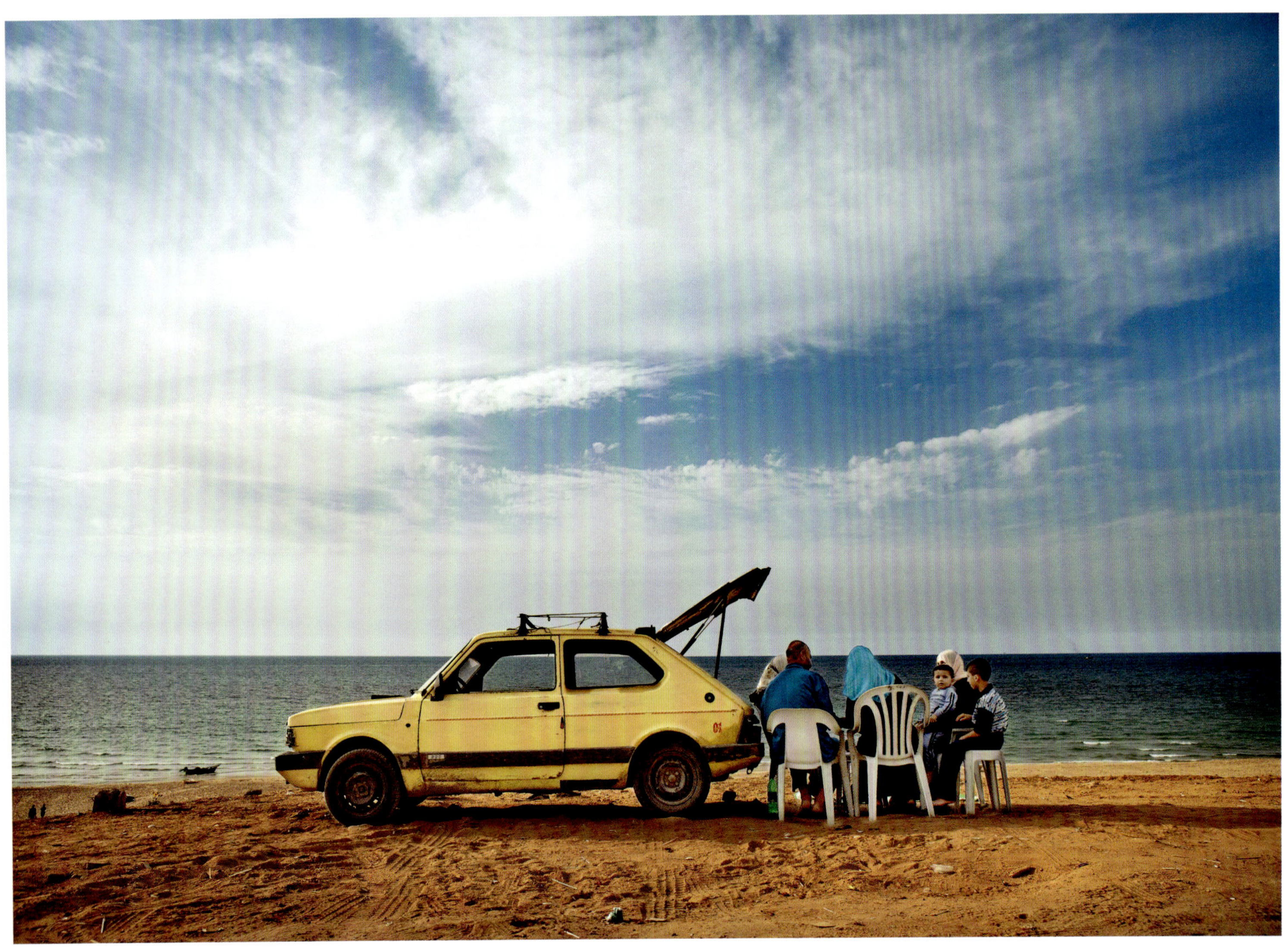

Tanya Habjouqa

The Jerusalem-based Tanya Habjouqa was born
in Amman, Jordan, in 1975 and educated in the
United States. Her early career began in Texas,
where she photographed Mexican migrant
communities and the results of urban poverty. She
then moved back to the Middle East, where she
now documents everyday life and social issues
throughout the Levant, a region that includes
Syria, Lebanon, Jordan, and Palestine, as well as
sections of Iraq and the Sinai Peninsula. Habjouqa
is a founding member of the photography collective
Rawiya. Her work has gained attention through
the exhibition *Women on the Verge* at the Empty
Quarter Gallery in Dubai (2012) and Photoquai 2013
in Paris. She has received many awards, including
the Clarion Award in 2007 and the SND Silver
Award in 2011 as well as a Magnum Foundation
Emergency Fund Grant in 2013.

*Jerusalem in Heels: Transsexuals of the Holy
Land* (2005–6) expresses the political and social
defiance of Palestinians and Israelis in photographs of Jerusalem's colorful "drag queens."
Another series, *Fragile Monsters: Arab Body
Building* (2009), focuses on the emotional side of
Arab body builders. Habjouqa's *Women of Gaza*
(2009) describes aspects of women's daily life at
a time of intense media attention to their rights in
Palestine under Hamas. The series *Wives of the
Syrian Revolution* (2012) comprises intimate photographs of Syrian women and children as refugees
in Jordan, constantly awaiting phone calls from
the men in their families.

Habjouqa's ongoing project *Occupied
Pleasures* (begun in 2009) describes moments of
respite for Palestinians coping with the limited
freedom of movement imposed by the Israeli
occupation of the Palestinian Territories. *Ladies
Who Rally* (2011) offers fascinating coverage of the
little-known story of female race-car drivers in
the Middle East. *Khan Ahmar: Bedouin Code* (2012)
reveals the vulnerability of a once-powerful culture, as a Palestinian Bedouin community battles
against the demolition of their homes and forced
eviction.

The twenty photographs in *Women of Gaza*
are not images typically associated with the
siege of Hamas in Gaza in 2009. Habjouqa's exploration of women's lives, taken throughout Gaza
over a period of two months, refute the chronic
misrepresentation of the Middle East, especially
its women. Although most women initially resisted
having their photographs taken, Habjouqa gained
their trust and was able to produce some of her
most powerful and poignant images of the plight
of the coastal community of Gaza as its residents
struggle to normalize life within the conditions
of oppression.

One of the untitled images shows a typical
scene in Gaza — a family car parked on the beach
for an informal get-together by the sea (plate 72).
The people of Gaza have little space in their living
quarters, and their freedom is limited, but they do

72–77. From *Women of Gaza* series, 2009
Each: 50.8 x 76.2 cm (20 x 30 in.)

have access to the large public expanses of the seashore. In another powerful portrait, a student wearing a *niqab* waits on a bench, holding a black bag with a small teddy bear hanging from it (plate 73). By capturing these humanizing details of fully covered women, Habjouqa challenges her own resentment of the rise of the *niqab*.

The photograph of an exercise class shows the limited public and private space available to women (plate 74). Three women, wearing long black garments and lighter-colored headscarves, turn away from the camera in their exercise routine, their feet remaining firmly planted on the floor. Their immobilized feet could be a metaphor for the limited freedom of movement in Gaza. The basketball court in which they exercise was provided by a women's organization concerned that there is no other dedicated place for such activities for women.

Another example from the series shows an educated young woman that the photographer met at the local university, swinging through the air at her uncle's farm (plate 75). She cannot go anywhere other than in her mind or on a private swing, yet she embraces the moment of pleasure and the sensation of freedom. In another photograph conveying young women's excitement, white *hijab*s frame the giddiness on the faces of schoolgirls on a motorboat from which a Palestinian flag flutters (plate 76). Palestinians can go six or seven nautical miles into the Mediterranean before reaching Israeli-restricted territories, and they embrace activities such as this five-minute ride on a class trip from a government school.

In a lively portrait, a university literature student is intent on photographing Habjouqa (plate 77). Her broad smile, bright red *hijab*, and pink phone against the rich greenery and red flowers contrast the discreet figure wearing a *niqab* in the background of the photograph. The vibrancy of the red-scarved young woman contradicts the stereotype of repressed women, and Palestinians in general, in Gaza. Habjouqa describes this young woman, an example of prosperous educated young women who face limited possibilities after graduating from college, as breathless with excitement about meeting someone from outside Gaza.

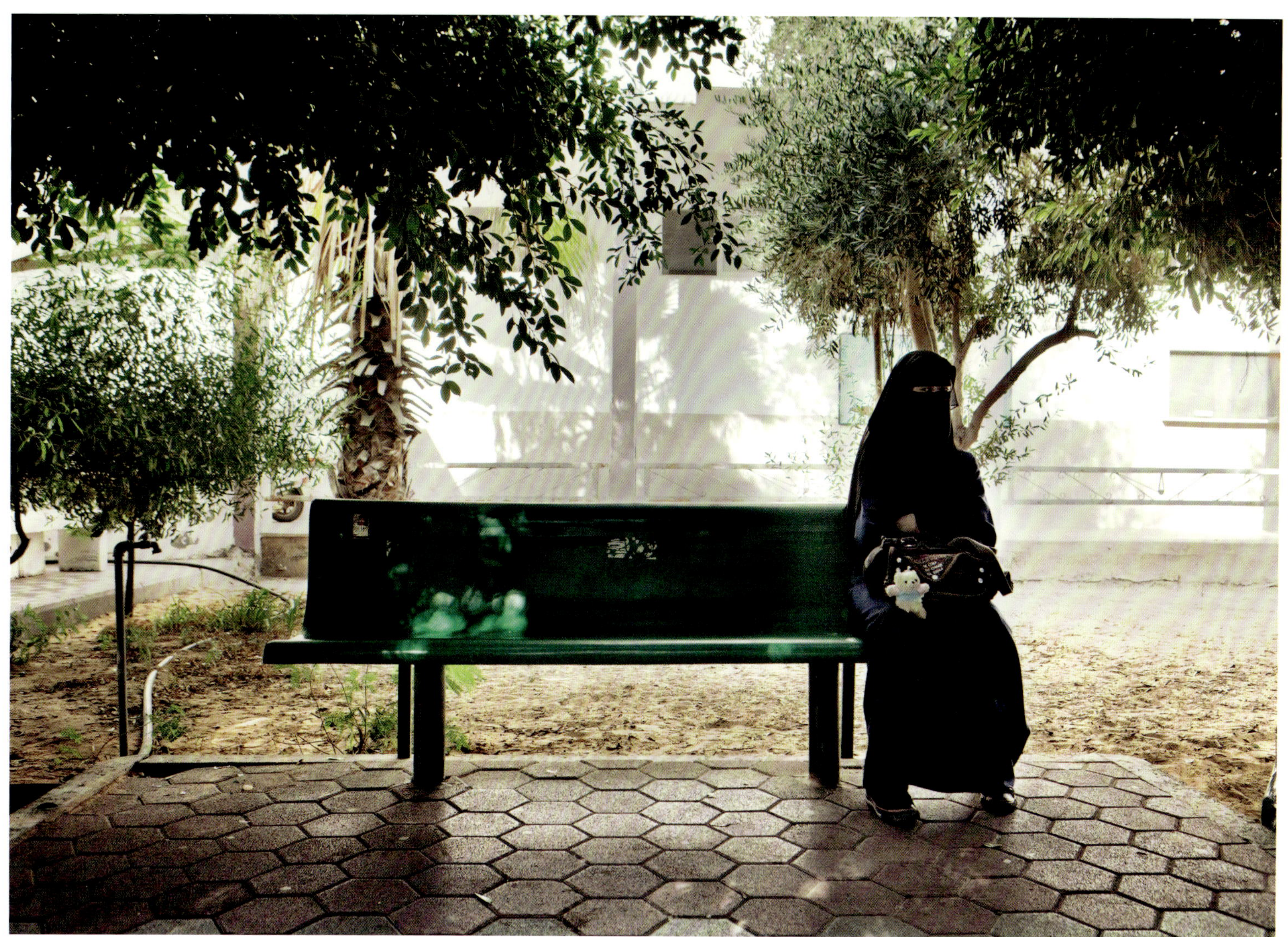

73

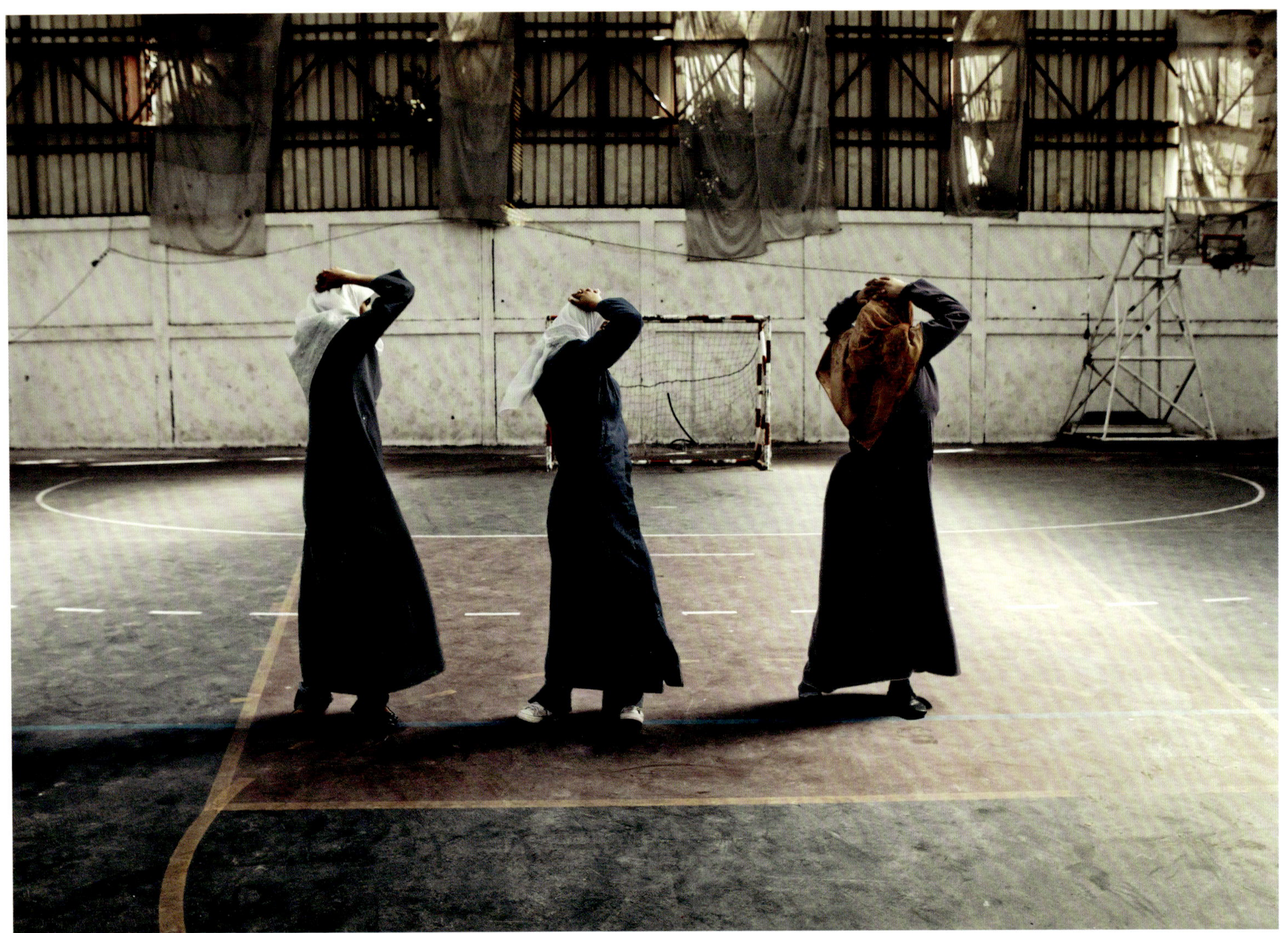

74

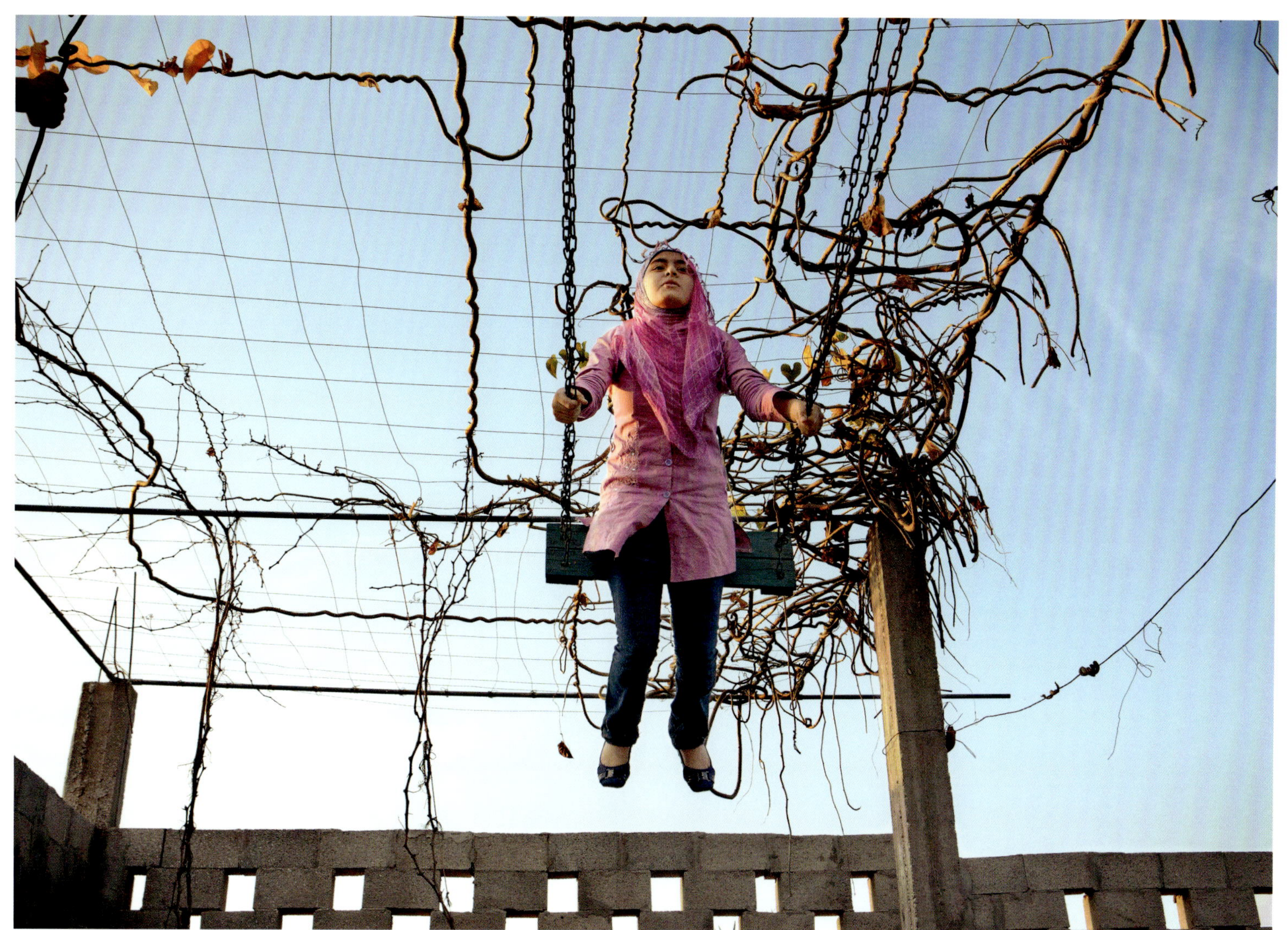

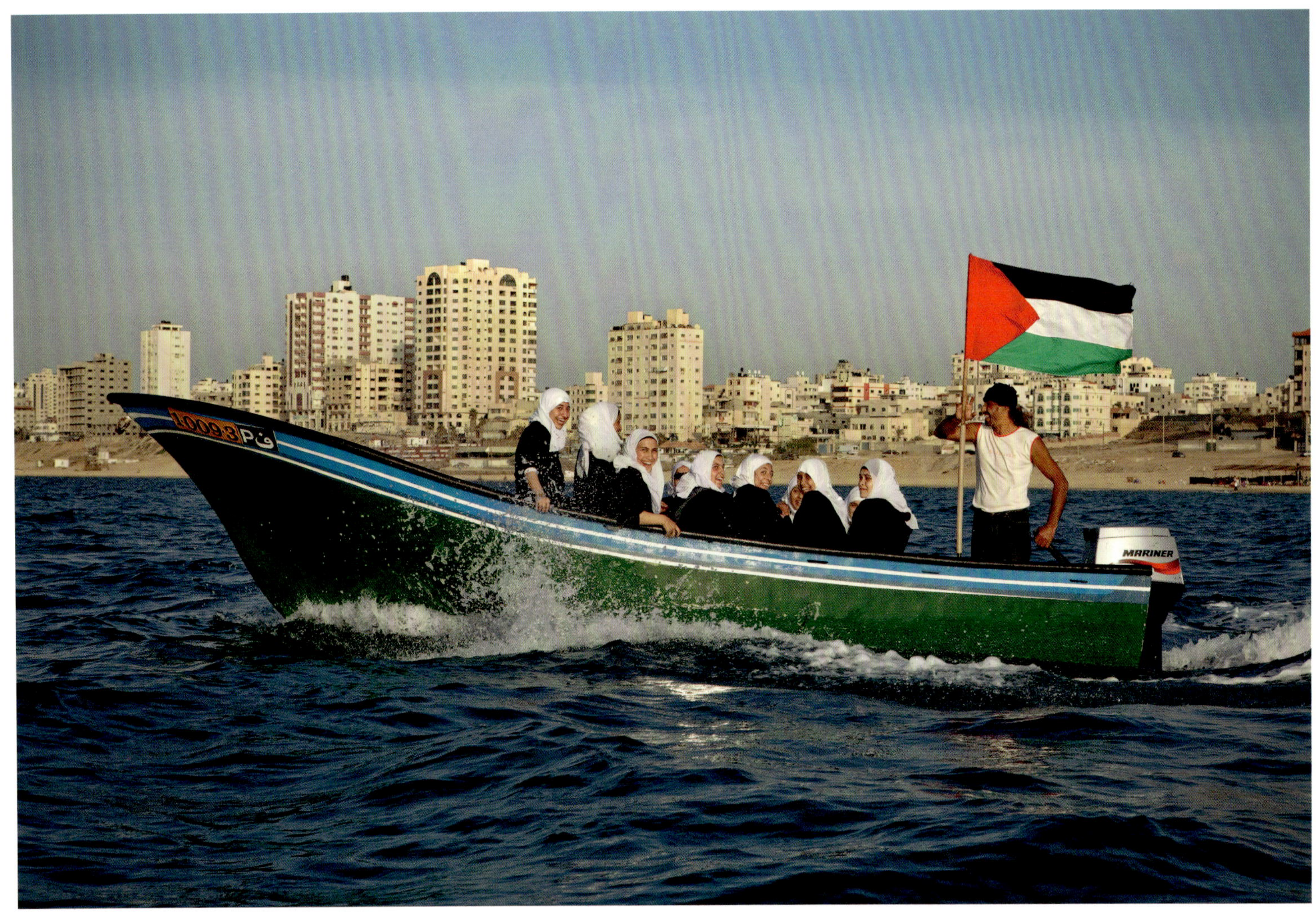

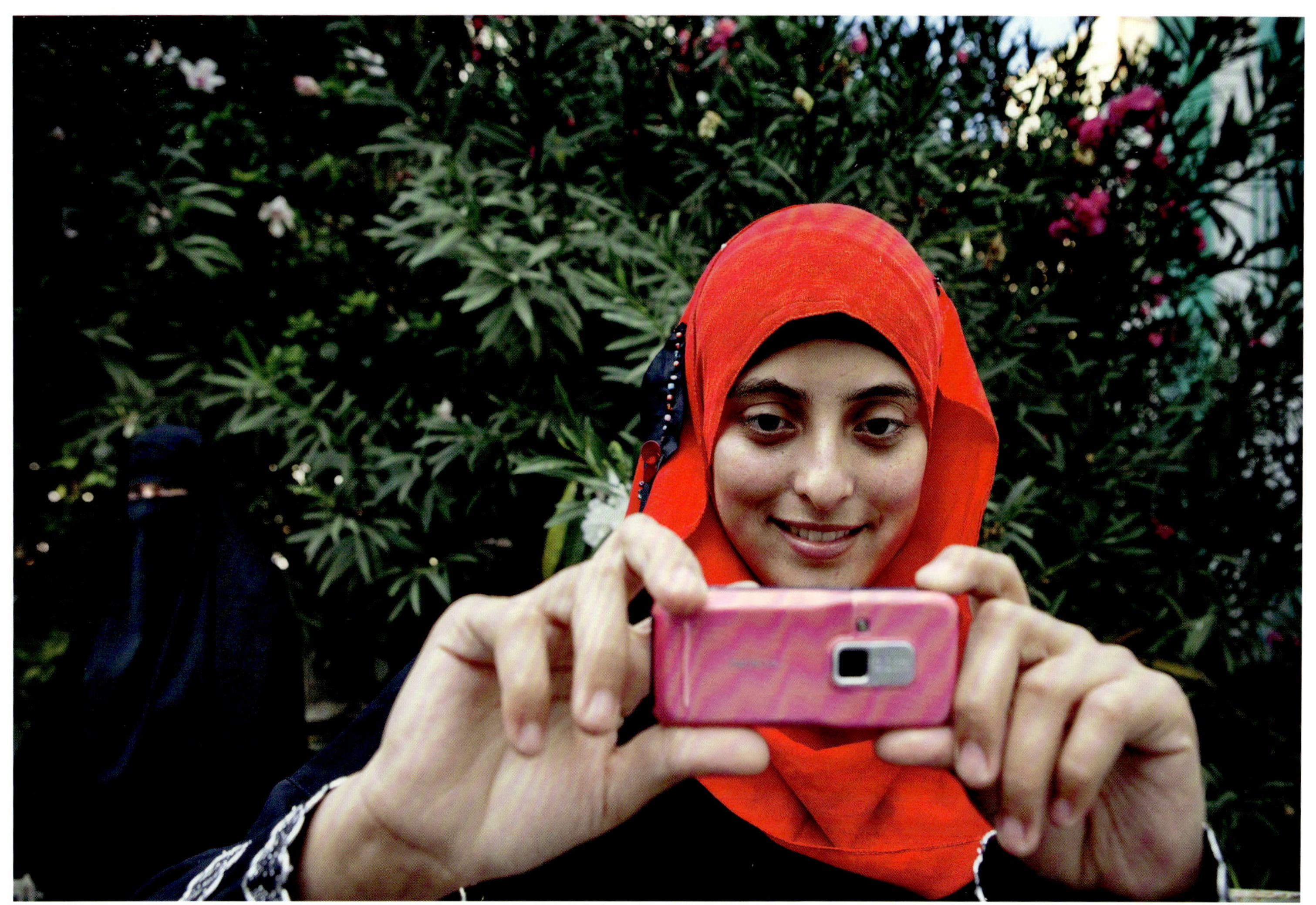

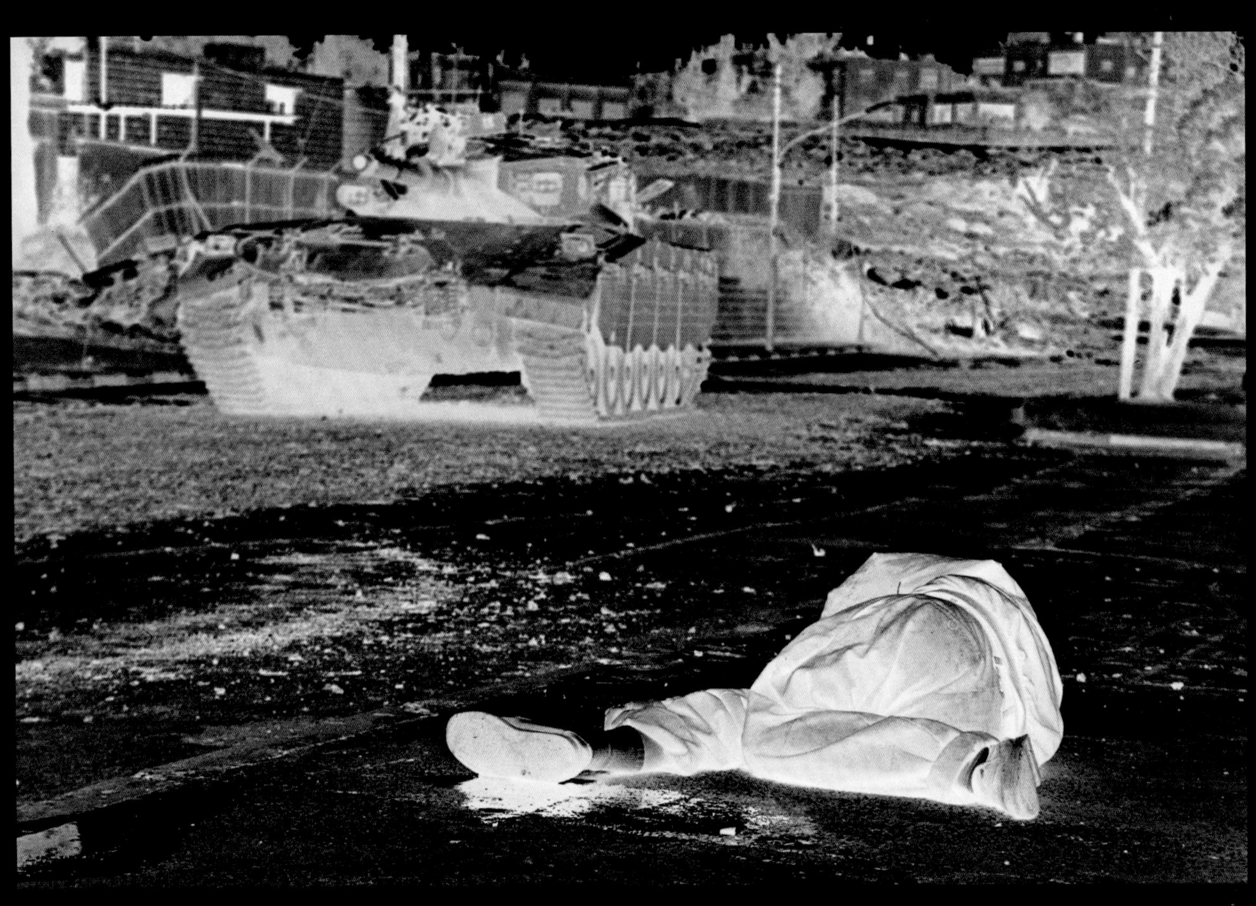

Rula Halawani

Rula Halawani was born in 1964 into a Palestinian family in the Mount of Olives district of East Jerusalem, and now lives and works where she grew up. She began studying photography as an undergraduate at the University of Saskatchewan, Canada, and pursued graduate work in photographic studies at the University of Westminster in the United Kingdom. After receiving a Master of Fine Arts, she returned to Palestine and began her early career as a photojournalist with the Reuters press agency. After covering a number of tragic events, including the death of a young Palestinian boy she knew, she left press photography. She was trained, according to the mission of Western photojournalism, to "get the picture," but, as she explained, "the relationship to what I was shooting was different. . . . The picture was not a separate thing or event to document. The pictures . . . were part of me, and I was part of them." Halawani became an independent photographer focusing on Palestinians, and went on to found the first photography program at Palestine's Birzeit University, where she is both a professor and program director. Her work has been exhibited widely, including in Amman, Jordan (2006); at the 12th Istanbul Biennial in 2011; in a large solo exhibition in 2008 at Le Botanique in Brussels, Belgium; and in London (2012 and 2013).

Upon leaving photojournalism, one of Halawani's first projects was *Negative Incursions*, a series of large-format photographs printed as negatives that she shot during the Israeli incursion into the West Bank in late March 2002. Following *Negative Incursions* came *Intimacy*, twenty-five close-ups of human hands at the Qalandia checkpoint between Ramallah and Jerusalem that

Palestinians pass through daily as they commute to and from work. The images of hands and identification cards passed between Palestinians and Israeli soldiers are impersonal, suggesting anonymity as well as the weight of living in occupied territories.

The prints that compose *The Wall* (2006) are extremely large, physically conveying the oppressiveness felt by Palestinians at the border between Israel and the Palestinian Territories. *Lifta* (2008) is a series of photographs of a "ghost city," the remaining ruins of one of the few Palestinian villages that was not fully demolished during the occupation. For *Presence and Impressions* (2009) Halawani prints enlargements of archival photographs of Palestinian villages before 1948, the year the state of Israel was created. She juxtaposes the enlargements with photographs she has taken of the sites recently, showing differences in the landscape that are striking, powerful, and disturbing. The series *Traces* (2012) features objects that Palestinians took from their homes when they were expelled in 1948 and which they now display in their current residences: keys, photographs, clothes they were wearing at the time, and other memorabilia. The projection series, *Testimonies* (2012), shows photographs of Palestinians who have died since 1948, which Halawani compares with her own conflicted personal history with

Israel: she was cured of a dermatological prob-
lem at a hospital run by her country's oppressor,
through the ironically named phototherapy.

The twenty-three photographs in *Negative
Incursions* were taken during a one-month period
during and after "Operation Defensive Shield," the
Israeli incursion into the West Bank in 2002 at
the time of the second Palestinian Intifada. In these
intense, surreal images printed large, and as negatives, Halawani has captured displaced persons,
destroyed homes, grieving mothers, and families
in the rubble of the aftermath. She describes her
purposes beyond the straightforward documentation of historical events: "As negatives, they
express the negation of our reality that the invasion
represented." In addition to the imposed darkness
of the negatives, each photograph has a thick black
border around it that refers to a television screen,
expressing Halawani's conviction about the
underrepresentation of the Palestinian plight in
the media.

Leaving the images to speak for themselves,
Halawani labels the photographs *Untitled*. *Untitled I*
presents the force and aggressiveness of a tank
charging into the city toward the photographer,
and hence toward the viewer. The position of the
left hand of the soldier aboard the tank echoes
that of Yasser Arafat, the Palestinian leader at
the time, in a freestanding poster to the left. The
delicate harmony of the two sets of hands visually
connects the opposing forces, adding tension to
the photograph. Like the poster of Arafat here,
those of a martyr in *Untitled XVII* appear almost like
television screens, another reference to media
attention, or lack thereof.

Untitled XIII is a haunting depiction of a woman
whose daughter had been shot dead in front of
her eyes, moments before her home was demolished. She extends her arms out as she shows
her daughter's fourth-year university schoolbooks.
The curtain of the window in the only standing
wall of her home seems to blow gently behind her,
while the foreground is a chaos of rubble and
wire cables. Grief also pervades *Untitled X*, where
three figures sit in the ruins of the their homes.
The self-containment of the woman on the left
contrasts with the gesture of the woman across
from her, who rests her head on her hand.

Untitled VI and *Untitled XIX* present comple-
mentary perspectives, literally from the ground. In
Untitled VI, the viewer is brought close to the people
who have been evacuated from a glass building
doomed to destruction and have dropped to the
ground with their hands clasped at the back of their
necks; their heads and the tank wheels are too
close, and similar in shape, for comfort. Viewed in
negative, the shards of glass on which they lie
resemble the rippling surface of water. *Untitled XIX*
was shot from the base of a huge pile of debris
with a figure standing on top. The negative creates
light passages among the ruins that evoke volcanic
fire, perhaps a metaphor for the region's underly-
ing conflicts.

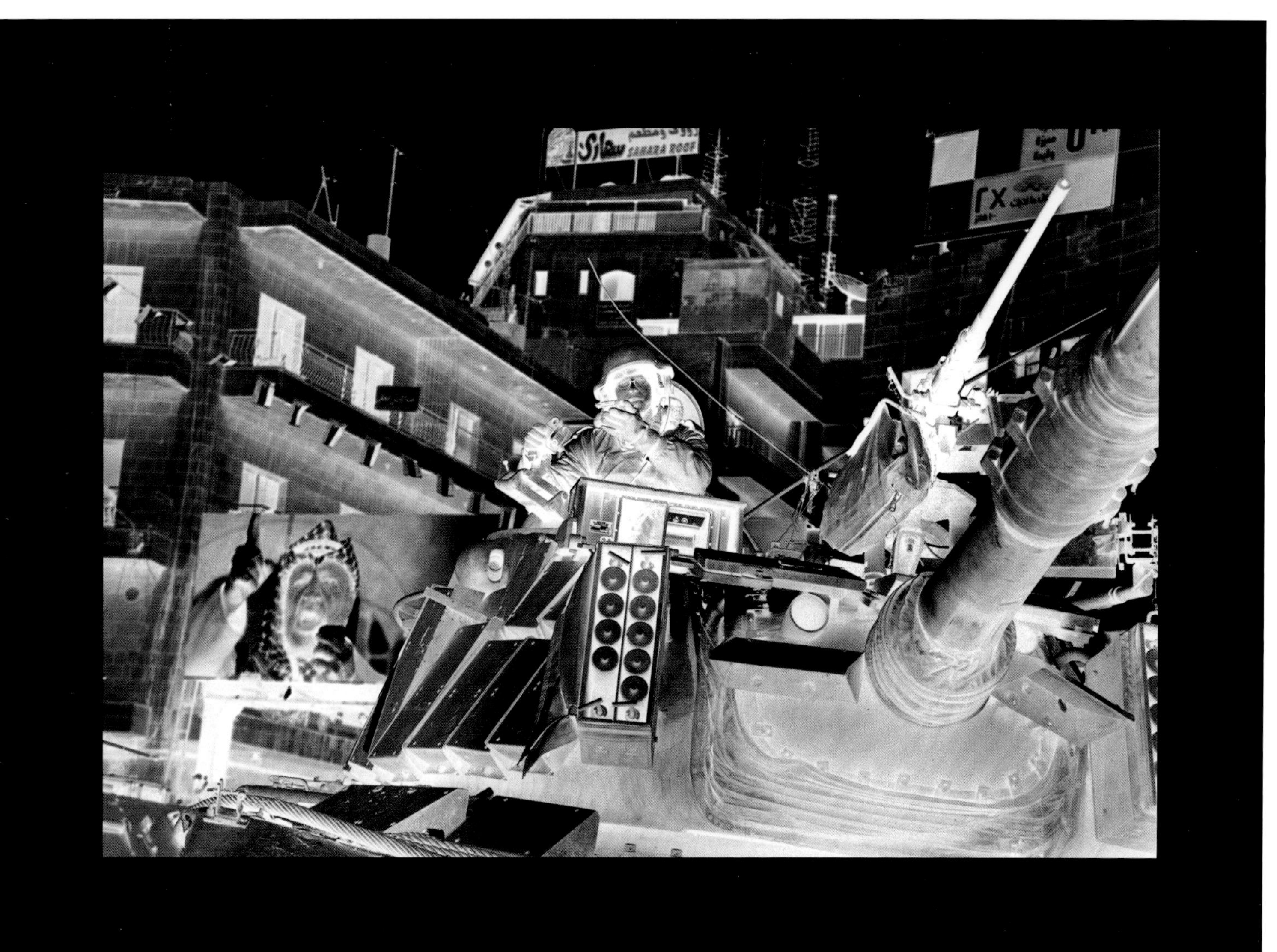

79. *Untitled I*, 2002
From *Negative Incursions* series
90 x 124 cm (about 35 x 49 in.)

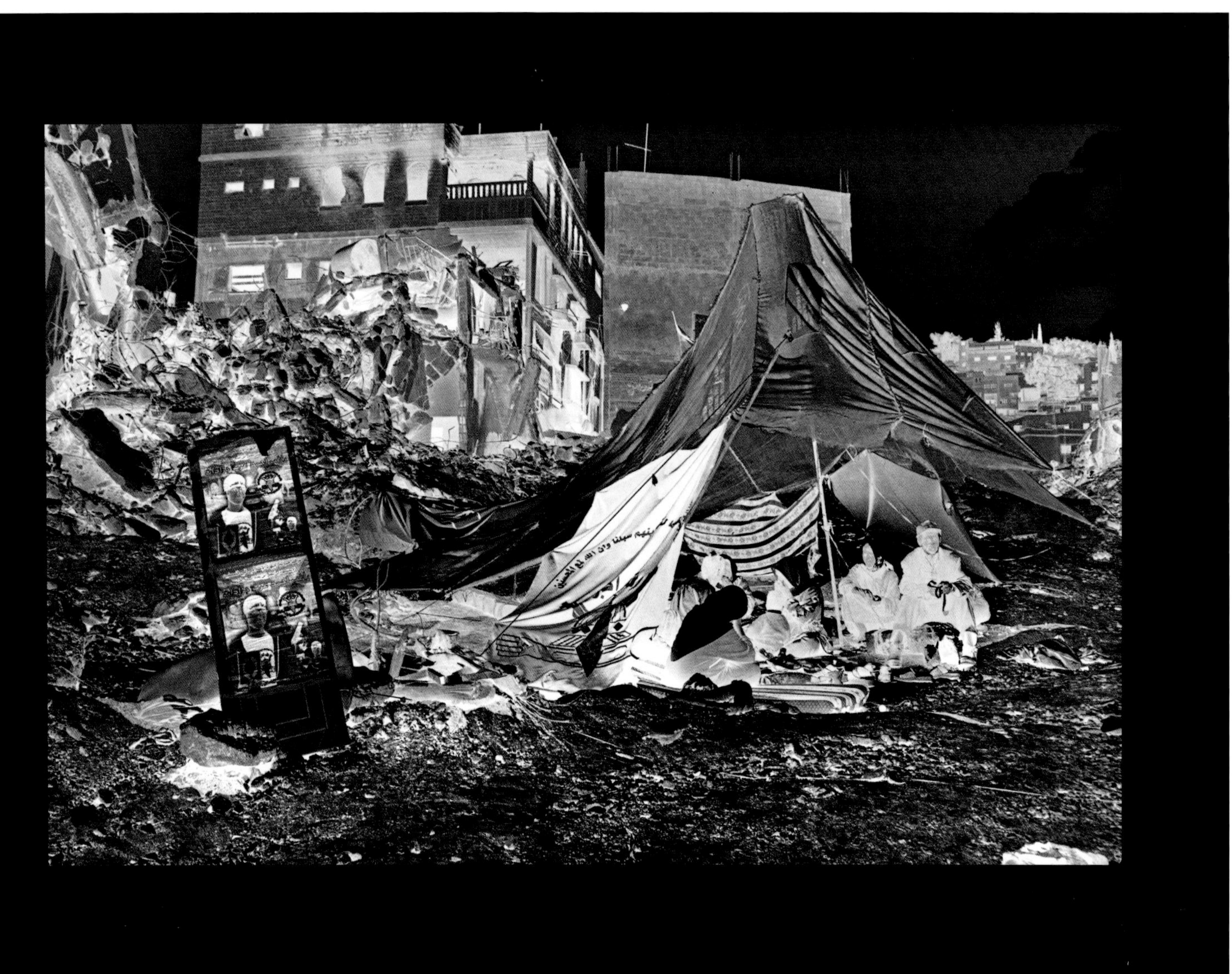

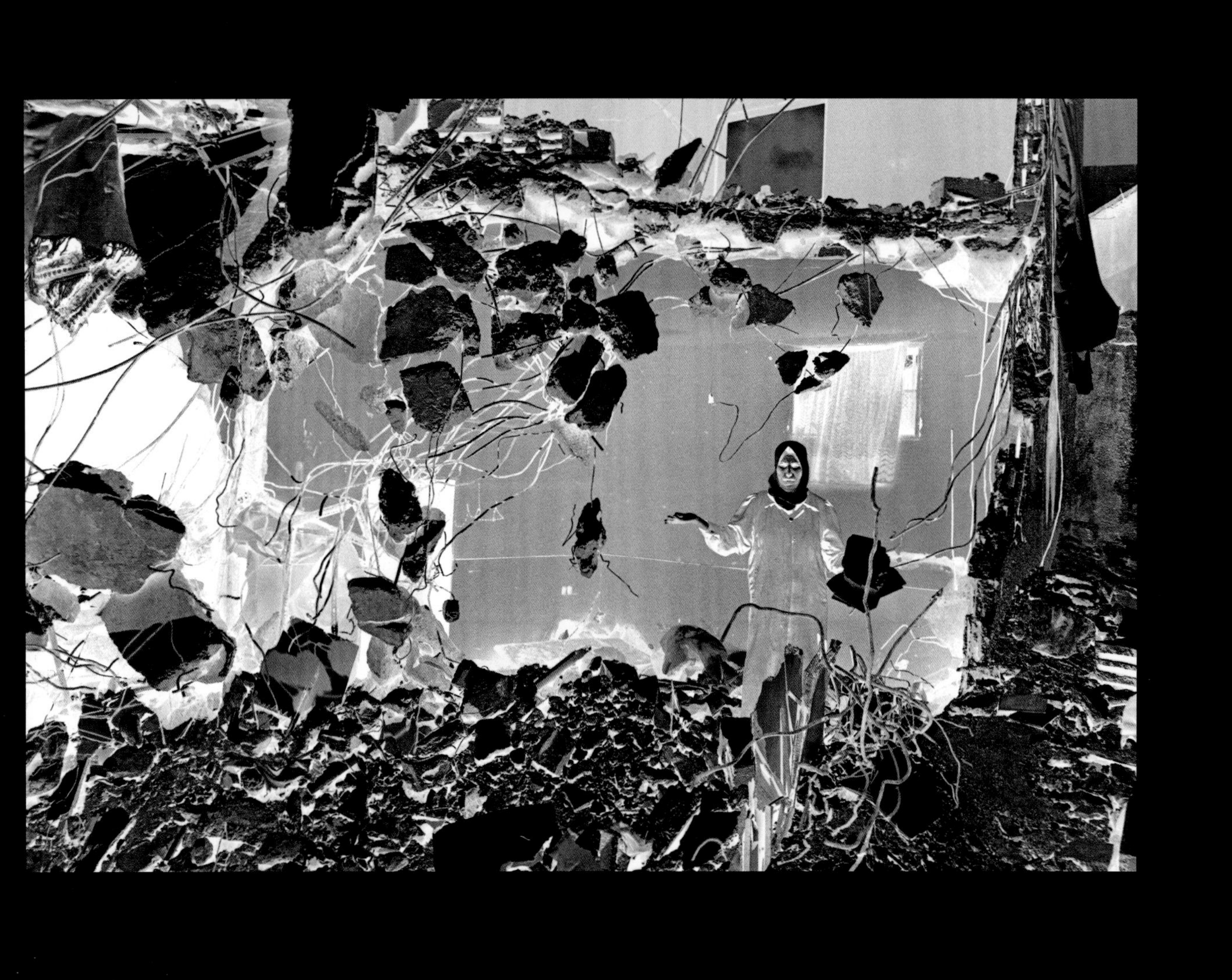

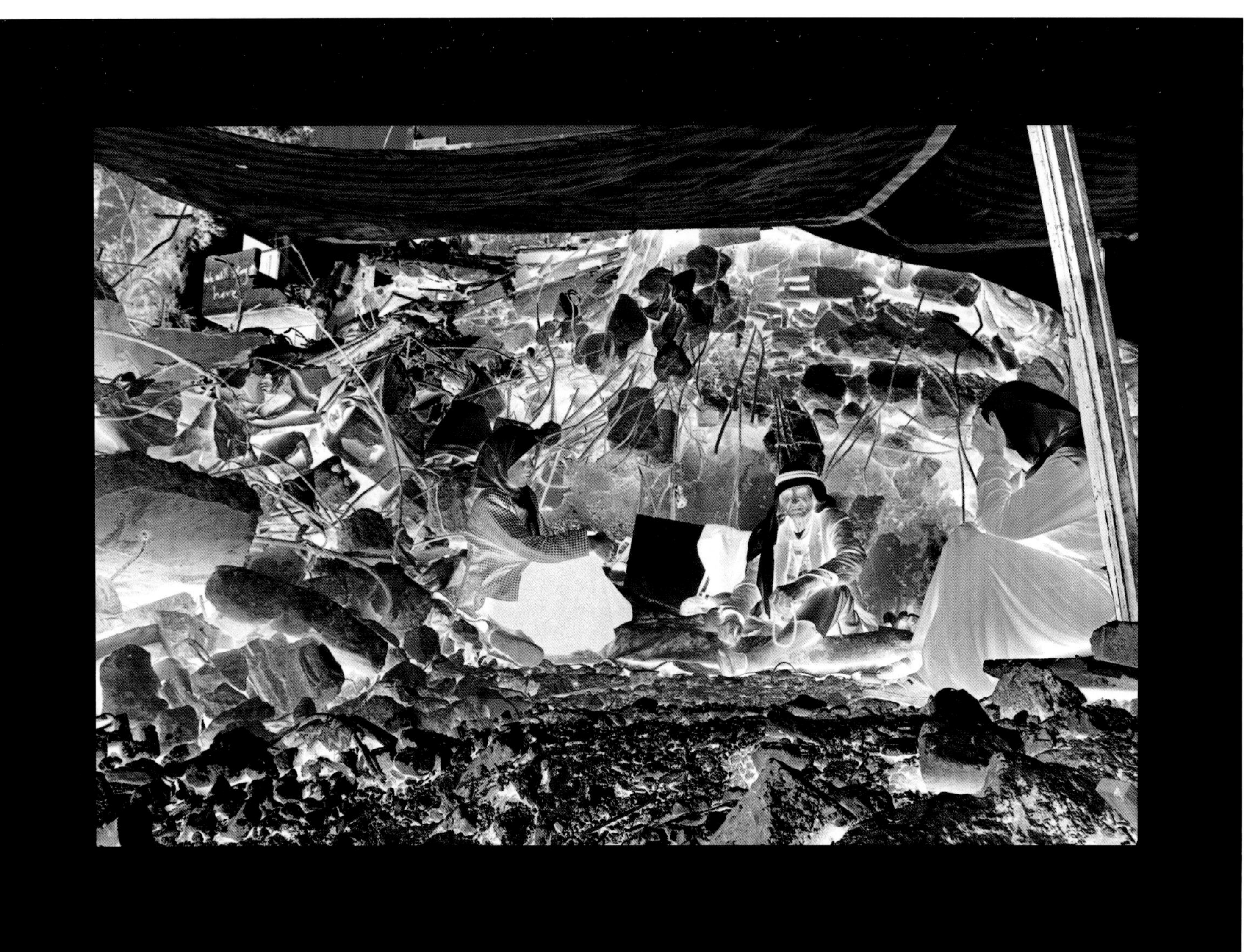

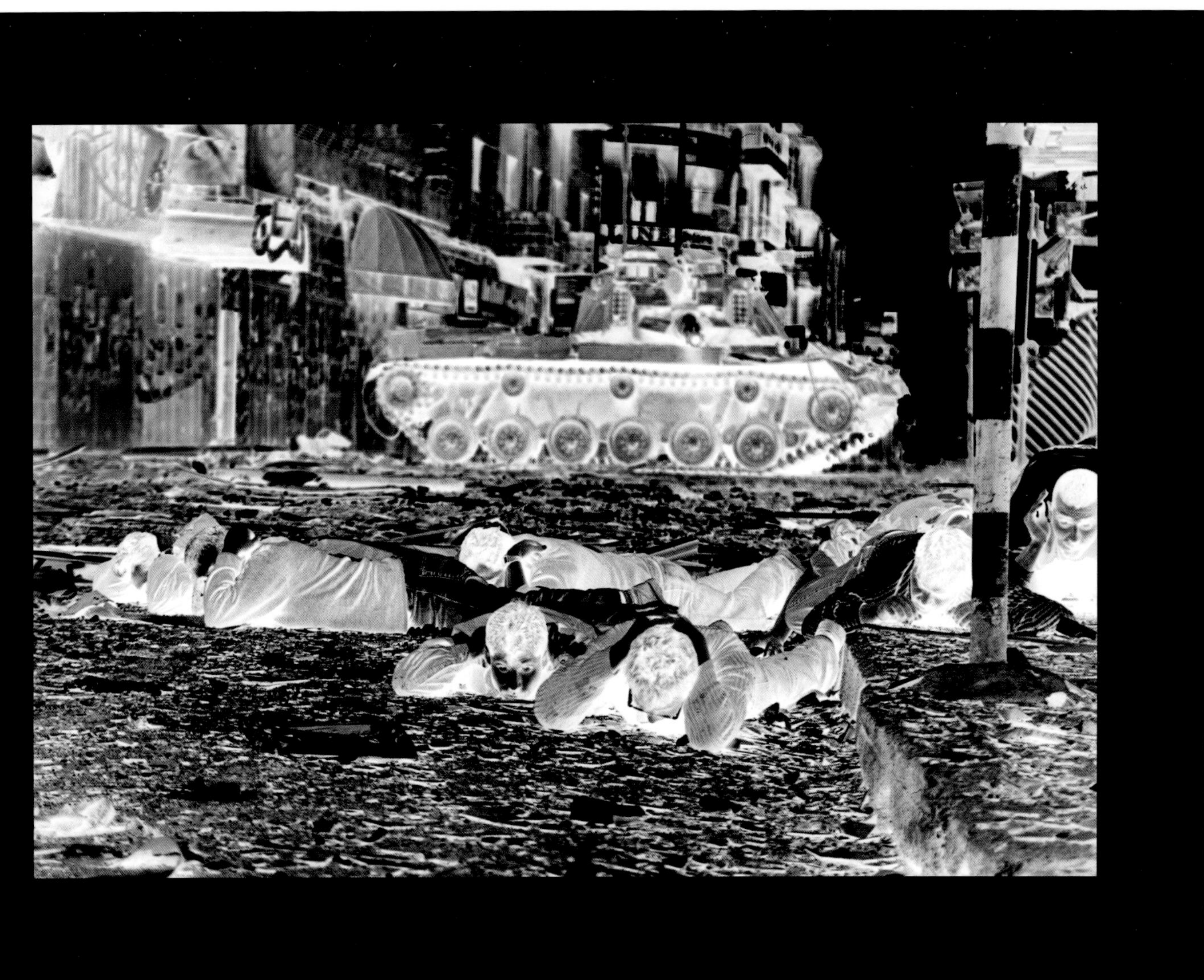

82. *Untitled X*, 2002
From *Negative Incursions* series
90 x 124 cm (about 35 x 49 in.)

83. *Untitled VI*, 2002
From *Negative Incursions* series
90 x 124 cm (about 35 x 49 in.)

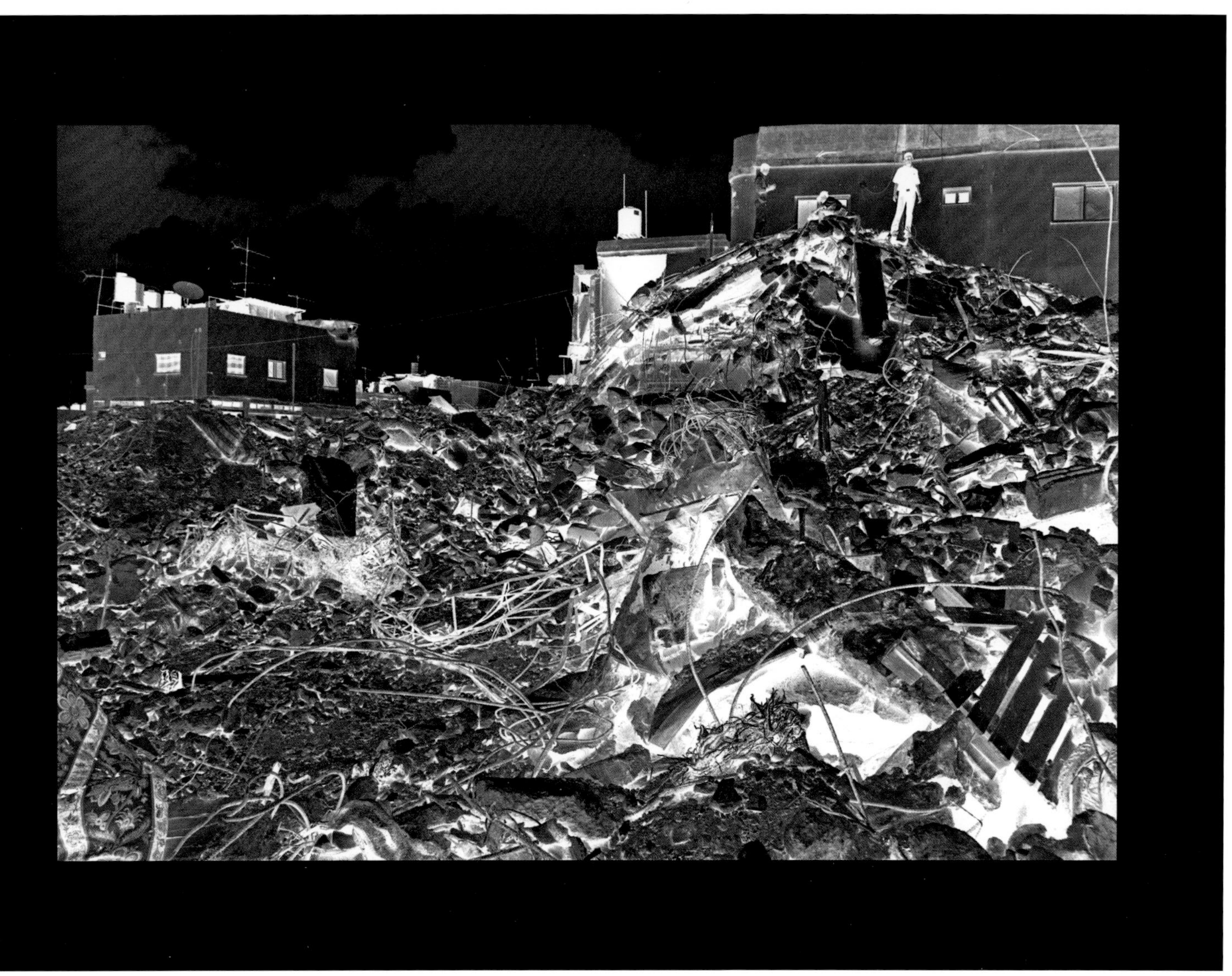

84. *Untitled XIX*, 2002
From *Negative Incursions* series
90 x 124 cm (about 35 x 49 in.)

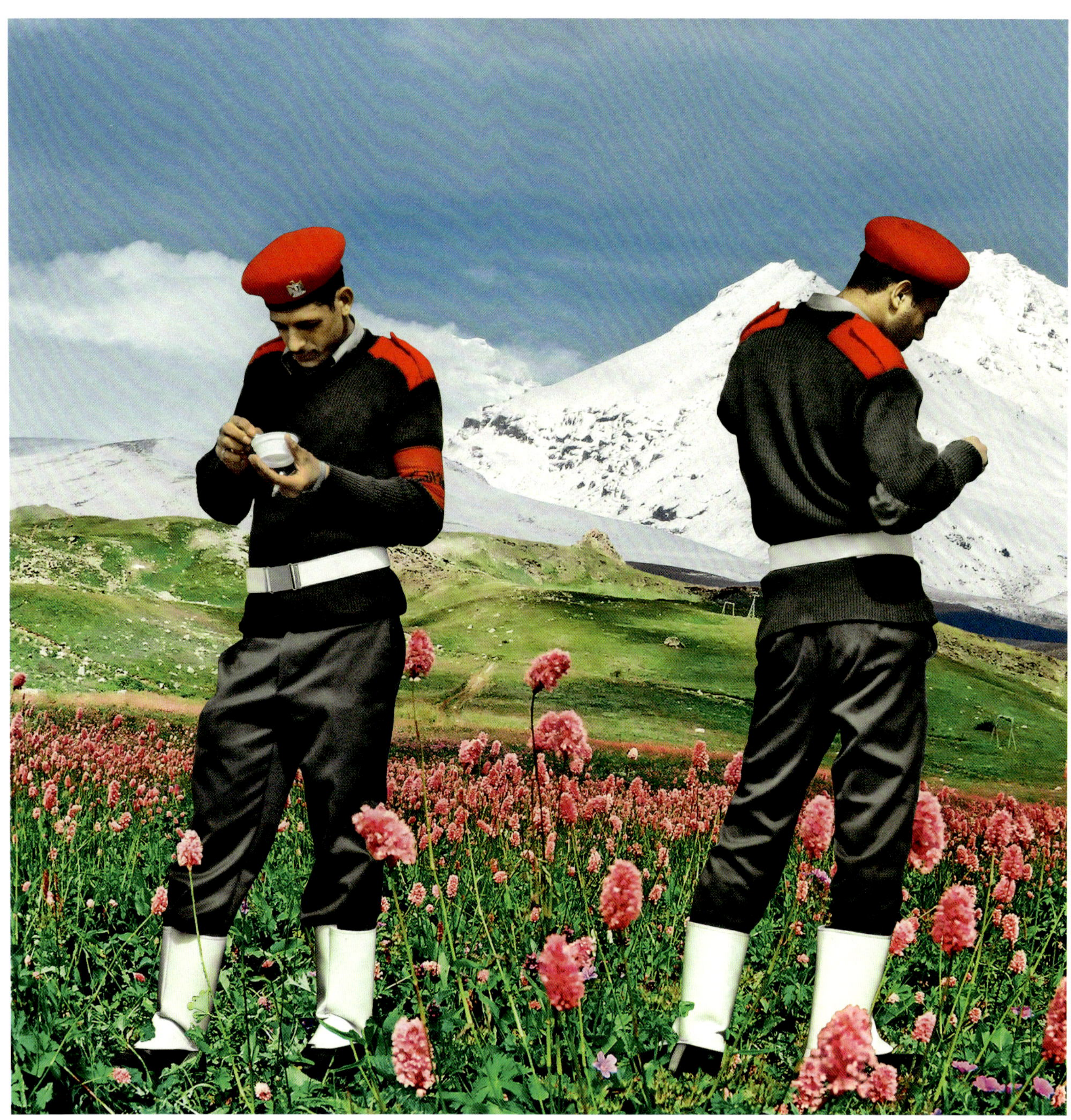

Nermine Hammam

Born in Cairo, Egypt, in 1967, Nermine Hammam was educated in the United Kingdom and the United States, where she received a Bachelor of Fine Arts in filmmaking from New York University's Tisch School of the Arts. She first worked with a film production company and later with the renowned Egyptian film director Youssef Chahine. Hammam also was a graphic designer for many years, creating the brand image for important Egyptian clients. She currently lives between Cairo and London. Her work has been exhibited widely and she has participated in international exhibitions such as X Biennale in Cuenca, Ecuador (2009); Photo Biennale in Thessaloniki, Greece (2009); and the Bamako Biennale for Photography in Mali (2011). She also received an honorable mention for the Julia Margaret Cameron Award in 2012, and first prize of the Freedom to Create Award and the Worldwide Photography Gala Awards in 2011.

Reflecting her early training in film and graphic design, Hammam forms narratives using digital manipulation and the layering of photographic elements — postcards from her personal collection, reproductions of Japanese screens, and her own photographs — to compose her imagery. Concerned with lens-based media's ability to manipulate reality, she explains: "The edge of the photograph can exclude as much as it includes. To me, this makes the photograph an inherently fictitious and unreliable record of both the past and the present."

Hammam's series include *Mitigation*, *Portraits*, *Ahoura*, *Escaton*, *Metanoia*, and *Anachrony*. *Cairo Year One*, made up of two parts — *Upekkha* (2011) and *Unfolding* (2012) — addresses the eighteen-day revolution of 2011 in Egypt and its aftermath, recording the progression from innocence and idealism to brutalization and polarity. The title of its first section, *Upekkha*, refers to the Buddhist concept of equanimity. The images show youthful Egyptian soldiers set in bucolic landscapes taken from postcards. Although intended to be shown as large-format prints, they have been exhibited in a smaller format closer to postcard size. Photographing the soldiers in Tahrir Square as they awaited the "military might" of the army arriving from their barracks in the desert, Hammam was surprised by the vulnerability of the young men. She sought to express this unexpected "military tenderness, virile coquetry, and masculine frailty. . . . I entered this traditionally male-dominated space, camera in hand, inverting conventional power relationships to 'shoot' the soldiers. Their response to my presence, as a woman, in their midst, has become part of the 'facts' documented in these images."

In *Dreamland I*, a soldier who stands looking up and to his right is placed against a backdrop of bright pink flowers that circle architectural columns, with a boat in the background. The soldier's photograph was taken in front of the Libyan embassy in Cairo, while people were yelling and throwing rocks around him. The young man stood calmly amid the chaos, as if in a dream, gently holding his gun. As Hammam explains: "The backgrounds emphasize the discordant presence of armed men among civilians in Tahrir:

85. *The Break*, 2011
From *Cairo Year One: Upekkha* series
60 x 60 cm (23 ⅝ x 23 ⅝ in.)

men of war in Paradise."[1] *The Break* features two soldiers, one facing toward and the other away from the viewer, as they eat a sweet snack in front of a majestic Alpine background as opposed to the original chaotic setting of Tahrir Square. The peaceful mountain scene and the soldiers' apparent relaxation introduce a delicacy and detachment again at odds with the social upheaval of Egypt.

The scenes shown in *Unfolding* create a dramatic contrast. This series of digital collages combines reproductions of seventeenth- and eighteenth-century Japanese screens with incidents of police brutality during the year following the Egyptian revolution. In Hammam's words: "By framing scenes of shocking pain, the Japanese screens also served to mock the artistic industry forming around the revolution—the paradoxical desire to stare, fascinated, and to look away, nauseated; the simultaneous longing to scream and remain silent."[2] The screens also refer to the distancing effect of contemporary screen media.

Fauna is the first of several works and features a woman wearing a *niqab* under attack on the ground, camouflaged by fragments of a Japanese screen. The source image, shot by the photojournalist Ahmed Ali for the AP syndicate, shows Egyptian army soldiers beating a protester during clashes near Cairo's downtown Tahrir Square.

The original news image in *A Leap in Faith* records Egyptian riot police battling with protesters in Tahrir Square over a tent city set up to commemorate revolutionary martyrs. The figure draped in the Egyptian flag to the left recalls the subject of Eugène Delacroix's *Liberty Leading the People*, painted to commemorate France's July Revolution of 1830.

Codes of My Kin includes an amateur frame grab of a video of a woman who has been arrested, violently beaten, and dragged on the ground with her *abaya* torn open to reveal her chest. The photograph, distributed by the Reuters news agency, has become an iconic image of the revolution—yet, as Hammam has observed, for many viewers the exposure of the woman's body and the provocative detail of her colored bra eclipsed the violence she suffered.

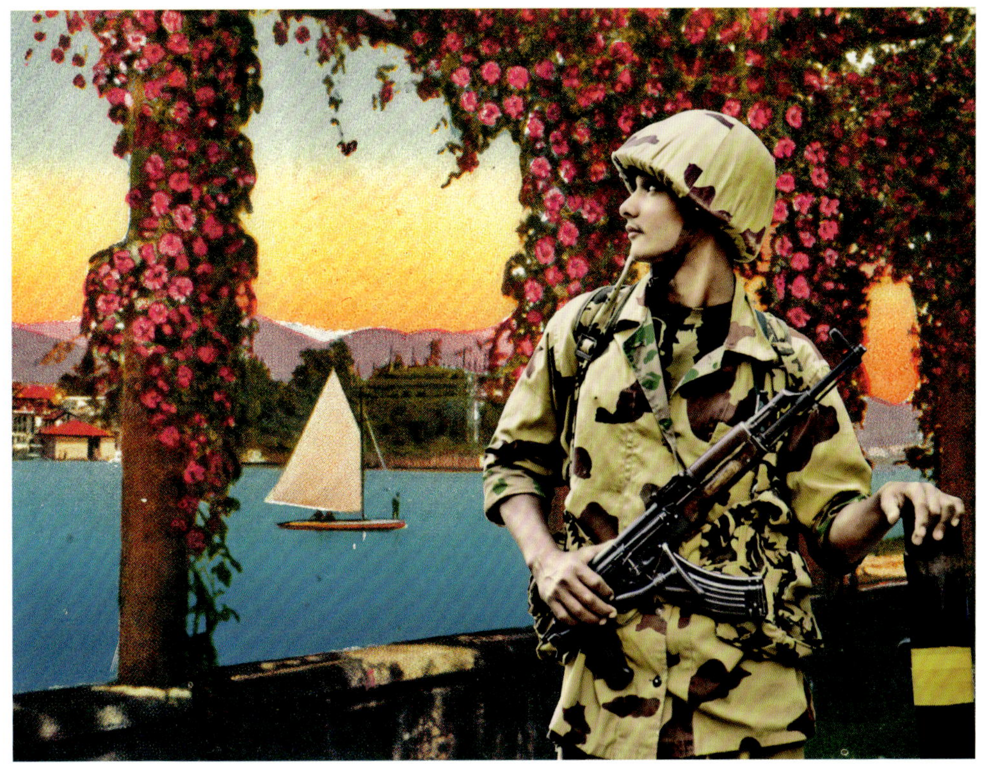

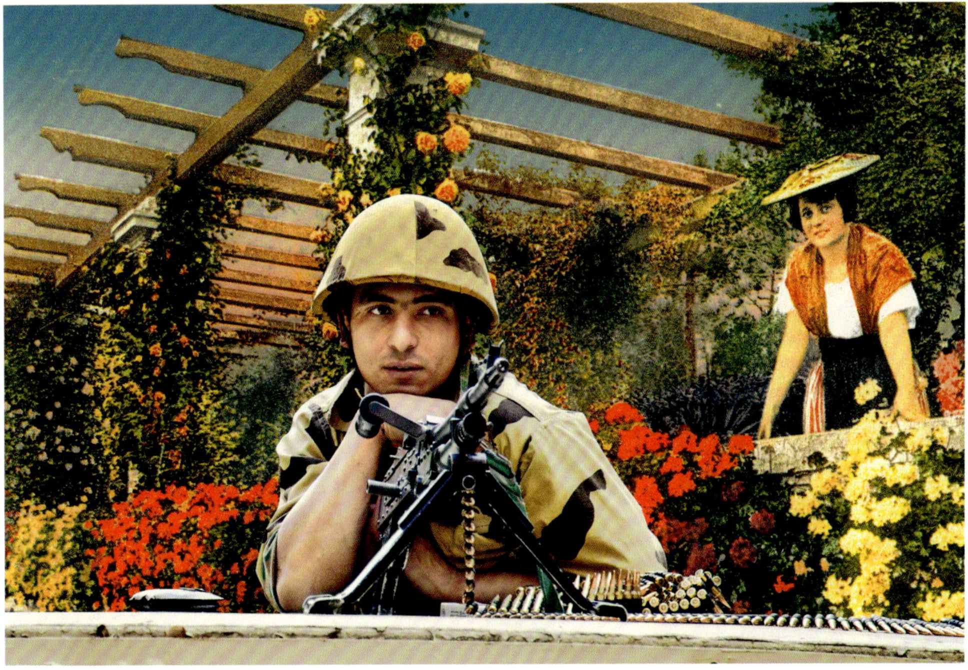

86. *Dreamland I*, 2011
From *Cairo Year One: Upekkha* series
67 x 90 cm (26 ⅜ x 35 ⅜ in.)

87. *Dreamland II*, 2011
From *Cairo Year One: Upekkha* series
60 x 90 cm (23 ⅝ x 35 ⅜ in.)

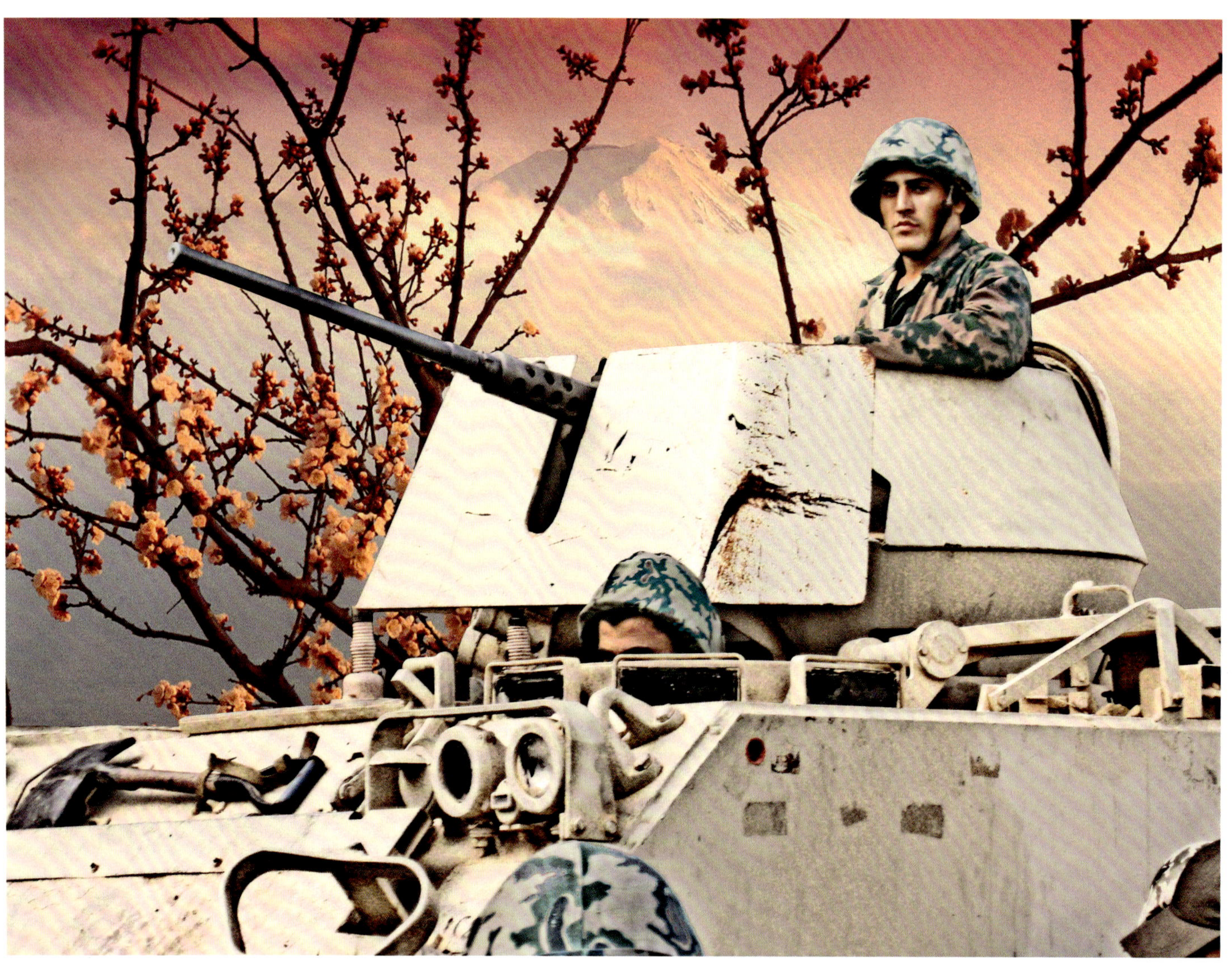

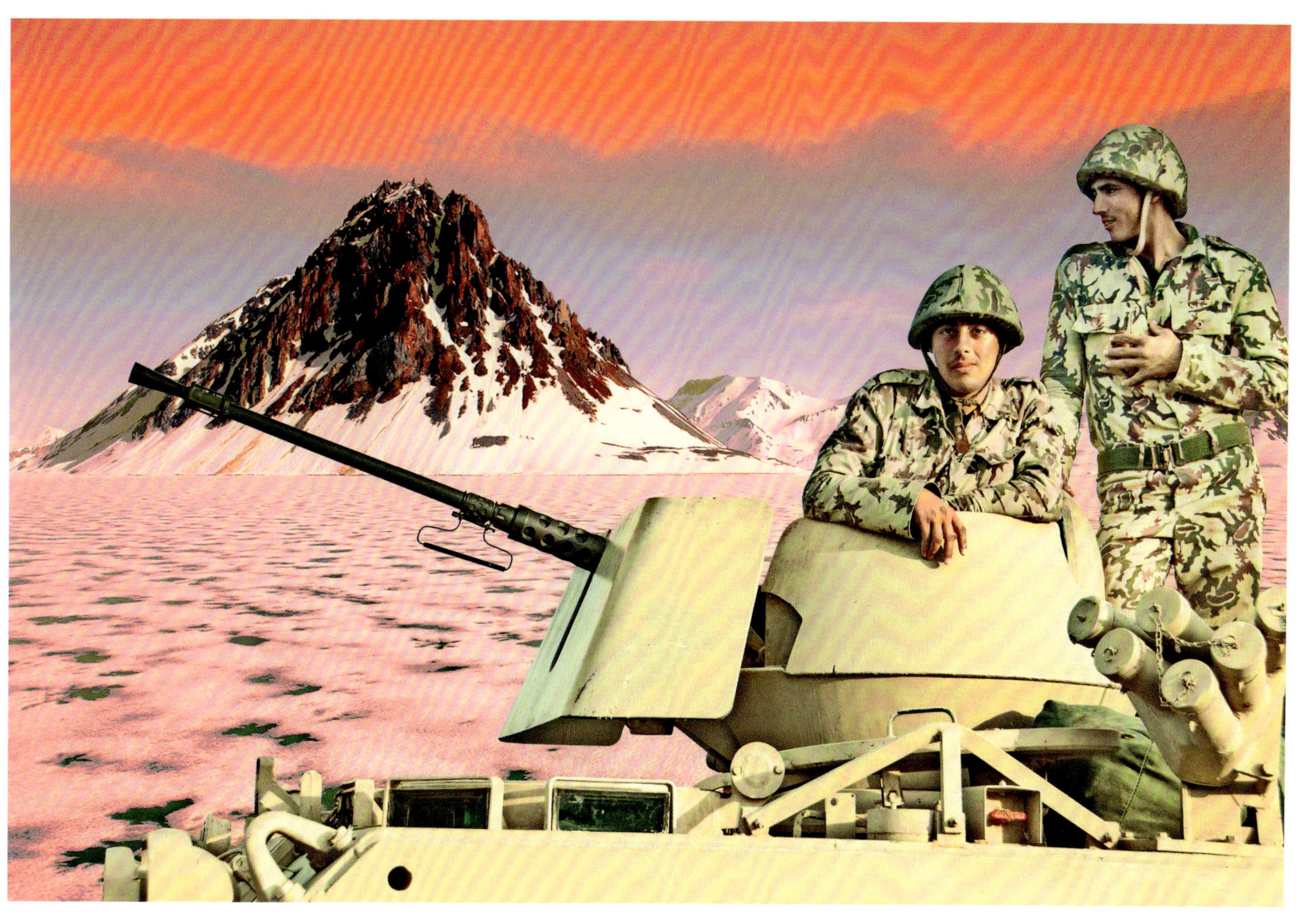

88. *Sham el Nasseem (Spring)*, 2011
From *Cairo Year One: Upekkha* series
62 x 84 cm (24 ⅜ x 33 ⅛ in.)

89. *At Dawn*, 2011
From *Cairo Year One: Upekkha* series
60 x 90 cm (23 ⅝ x 35 ⅜ in.)

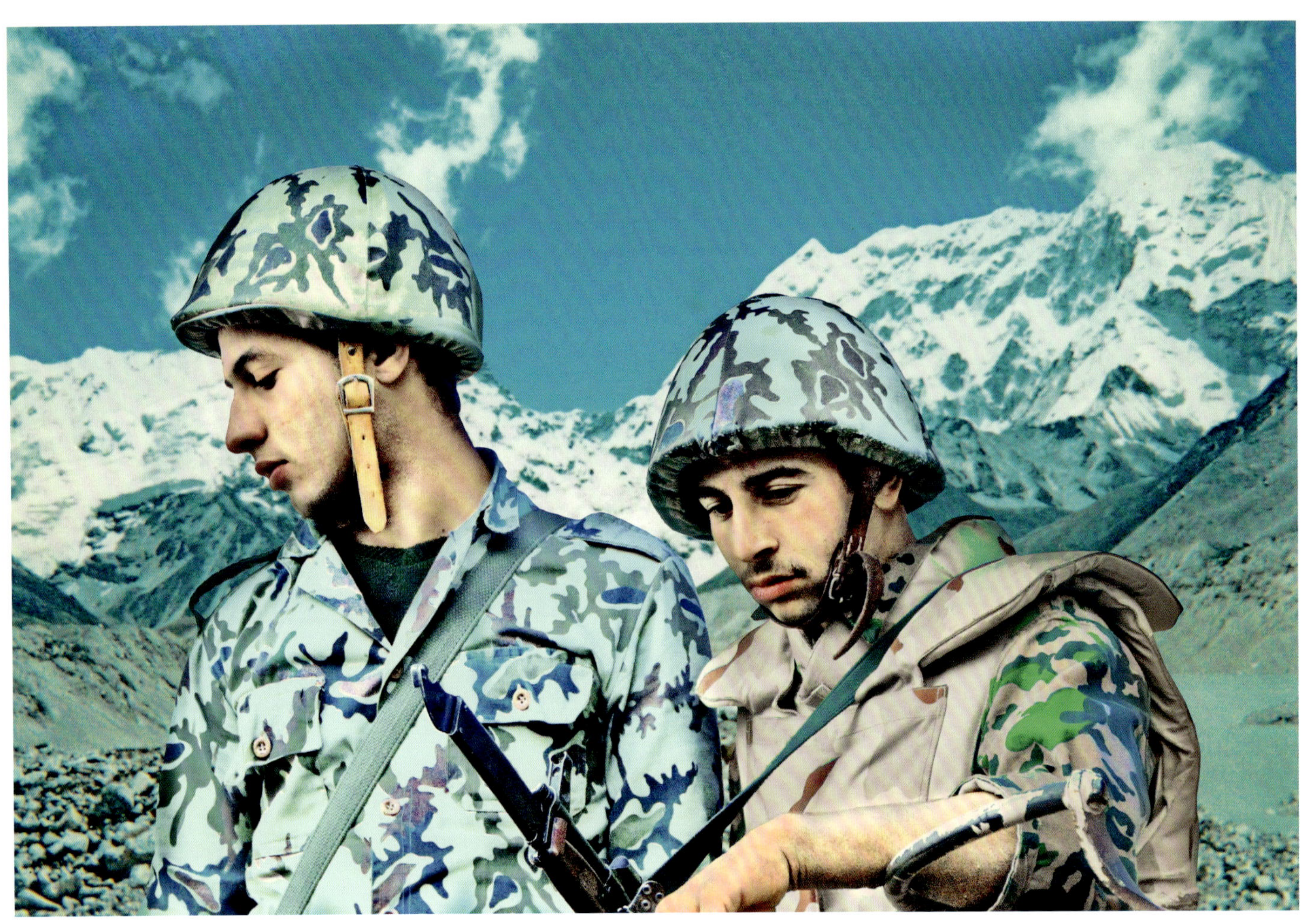

90. *Armed Innocence II*, 2011
From *Cairo Year One: Upekkha* series
62 x 84 cm (24 ⅜ x 33 ⅛ in.)

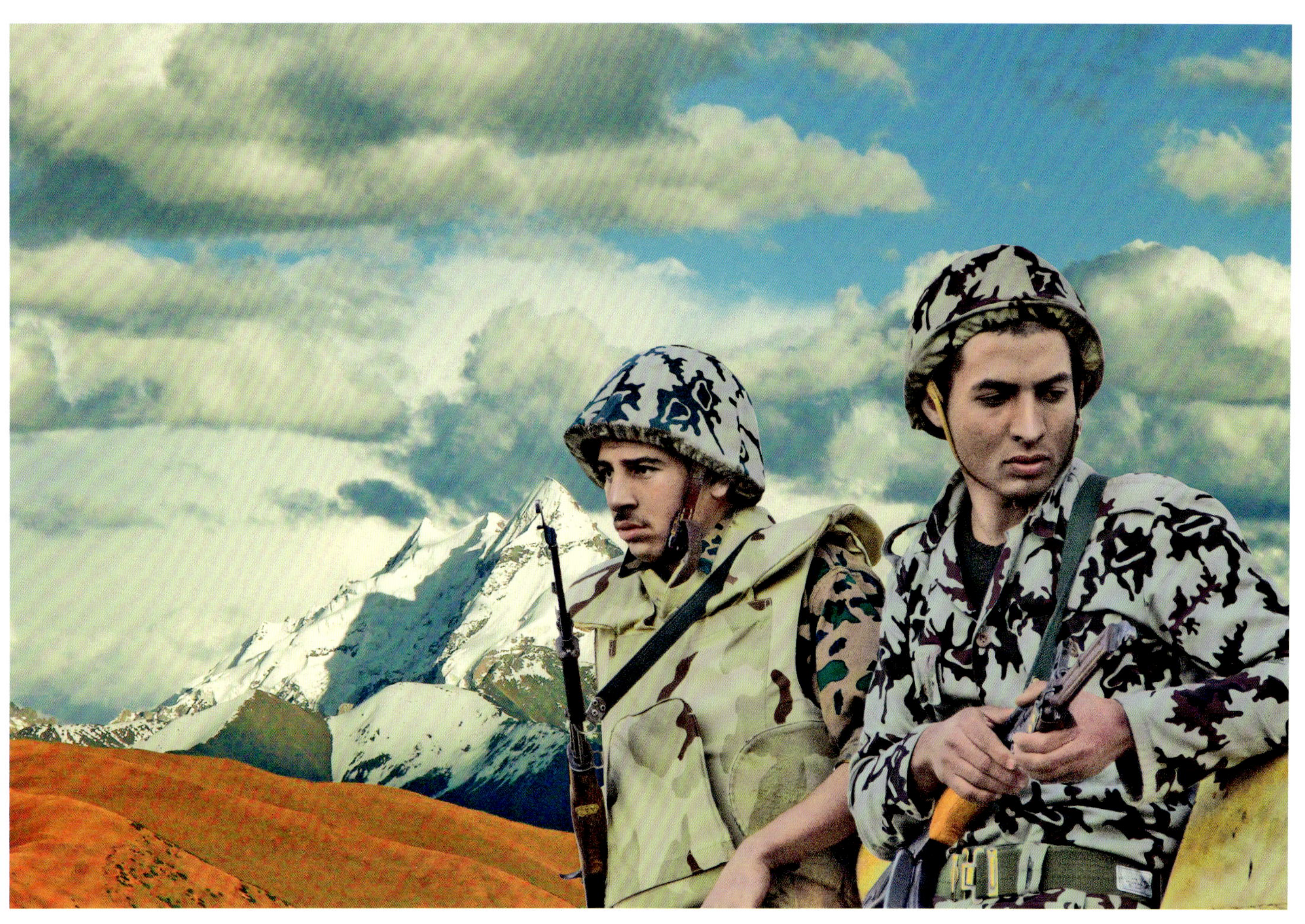

91. *Armed Innocence I*, 2011
From *Cairo Year One: Upekkha* series
62 x 84 cm (24 ⅜ x 33 ⅛ in.)

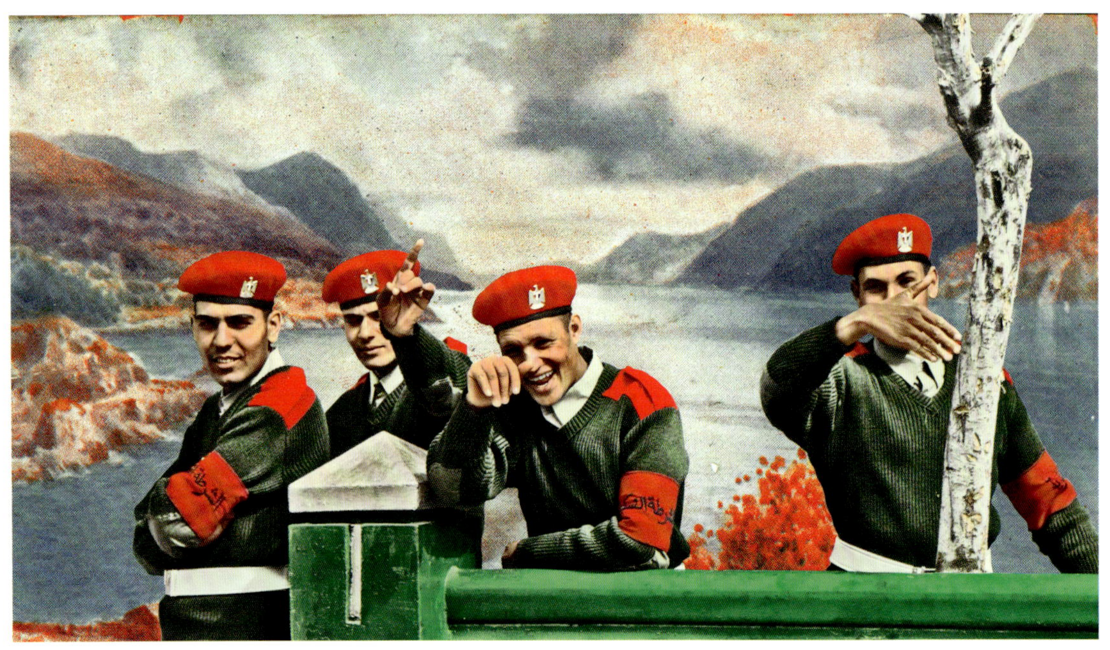

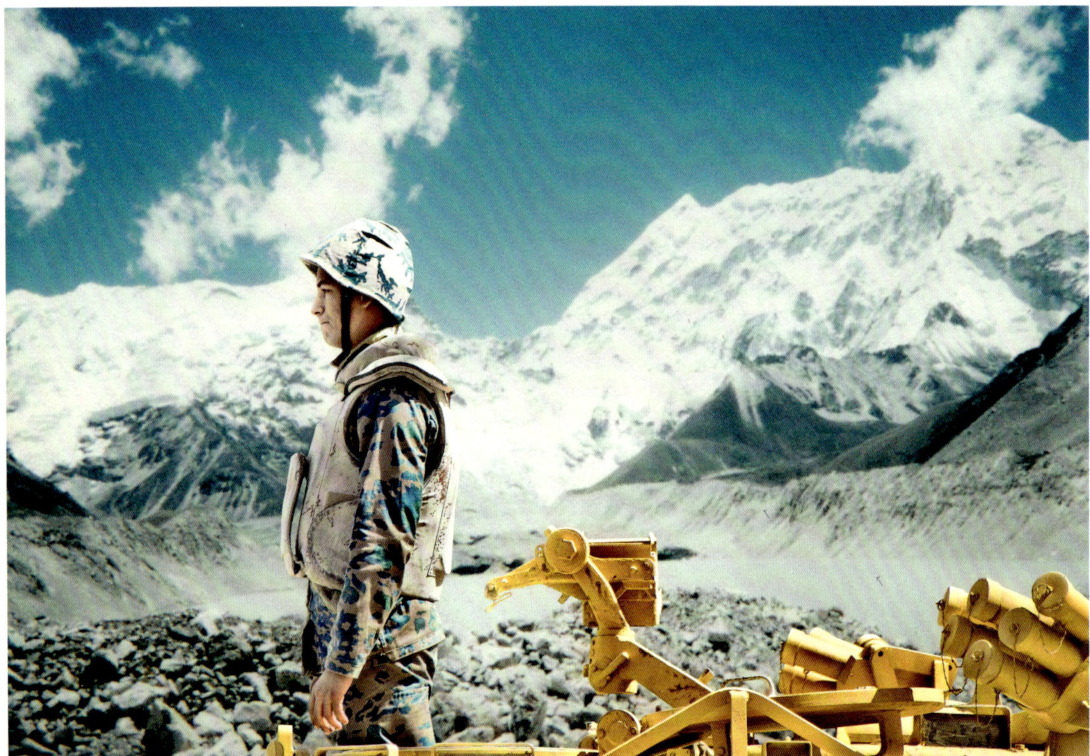

92. *Stop, Come, Go, Continue*, 2011
From *Cairo Year One: Upekkha* series
50 x 90 cm (19 ⅝ x 35 ⅜ in.)

93. *Where To From Here?* 2011
From *Cairo Year One: Upekkha* series
60 x 90 cm (23 ⅝ x 35 ⅜ in.)

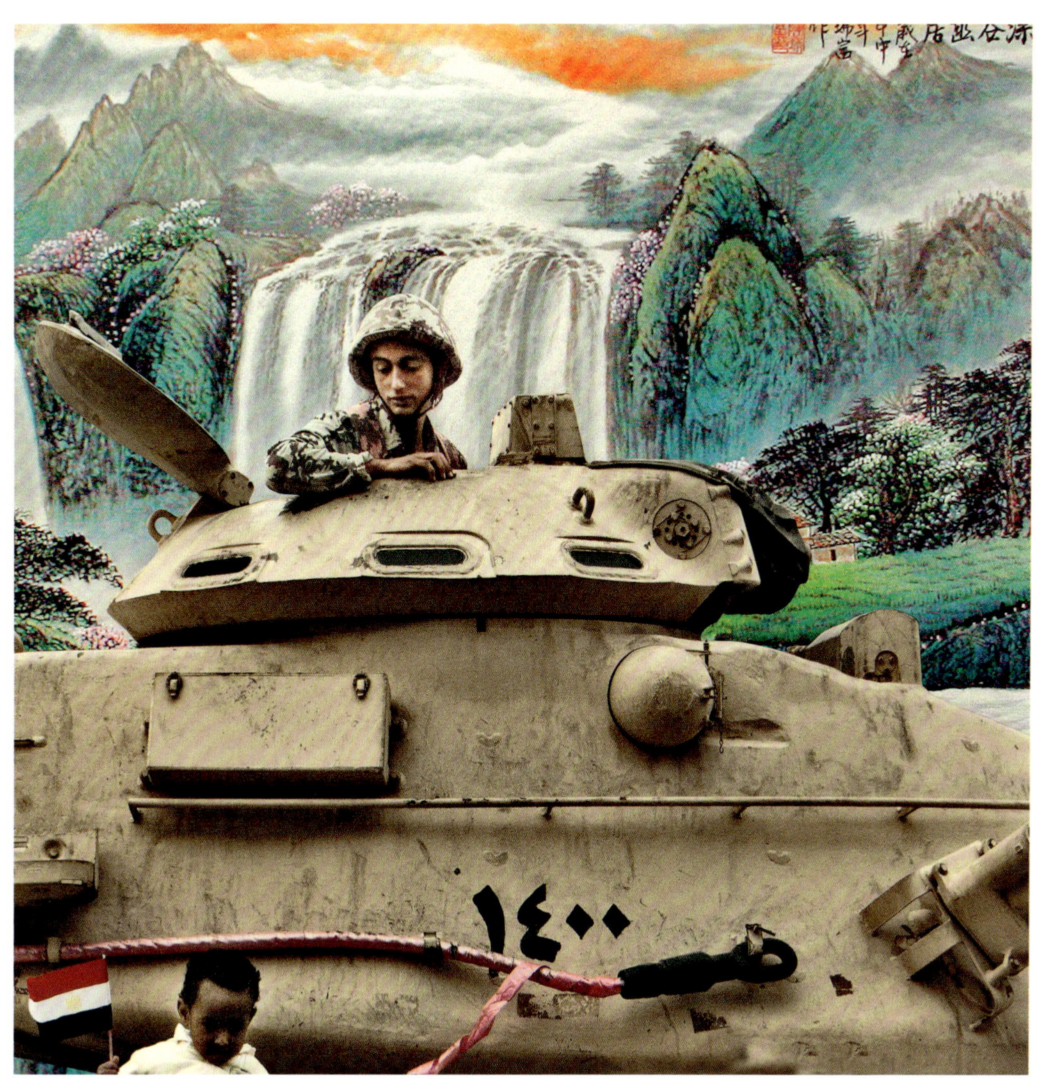

94. *The Fall*, 2011
From *Cairo Year One: Upekkha* series
50 x 50 cm (19 ⅝ x 19 ⅝ in.)

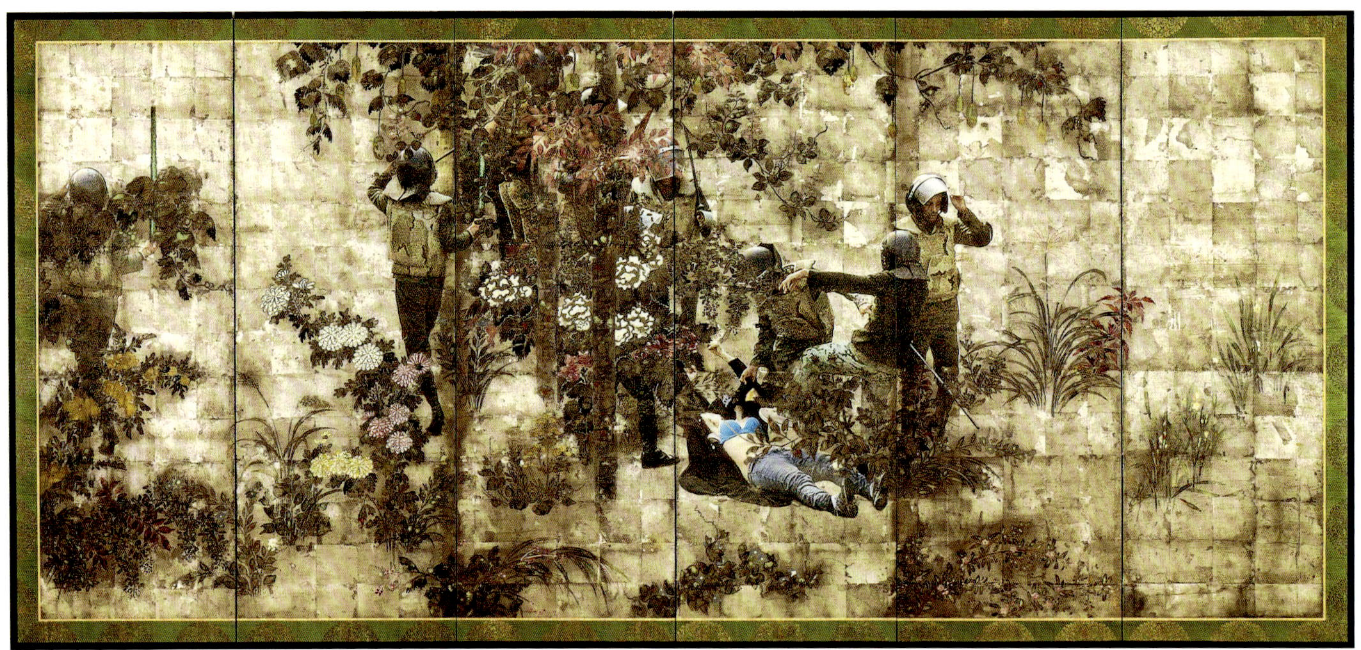

95. *Codes of My Kin*, 2012
From *Cairo Year One: Unfolding* series
22 x 53 cm (8 ⅝ x 20 ⅞ in.)

96. *Fauna*, 2012
From *Cairo Year One: Unfolding* series
20 x 26 cm (7 ⅞ x 10 ¼ in.)

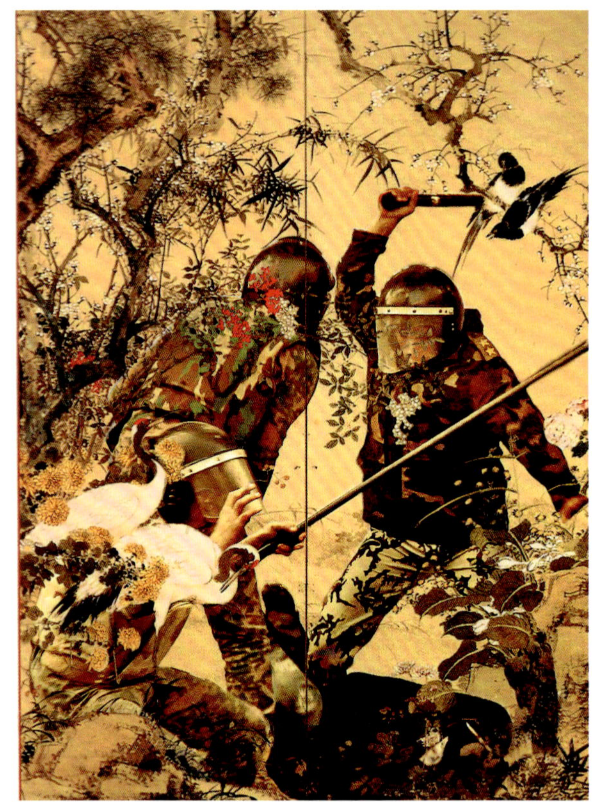

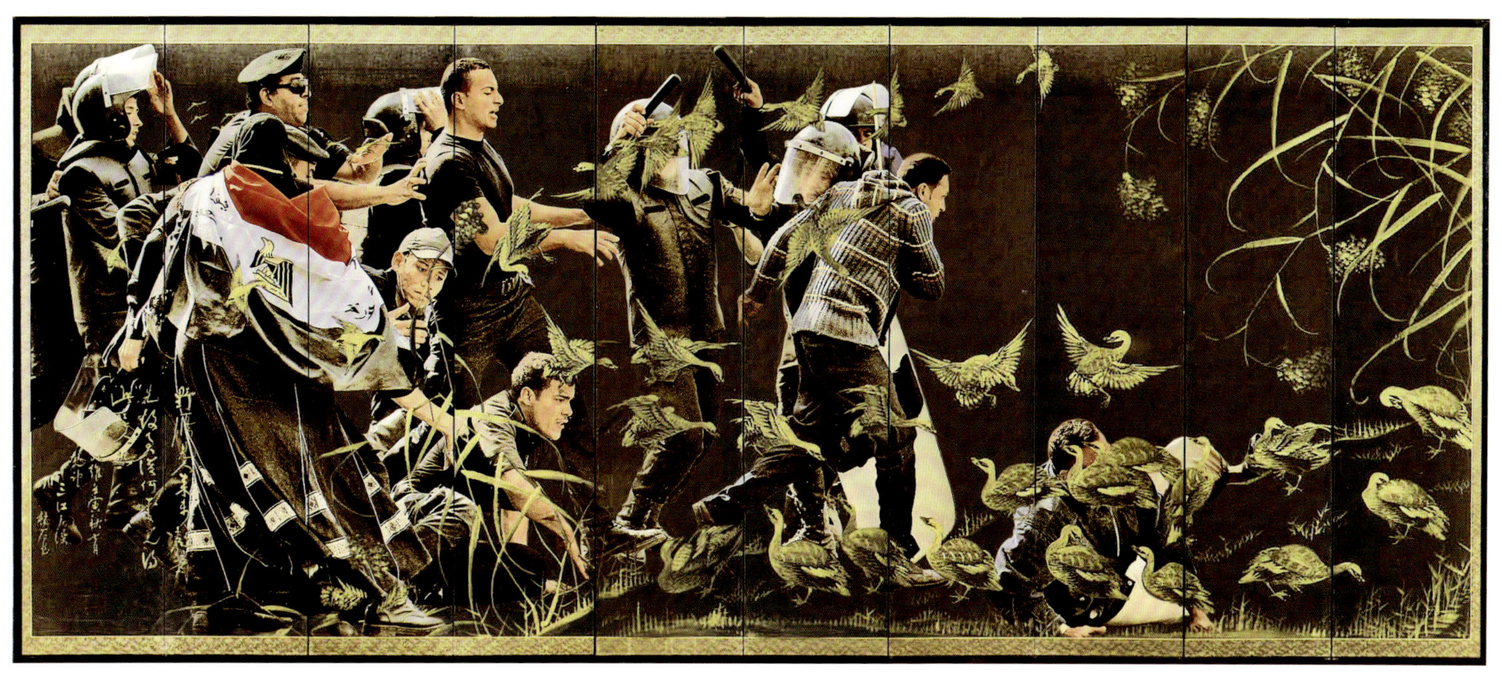

97. *A Leap in Faith*, 2012
From *Cairo Year One: Unfolding* series
22 x 53 cm (8 ⅝ x 20 ⅞ in.)

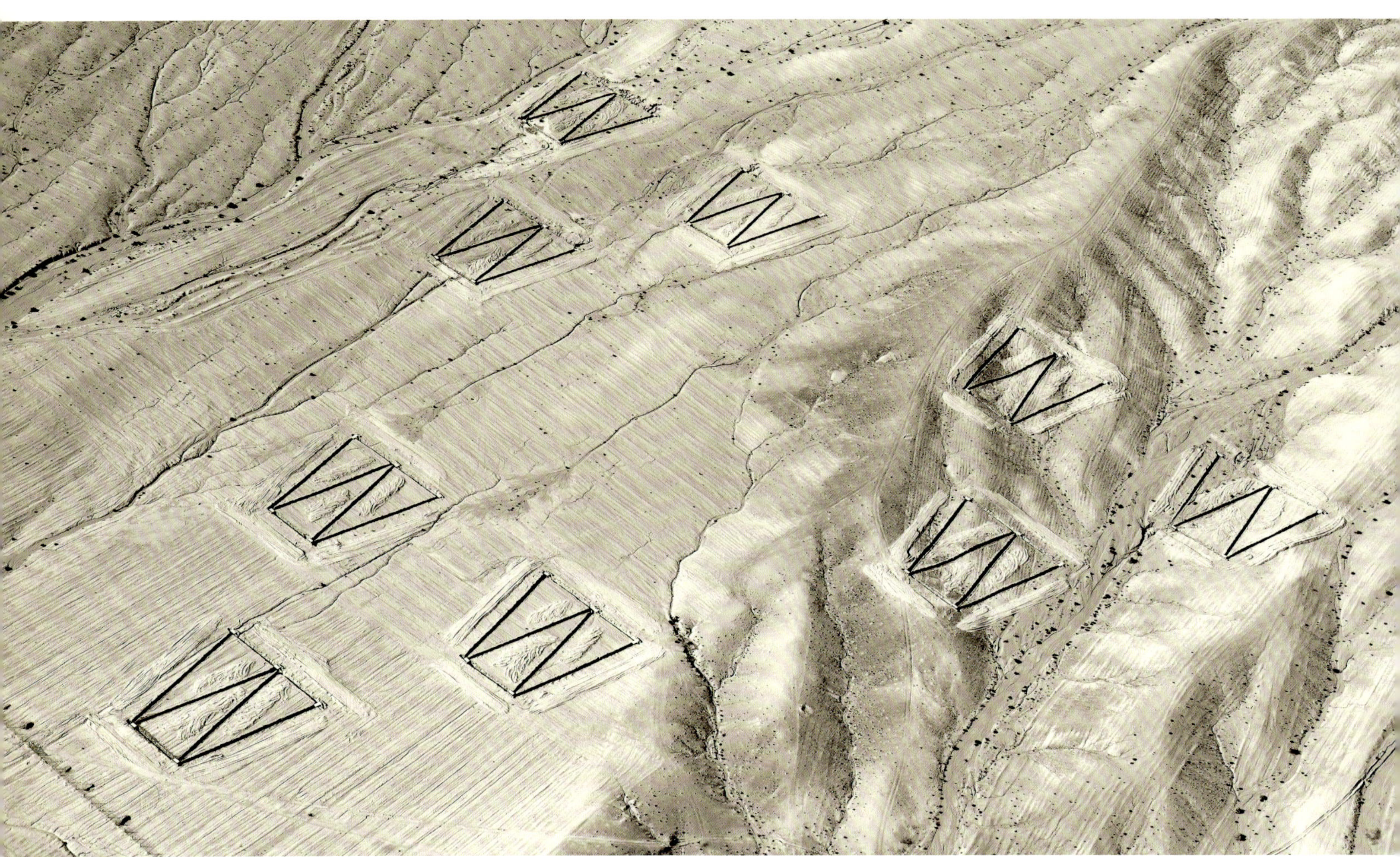

Jananne Al-Ani

Jananne Al-Ani was born in Kirkuk, Iraq, in 1966 to an Irish mother and an Iraqi father. She studied fine art and photography in London, where she currently lives and works. Her work has received many awards, including the Abraaj Capital Art Prize (2011). Al-Ani's photographs, videos, and films have been exhibited widely, and she has had several solo shows, including those at the Imperial War Museum in London (1999); the Smithsonian Freer and Sackler Galleries of Art (1999 and 2012); Tate Britain (*Art Now*, 2005); Darat al Funun, Amman (2010); and the Beirut Art Center (2013). She co-curated the traveling exhibition *Veil* (2003–4, U.K. and Sweden), which broadened the debate on the subject of the veil in a complex and provocative way.[1]

Al-Ani's work questions representation and documentation of the Middle East, both its people and its land. The use of digital and satellite images in the 1991 Desert Storm campaign of the first Gulf War changed her thinking about the photographic medium. She believes the Western media's "portrayal of the population, the culture, and, crucially, the landscape of the Middle East . . . revealed that the nineteenth-century Orientalist stereotype of the Arab and the desert remained firmly embedded in Western consciousness. The site of the war was shown to be a desert, a place with no history and no population — an empty space, a blank canvas."[2] Al-Ani addresses this misrepresentation in *Untitled (Gulf War Work)* (1991), which juxtaposes four rows of five small photographs: images of Mesopotamian archaeological artifacts, her own family snapshots, formal portraits, and press images of the war. The inclusion of her family was Al-Ani's way of personalizing and humanizing the war, as well as adding to it a more complex historical narrative. This project, which she describes as a way to bring the body back into the empty landscape portrayed in Western media, is a point of origin for much of her work.

Following this piece, Al-Ani produced a series of photographic works with herself, her mother, and her three sisters as protagonists, which examines the Western fascination with the veil in Orientalist painting and photography. In an untitled diptych from 1996, the five women are progressively veiled and unveiled, their heads and shoulders gradually appearing and disappearing. The large-scale photographs are displayed facing each other so as to disrupt the voyeuristic relationship between the viewer and subject and force the audience to become aware of itself engaged in the process of looking (see plates 2–3).[3]

Several video pieces followed, featuring a chorus of female "talking heads." *A Loving Man* (1996–99), *1001 Nights* (1998), and *She Said* (2000) all adopt a confessional mode, making enigmatic use of biography, manipulating language, and fragmenting narrative. *Muse* (2004) represented a departure for Al-Ani, as the first work she shot outside the studio, in a landscape, in which a male protagonist occupies center stage.

Her series *The Aesthetics of Disappearance: A Land Without People* explores the disappearance of the body in the real and imagined landscapes of the Middle East and includes the two large-scale

98–103. *Aerial I–Aerial VI*, 2011
Production stills from
Shadow Sites II

film works *Shadow Sites I* (2010) and *Shadow Sites II* (2011). In response to the development of aerial photography during the first half of the twentieth century and the subsequent production of complex reconnaissance and satellite imaging devices used during the 1991 Desert Storm campaign and the 2003 Gulf War, the *Shadow Sites* films adopt the vantage point of such missions while taking an altogether different viewpoint of the ground surveyed. They feature land that bears traces of natural and man-made activity as well as ancient and contemporary structures. Seen from above, the landscape appears abstracted: buildings are flattened and inhabitants are made invisible to the human eye. In *Shadow Sites II*, the aerial photographs projected sequentially onto the wall seem to melt into one another, accompanied by the noise of an airplane motor that sounds alarmingly like a drone. From one frame to the next, as the viewer is drawn in closer and closer to the landscape below, previously invisible details are revealed.

Al-Ani describes the project: "After a three-year period of research and development, I have produced a new body of photographic and moving image work, which explores the disappearance of the body in the contested and highly charged landscapes of the Middle East by examining what happens to the evidence of atrocity and genocide and how it affects our understanding of the often beautiful landscapes into which the bodies of victims disappear." These images, while referring to contemporary war reportage and military surveillance, are also reminiscent of the aerial reconnaissance photographs of the Western Front taken by Edward Steichen while working for the Aerial Expeditionary Force during World War I, which Al-Ani discovered in the course of her extensive archival research. She describes Steichen's photographs as "strikingly beautiful images of landscapes obliterated by shelling and crisscrossed by trenches, but abstracted to such a degree as to have become exquisite and minimal works of art."

The *Shadow Sites* films share the complexity of powerful and beautiful images of ancient and contemporary landscapes and structures that testify to loss and to history. The combined technologies of flight and photography expose both natural and man-made activity on the land. The seemingly abstracted landscapes are "shadow sites" because only when the sun is low can the details of the landscape, archaeological sites, and settlements be seen from the air. The earth becomes a sensitive surface akin to photographic film, bearing the latent image of the historical past, "the landscape itself exposing signs of survival and loss and becoming the bearer of particularly resilient and recurring memories."[4]

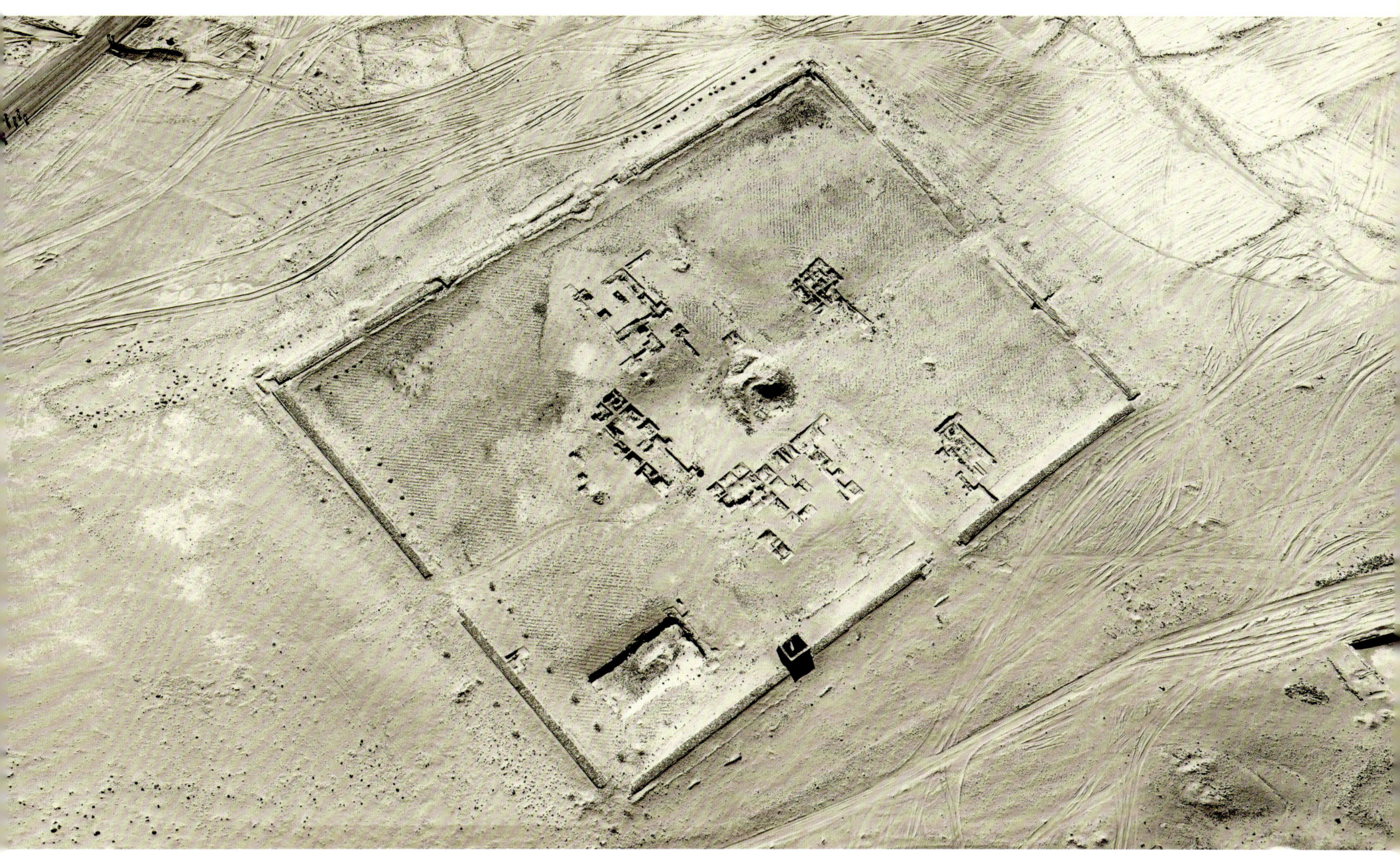

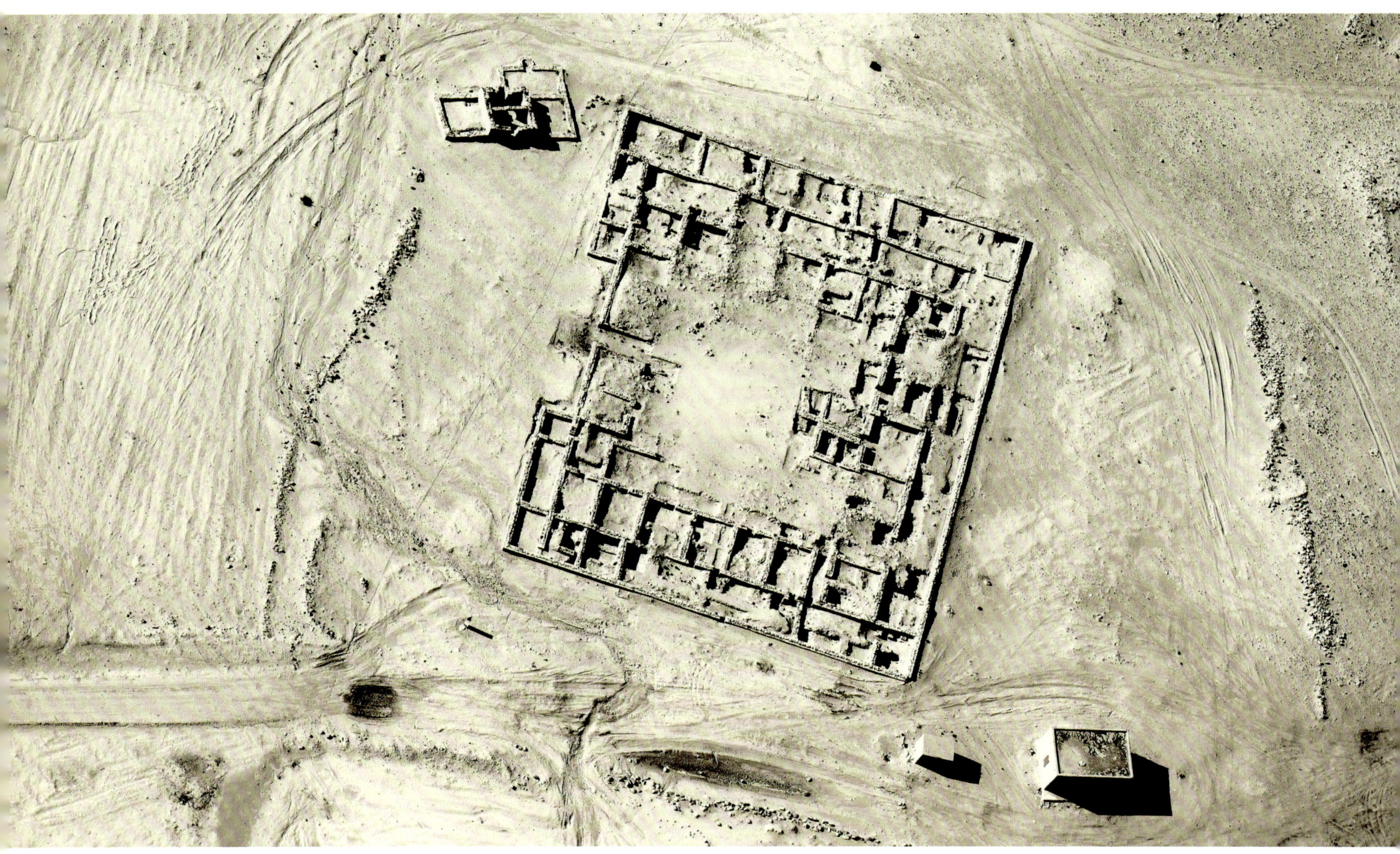

100

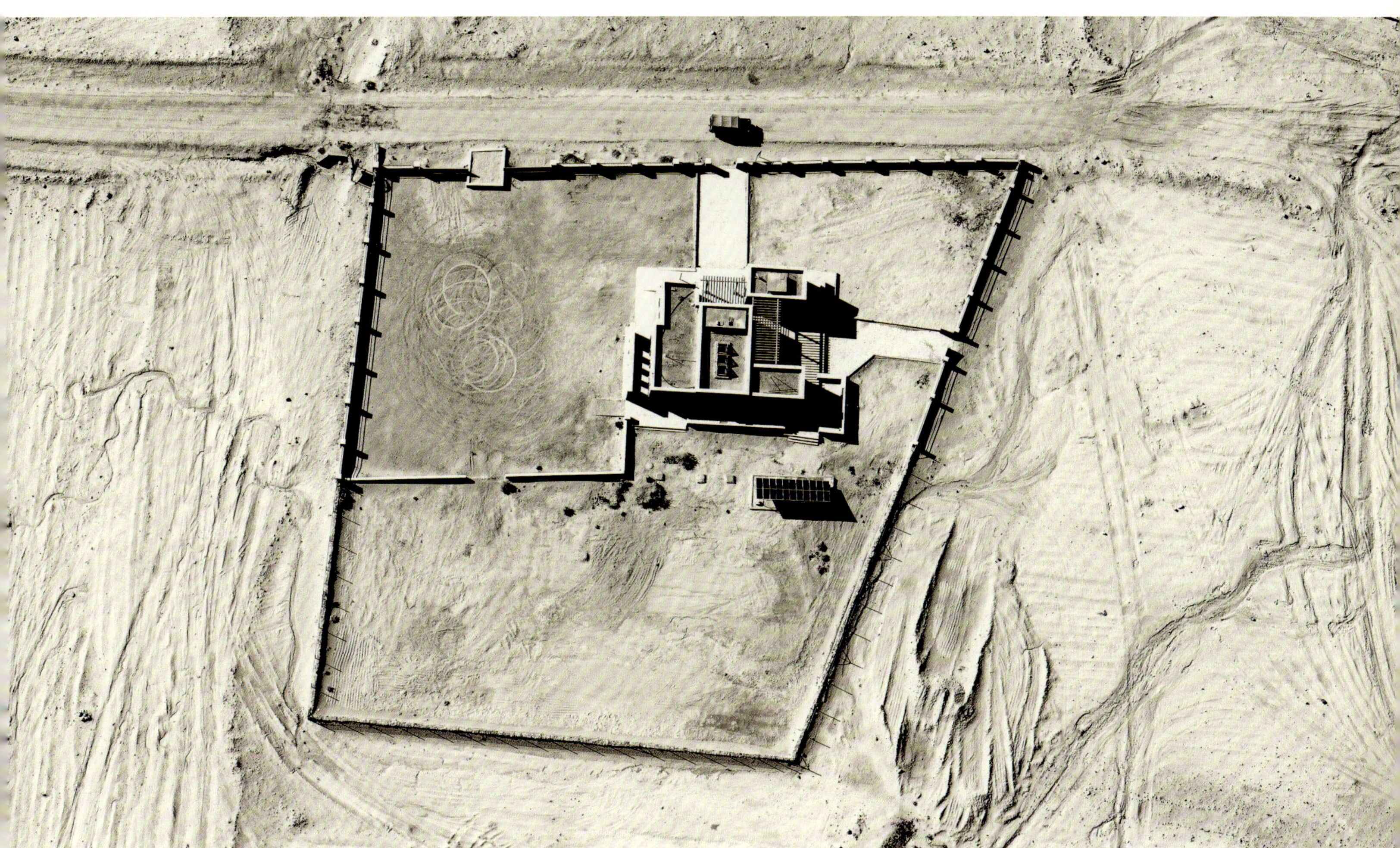

101

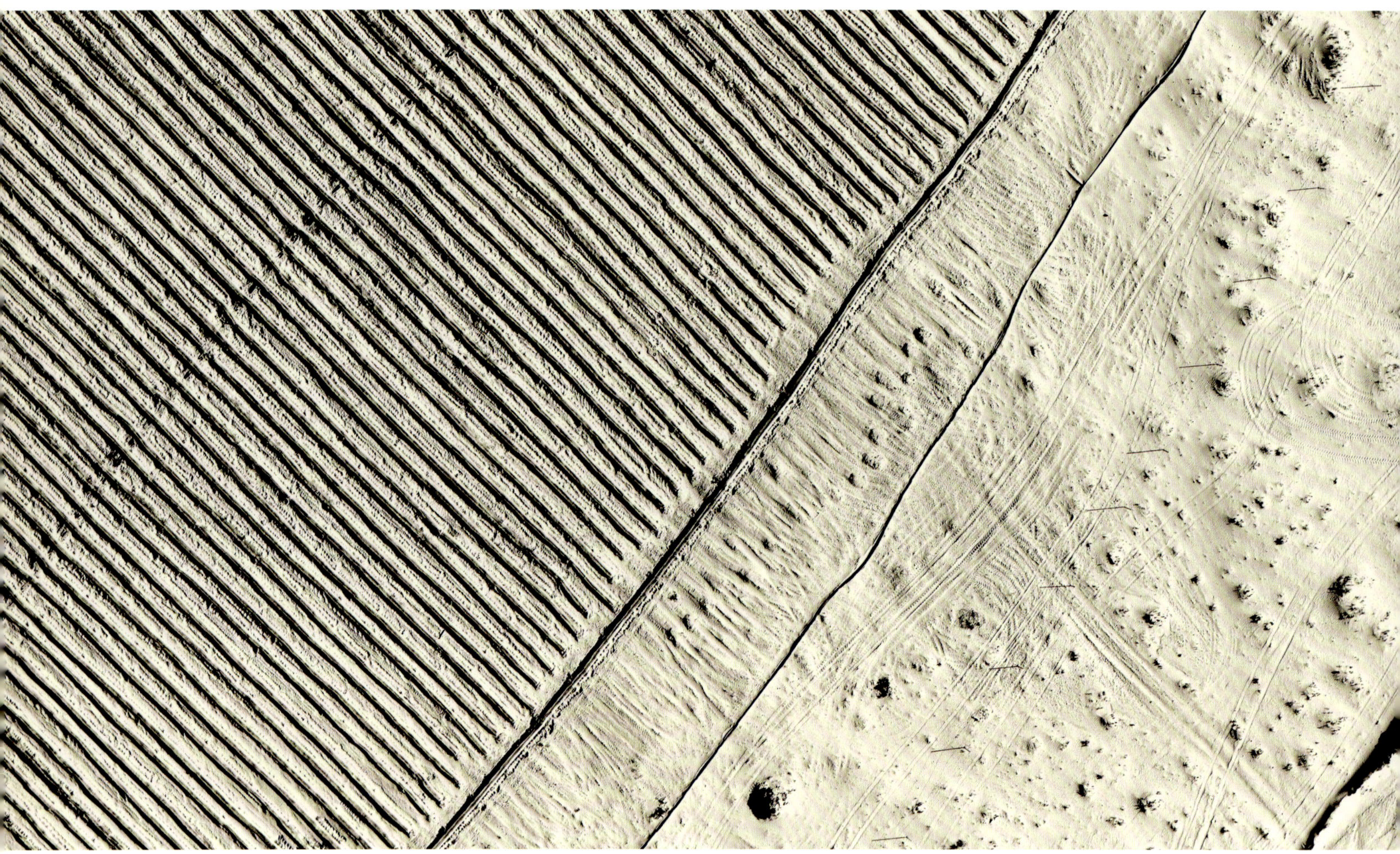

102

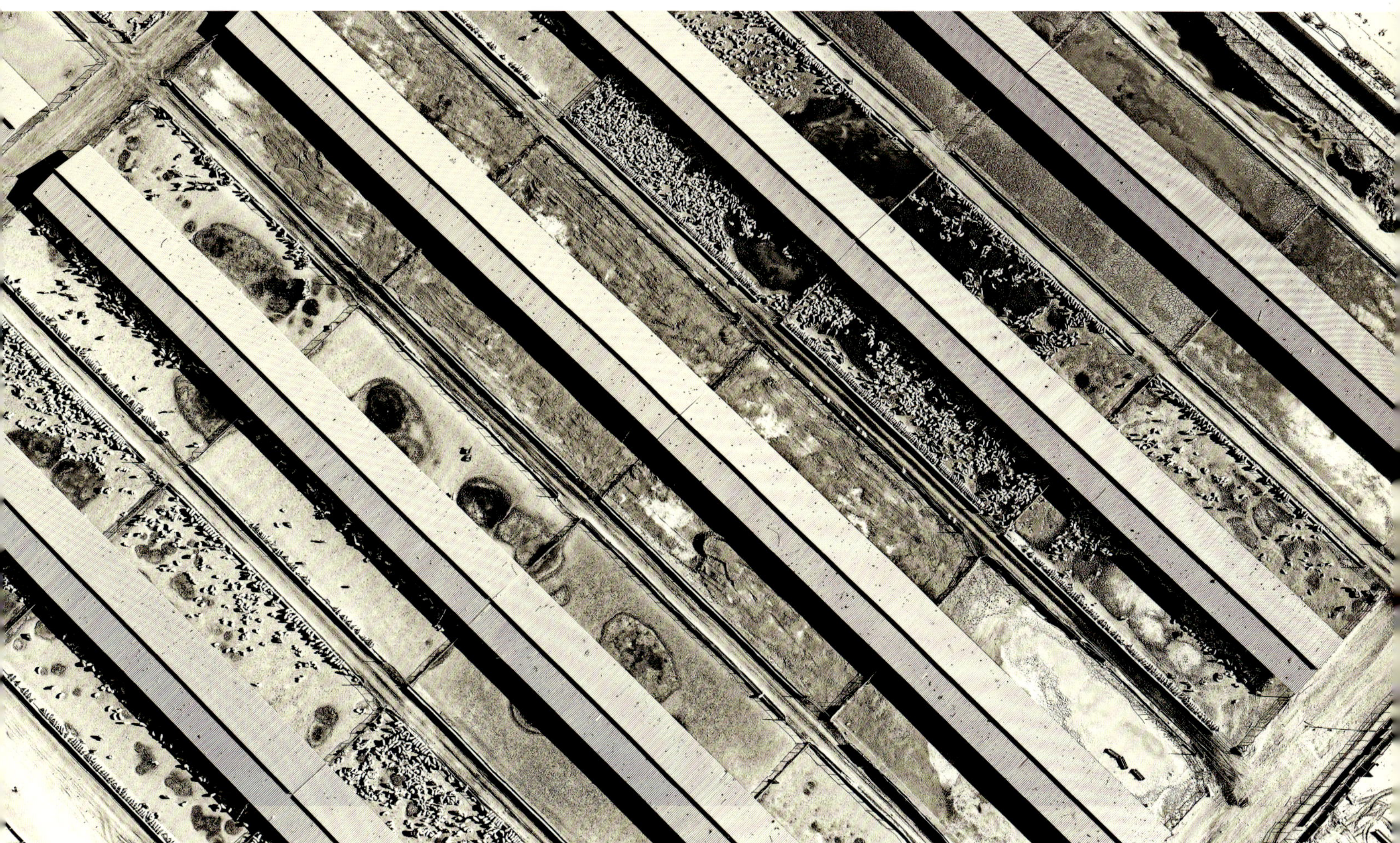

103

104. Installation photograph of
Shadow Sites II, 2011

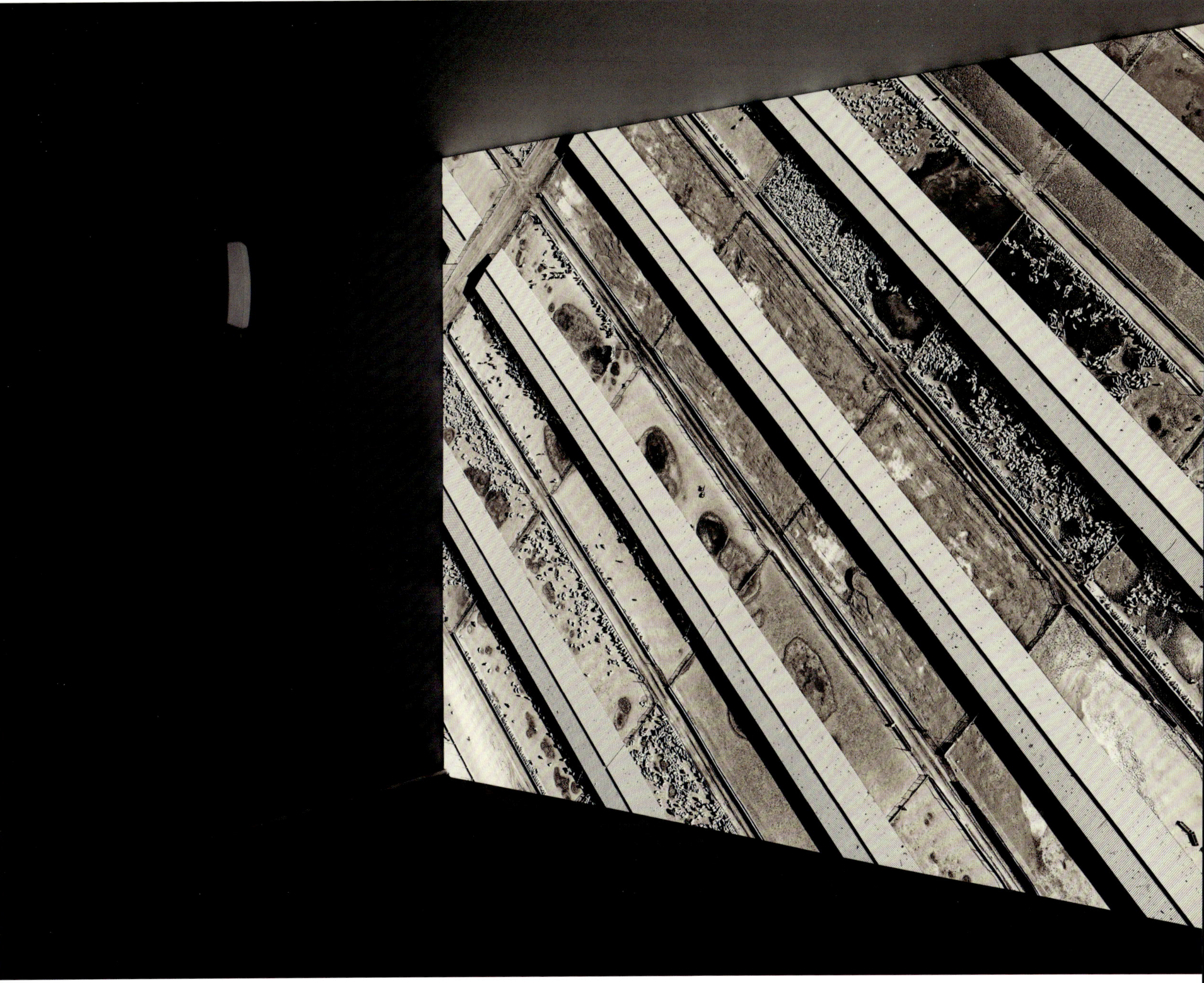

pages 9–19

1 See Michket Krifa, ed., *Femmes d'images, fragments d'intimité* (Paris: AFAA, 2006); Michket Krifa, ed., *Femmes d'images, espace privé* (Tunis: Institut français de coopération, 2007).

2 Samuel Herzog, "Art local: Perception globale," in *Créations artistiques contemporaines en pays d'Islam: Des arts en tensions* (Paris: Editions Kimé, 2006), 567.

3 For instance, in the exhibition *Le corps comme territoire* at the photography festival Rencontres d'Arles, Arles, France (2002).

4 Fatima Mernissi, *Le harem et l'Occident* (Paris: Albin Michel, 2001), 9.

5 Roland Barthes, *Camera Lucida: Reflections on Photography*, trans. Richard Howard (New York: Hill and Wang, 1981), 153.

pages 21–35

1 The contested term "Middle East," originally coined by the British government and popularized by a U.S. naval strategist, is used in this essay to refer to a geographical region, though the photographers come from Iran and the Arab world alone.

2 Venues that have contributed to the increased attention to art from the Middle East include long-established galleries that focus on Arab and/or Iranian art, such as Rose Issa Projects in London, the Silk Road Gallery in Tehran, Darat Al Fannun in Amman, and The Townhouse Gallery in Cairo. Among more recently founded organizations that have provided new exhibition platforms are the Contemporary Image Collective (CIC) in Cairo, 2004; FANOOS in Tehran, 2008; the Beirut Art Center, 2009; and MATHAF: Arab Museum of Modern Art in Doha in 2010. They are joined by private collections such as the Nadour Collection, established in 2008; and the Khalid Shoman Foundation, incorporated in 2002. The international art fair Art Dubai, founded in 2007, now plays a major role in the contemporary art market.

"Arab Spring" is a term coined shortly after a wave of rebellions in the Arab world began in Tunisia on December 18, 2010. Initially referring to the uprisings of the spring of 2011, the term describes activities that have continued in the region in subsequent years.

3 Among the foremost commentators on photography in the Arab world, Krifa was one of the first to make this observation. Michket Krifa, "A Short Inventory," in *Nazar: Photographs from the Arab World* (New York: Aperture, 2004), 10. See also her Foreword to this volume.

4 The Iranian Newsha Tavakolian and the Jordanian Tanya Habjouqa, both included in this volume, were founding members of Rawiya.

5 Nat Muller addresses the complications of presenting a survey of contemporary art from the Middle East in her "Contemporary Art in the Middle East," in Paul Sloman, ed., *Contemporary Art in the Middle East* (London: Blackdog Publishing, 2009), 12. The term "Islamic art" has been used to describe contemporary secular art made in places under Islamic influence or rule. I have chosen to refer instead to the artists' geographic origins. For more discussion on this topic, see Fereshteh Daftari, "Islamic or Not," in *Without Boundary: Seventeen Ways of Looking*, exh. cat. (New York: Museum of Modern Art, 2006), 10–27, and Glenn D. Lowry, "Oil and Sugar: Contemporary Art and Islamic Culture," Eva Holtby Lecture on Contemporary Culture, vol. 3 (Toronto: Institute for Contemporary Culture at the Royal Ontario Museum, 2009). See also Nasser Rabbat, "What's in a Name? The New 'Islamic Art' Galleries at the Met," *Artforum* 50, no. 8 (January 2012), accessed online.

6 Pioneering photographers in the region, particularly in the nineteenth century, include Frederic Goupil-Fesquet, Maxime du Camp, Auguste Salzmann, James Robertson and Francis Frith.

7 See Issam Nassar, "Early Photography in the Eastern Arab World," *Nazar: Photographs from the Arab World* (New York: Aperture, 2004), 14–15.

8 See Van Leo, Armand, and Alban, *Portraits du Caire*, with a preface by Mounira Khemir (Arles: Actes Sud / Fondation arabe pour l'image, 1999).

9 See Rose Issa, "Interwoven Temporalities," in Rose Issa and Michket Krifa, eds., *Arab Photography Now* (Heidelberg: Kehrer Verlag, 2011), 13.

10 Jalali has had a significant influence on three of the photographers in *She Who Tells a Story* (Shadi Ghadirian, Gohar Dashti, and Newsha Tavakolian).

11 For instance, the film directors Samira Makhmalbaf, Rakhshan Bani Etemad, Mania Akbari, and Forouq Farrokhzad, some of whom emerged as early as the 1950s and '60s. Interview with Rose Issa in Sloman, ed., *Contemporary Art in the Middle East*, 198.

12 The Iranian-born professor Hamid Naficy has observed that "the rise of differently situated women directors is emblematic and constitutive of the forceful emergence of women into the public space in many spheres, including politics, cinema, television, press, and performing and visual arts." Hamid Naficy, "Poetics and Politics of Veil, Voice and Vision in Iranian Post-revolutionary Cinema," in David A. Bailey and Gilane Tawadros, eds., *Veil: Veiling, Representation and Contemporary Art*, exh. cat. (Cambridge: MIT Press, 2003), 138.

13 Omid Rouhani, "Pionnières," *art press* 2, no. 17 (May–July 2010): 54.

14 Unless otherwise noted, quotations of or references to statements by the artists in this book are from personal communications or interviews with the author.

15 Hammam stresses, however, that she rejects the preconceived notion that women are more oppressed than men in Egypt.

16 For discussion of the Orientalist debate in the context of contemporary art in the Middle East, see the appendix in Sloman, ed., *Contemporary Art in the Middle East*, which includes essays by scholar Zachary Lockman and interviews with

significant figures in the contemporary art world. For a discussion of the representation of women in historically unequal power relationships, see Sarah Graham-Brown's comprehensive study *Images of Women: The Portrayal of Women in Photography of the Middle East, 1860–1950* (New York: Columbia University Press, 1988).

17 Jananne Al-Ani, "Acting Out," in Bailey and Tawadros, *Veil*, 93.

18 See ibid., 106. Al-Ani was co-curator of the exhibition *Veil*, which was organized by the Institute of International Visual Arts in association with the Iran Heritage Foundation and held in Walsall, Liverpool, and Oxford, U.K., in 2003–4. In conversation, the artist has further pointed out that the veil is not unique to Muslim culture and appears widely in the representations of many others, including Christianity. See also ibid., 18.

19 Both Neshat and Essaydi emigrated to the United States, and the Iraqi-Irish Al-Ani lives in London. Other photographers in this publication (Rania Matar, Tanya Habjouqa, Boushra Almutawakel, and Nermine Hammam) have also lived for significant periods of time in other cultures.

20 Neshat and Al-Ani have significantly changed their artistic orientation since the 1990s, while Essaydi's work has remained in constant dialogue with the history of visual Orientalism.

21 See Kelly Baum, "Art, Precarity, and Biopolitics," in Judith Brodsky and Ferris Olin, eds., *The Fertile Crescent: Gender, Art, and Society* (New Brunswick: Rutgers University Institute for Women and Art, 2012), 45.

22 As the curators David A. Bailey and Gilane Tawadros point out, "in some ways, Neshat's works can be seen as protagonists entering the stage on which the veil and veiling have been embroiled in the history of the struggle against colonialism and, more recently neo-colonialism." Bailey and Tawadros, *Veil*, 35.

23 Lalla Essaydi, interview with the author, New York, September 28, 2012, transcription, Museum of Fine Arts, Boston.

24 It is important to note that while the Quran, the sacred book of Islam, recommends modesty, it does not require the *hijab*. The doctrine that women cover themselves is related to an interpretation of the *hadith*, sacred texts written after the Quran. The *hijab* is not systematically imposed on Muslim women; for some, it reflects a personal religious choice, and for others, an aesthetic preference. Almutawakel was inspired by a parallel that Egyptian feminist writer Nawal Elsadawi has drawn between the wearing of makeup and headscarves.

25 On this issue, see Ramin Sadighi, "La musique et la loi," *art press* 2, no. 17 (May–July 2010): 102.

26 Rose Issa, "Still Revelations," *Iranian Photography Now* (Ostfildern: Hatje Cantz Verlag, 2008), 13.

27 Marta Weiss, "Recording, Reframing, and Resisting," in Marta Weiss, Venetia Porter, Kate Best, and Stephen Deucher, *Light from the Middle East: New Photography*, exh. cat. (London: Steidl Verlag, 2012).

28 Venetia Porter discusses another artist's appropriation of this image in a painting, which was ultimately banned at Art Dubai in 2012, in "Behind the Image," ibid., 122.

29 While Hammam uses "found images," the Tunisian-Belgian photographer Karim Ben Khelifa explains that to avoid hostility and blend in with protesters in Yemen during the Arab Spring, he chose to use his iPhone as a camera.

30 The political and cultural change throughout the region beginning in 2009, particularly in Iran and several Arab countries, has had a direct effect on photographers' work. Tavakolian has shifted more toward fine-art photography, and Hammam now tends to appropriate images from the media rather than making her own. The changes in Ghadirian's and Dashti's work after 2009 may also respond to the restrictions that were placed on photographers' work.

31 Al-Ani's starting point for this project was forensic work conducted by the anthropologist Margaret Cox in Kosovo in the 1990s for the purposes of the prosecution of war crimes, involving evidence that emerged from the unearthing of mass graves and the study of natural elements at genocide sites. Al-Ani was also inspired by the cultural theorist Paul Virilio's 1980 seminal text "The Aesthetics of Disappearance," as she explains in Sharmini Pereira, ed., *Footnote to a Project: The 2011 Abraaj Capital Art Prize* (London: Abraaj Capital Art Prize, 2011), 105–207.

page 39

1 *http://lallaessaydi.com*, accessed 4/1/2013.

2 Ibid.

pages 43–44

1 Q&A: Boushra Almutawakel, "Challenging the Norm," *The Economist*, "Prospero: Books, Arts, and Culture" blog, posted Aug. 16, 2012 (*www.economist.com/blogs/prospero*).

2 Ibid.

page 51

1 Rania Matar, *Ordinary Lives* (New York: Quantuck Lane Press, dist. W. W. Norton, 2009), 124.

2 Quotations from the artist are from her website, *www.raniamatar.com*, accessed 11/1/2012.

page 59

1 Arthur C. Danto and Marina Abramović, *Shirin Neshat* (New York: Rizzoli, 2010), 19.

page 69

1 See Venetia Porter et al., *Hajj: Journey to the Heart of Islam*, exh. cat. (Cambridge, Mass.: Harvard University Press, 2012).

page 93

1 From the artist's website, *www.gohardashti.com*, accessed 11/1/2012.

page 130

1 Omar Al-Quattan and Rose Issa, *Nermine Hammam: Cairo Year One*, exh. cat. (London: The Mosaic Rooms/Rose Issa Projects, 2012), 12.

2 Ibid., 26–28.

pages 141–42

1 See David A. Bailey and Gilane Tawadros, eds., Veil: *Veiling, Representation, and Contemporary Art*, exh. cat. (Cambridge, Mass.: MIT Press, 2003).

2 Jananne Al-Ani, "Acting Out," ibid., 92.

3 The artist states that an important reference for these images is *The Colonial Harem* (Minneapolis: University of Minnesota Press, 1986), in which Malek Alloula examines postcards of Algerian women produced during the French occupation: "Alloula draws a compelling analogy between the gaze of the veiled woman and that of the photographer. It was this confrontation between the photographer (the viewer) and the veiled woman (the subject of the photograph) which I try to draw attention to in this work. The work attempted to find a new and radical space in which to think about the image of the veil that would challenge its popular stereotypes either as a sign of the oppression of Muslim women or as a highly sexualized and seductive prop in an Orientalist fantasy." These stereotypical understandings of the veil shifted after 9/11 and the emergence of radical Islam: "Once the image of veiled Chechen hostage takers and Palestinian suicide bombers started to infiltrate the news, a new mythology began to emerge in which the veiled Muslim woman became a terrifying and dangerous agent—one of the reasons it became impossible for me to continue to use the actual veil in my work and that led me to consider all the other ways in which the idea or metaphor of the veil and veiling could function in a visual context." Personal communication, March 21, 2013.

4 Sharmini Pereira, ed., *Footnote to a Project: The 2011 Abraaj Capital Art Prize* (London: Abraaj Capital Art Prize, 2011), 191.

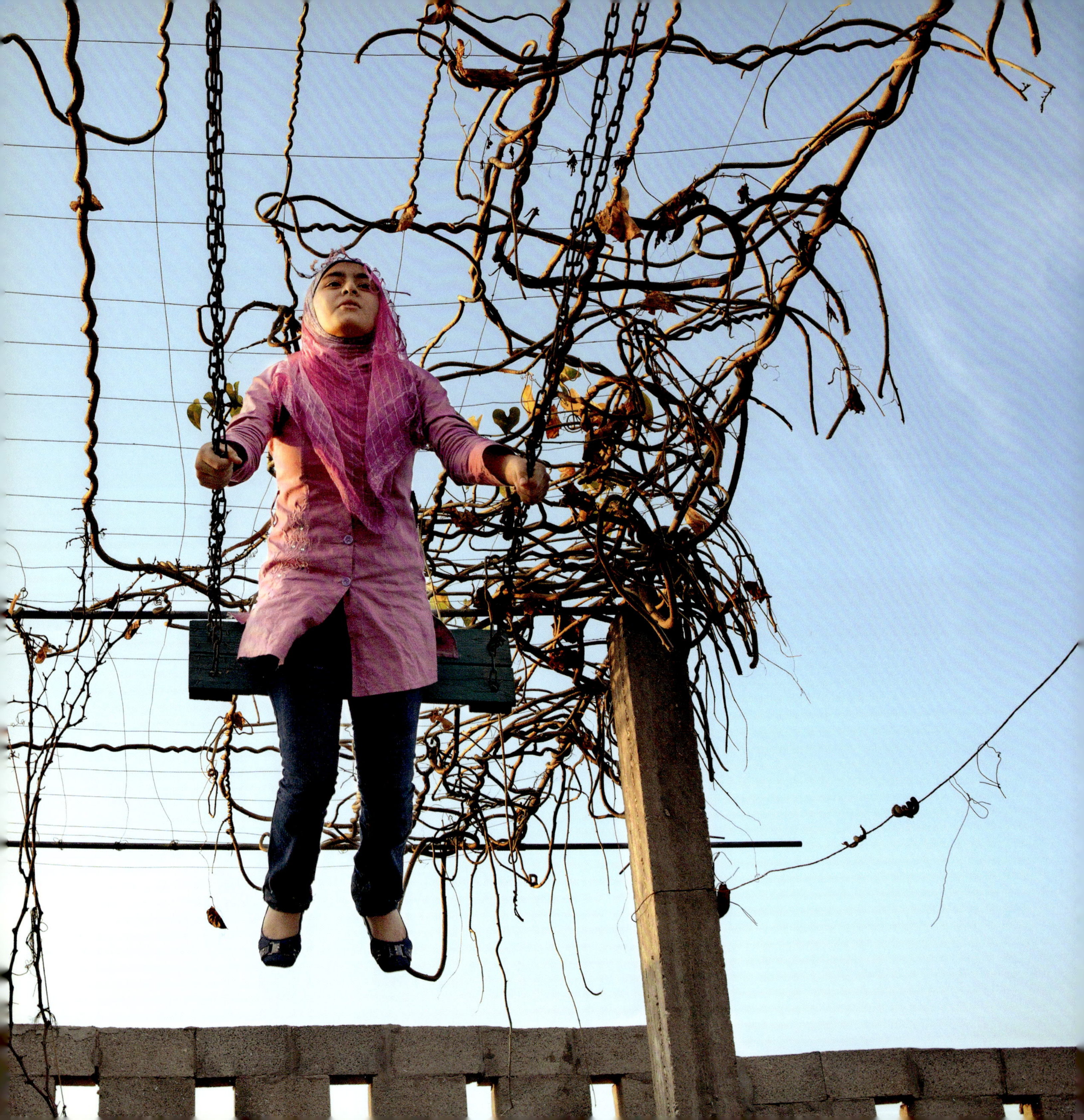

Shirin Neshat (b. 1957)
1. *Identified*, 1995
From *Women of Allah* series
Gelatin silver print with pen and ink
Framed: 132.1 x 88.9 cm (52 x 35 in.)
Collection of Michael Mattis and
Judith Hochberg
Courtesy of Gladstone Gallery,
New York and Brussels
Photograph: Cynthia Preston

Jananne Al-Ani (b. 1966)
2–3. Untitled, 1996
Gelatin silver prints
Each: 122 x 182 cm (48 x 71 ⅝ in.)
Smithsonian Freer/Sackler Galleries of Art
Courtesy of the artist and Rose Issa
Projects

Shadi Ghadirian (b. 1974)
4, 7–8. From *Qajar* series, 1998
Gelatin silver prints
Each: 40 x 30 cm (about 16 x 12 in.)
Courtesy of the artist

6 and 9. From *Qajar* series, 1998
Gelatin silver prints
Each: 40 x 30 cm (about 16 x 12 in.)
Museum of Fine Arts, Boston
Horace W. Goldsmith Fund for
Photography and Abbott Lawrence Fund,
2013.570–71

Shirin Neshat (b. 1957)
5. Untitled, 1996
From *Women of Allah* series
Gelatin silver print with pen and ink
167.6 x 132.1 cm (66 x 52 in.)
Collection of Lucille and Richard
Spagnuolo
Courtesy of Gladstone Gallery,
New York and Brussels
Photograph: Larry Barns

10. *Speechless*, 1996
From *Women of Allah* series
Gelatin silver print with pen and ink
167.6 x 132.1 cm (66 x 52 in.)
Los Angeles County Museum of Art,
purchased with funds provided by
Jamie McCourt through the 2012
Collector's Committee
Courtesy of Gladstone Gallery,
New York and Brussels

11. *I Am Its Secret*, 1993
From *Women of Allah* series
Gelatin silver print with pen and ink
33 x 22.9 cm (13 x 9 in.)
Collection of Michael Mattis and
Judith Hochberg
Courtesy of Gladstone Gallery,
New York and Brussels
Photograph: Plauto

12. *Mystified*, 1997
From the film *Turbulent*
Gelatin silver print with pen and ink
94 x 139.7 cm (37 x 55 in.)
Courtesy of Galerie Jérôme de
Noirmont, Paris

Lalla Essaydi (b. 1956)
13. *Converging Territories #29*, 2004
Chromogenic print
142.2 x 111.8 cm (56 x 44 in.)
Museum of Fine Arts, Boston
2005.30

14. *Bullets Revisited #3*, 2012
Triptych, three chromogenic prints
on aluminum
Overall: 1.68 x 3.81 m (5 ½ x 12 ½ ft)
Courtesy of the artist and
Howard Yezerski Gallery

Boushra Almutawakel (b. 1969)
15. Untitled, 2001
From *The Hijab* series
Chromogenic print
120 x 100 cm (47 ¼ x 39 ⅜ in.)
Courtesy of the artist

16–24. *Mother, Daughter, Doll* series, 2010
Chromogenic prints
Each: 60 x 40 cm (about 24 x 16 in.)
Museum of Fine Arts, Boston
Museum purchase with funds donated by
Richard and Lucille Spagnuolo,
2013.556–64

Rania Matar (b. 1964)
25. *Christilla, Rabieh, Lebanon*, 2010
From *A Girl and Her Room* series
Pigment print
86.4 x 122 cm (34 x 48 in.)
Courtesy of the artist and Carroll
and Sons, Boston

26. *Alia, Beirut, Lebanon*, 2010
From *A Girl and Her Room* series
Pigment print
86.4 x 122 cm (34 x 48 in.)
Courtesy of the artist and Carroll
and Sons, Boston

27. *Reem, Doha, Lebanon*, 2010
From *A Girl and Her Room* series
Pigment print
86.4 x 122 cm (34 x 48 in.)
Courtesy of the artist and Carroll
and Sons, Boston

28. *Stephanie, Beirut, Lebanon*, 2010
From *A Girl and Her Room* series
Pigment print
86.4 x 122 cm (34 x 48 in.)
Courtesy of the artist and Carroll
and Sons, Boston

29. *Mariam, Bourj al Shamali Palestinian
Refugee Camp, Tyre, Lebanon*, 2009
From *A Girl and Her Room* series
Pigment print
86.4 x 122 cm (34 x 48 in.)
Courtesy of the artist and Carroll
and Sons, Boston

30. *Bisan, Bethlehem, West Bank*, 2009
From *A Girl and Her Room* series
Pigment print
86.4 x 122 cm (34 x 48 in.)
Courtesy of the artist and Carroll
and Sons, Boston

Shirin Neshat (b. 1957)
31. *Roja*, 2012
From *Book of Kings* series (Patriots)
Gelatin silver print with pen and ink
152.4 x 114.3 cm (60 x 45 in.)
Museum of Fine Arts, Boston
Charles Bain Hoyt Fund and Francis
Welch Fund, 2013.554

32. *Ahmed*, 2012
From *Book of Kings* series (Masses)
Gelatin silver print with pen and ink
101.6 x 76.2 cm (40 x 30 in.)
Courtesy of Galerie Jérôme de
Noirmont, Paris

33. *Marjan*, 2012
From *Book of Kings* series (Masses)
Gelatin silver print with pen and ink
101.6 x 76.2 cm (40 x 30 in.)
Courtesy of Galerie Jérôme de
Noirmont, Paris

34. *Taraneh*, 2012
From *Book of Kings* series (Masses)
Gelatin silver print with pen and ink
101.6 x 76.2 cm (40 x 30 in.)
Courtesy of Galerie Jérôme de
Noirmont, Paris

35. *Kouross*, 2012
From *Book of Kings* series (Masses)
Gelatin silver print with pen and ink
101.6 x 76.2 cm (40 x 30 in.)
Courtesy of Gladstone Gallery,
New York and Brussels

36. *Mosaeb*, 2012
From *Book of Kings* series (Masses)
Gelatin silver print with pen and ink
101.6 x 76.2 cm (40 x 30 in.)
Courtesy of Gladstone Gallery,
New York and Brussels

37. *Ava*, 2012
From *Book of Kings* series (Masses)
Gelatin silver print with pen and ink
101.6 x 76.2 cm (40 x 30 in.)
Courtesy of Gladstone Gallery,
New York and Brussels

38. *Divine Rebellion*, 2012
From *Book of Kings* series
Gelatin silver print with acrylic
157.5 x 124.5 cm (62 x 49 in.)
Courtesy of Galerie Jérôme de
Noirmont, Paris

Newsha Tavakolian (b. 1981)
39. Untitled, 2010
From *Listen* series
Chromogenic print
100 x 120 cm (39 ⅜ x 47 ¼ in.)
Courtesy of the artist and East Wing
Contemporary Gallery

40. *Maral Afsharian*, 2010
From *Listen* series
Chromogenic print
60 x 80 cm (23 ⅝ x 31 ½ in.)
Courtesy of the artist and East Wing
Contemporary Gallery

41. *Mahsa Vahdat*, 2010
From *Listen* series
Chromogenic print
60 x 80 cm (23 ⅝ x 31 ½ in.)
Courtesy of the artist and East Wing
Contemporary Gallery

42. *Azita Akhavan*, 2010
From *Listen* series
Chromogenic print
60 x 80 cm (23 ⅝ x 31 ½ in.)
Courtesy of the artist and East Wing
Contemporary Gallery

43. *Ghazal Shakari*, 2010
From *Listen* series
Chromogenic print
60 x 80 cm (23 ⅝ x 31 ½ in.)
Courtesy of the artist and East Wing
Contemporary Gallery

44. *Sayeh Sodaifi*, 2010
From *Listen* series
Chromogenic print
60 x 80 cm (23 ⅝ x 31 ½ in.)
Courtesy of the artist and East Wing
Contemporary Gallery

45. *Sahar Lotfi*, 2010
From *Listen* series
Chromogenic print
60 x 80 cm (23 ⅝ x 31 ½ in.)
Courtesy of the artist and East Wing
Contemporary Gallery

46. Installation photograph of *Listen*, 2010
From *Listen* series
Six-screen video
Courtesy of the artist and East Wing
Contemporary Gallery

47. *When I Was Twenty Years Old*
(for Maral Afsharian), 2010
From *Listen* series
Chromogenic print mounted on aluminum
31 x 31 cm (12 ¼ x 12 ¼ in.)
Courtesy of the artist and East Wing
Contemporary Gallery

48. *I Am Eve* (for Mahsa Vahdat), 2010
From *Listen* series
Chromogenic print mounted on aluminum
31 x 31 cm (12 ¼ x 12 ¼ in.)
Courtesy of the artist and East Wing
Contemporary Gallery

49. *This Is Not in the Dream of Eastern
Women* (for Azita Akhavan), 2010
From *Listen* series
Chromogenic print mounted on aluminum
31 x 31 cm (12 ¼ x 12 ¼ in.)
Courtesy of the artist and East Wing
Contemporary Gallery

50. *Glass Ceilings* (for Ghazal Shakari), 2010
From *Listen* series
Chromogenic print mounted on aluminum
31 x 31 cm (12 ¼ x 12 ¼ in.)
Courtesy of the artist and East Wing
Contemporary Gallery

51. *Again, I Stayed Behind, in the Empty Cold*
(for Sayeh Sodaifi), 2010
From *Listen* series
Chromogenic print mounted on aluminum
31 x 31 cm (12 ¼ x 12 ¼ in.)
Courtesy of the artist and East Wing
Contemporary Gallery

52. *Don't Forget This Is Not You*
(for Sahar Lotfi), 2010
From *Listen* series
Chromogenic print mounted on aluminum
31 x 31 cm (12 ¼ x 12 ¼ in.)
Courtesy of the artist and East Wing
Contemporary Gallery

Shadi Ghadirian (b. 1974)
53. *Nil, Nil #4*, 2008
Chromogenic print
110 x 75 cm (about 45 x 30 in.)
Courtesy of the artist

54. *Nil, Nil #1*, 2008
Chromogenic print
75 x 75 cm (about 30 x 30 in.)
Courtesy of the artist

55. *Nil, Nil #14*, 2008
Chromogenic print
75 x 110 cm (about 30 x 45 in.)
Courtesy of the artist

56. *Nil, Nil #8*, 2008
Chromogenic print
75 x 110 cm (about 30 x 45 in.)
Courtesy of the artist

57. *Nil, Nil #11*, 2008
Chromogenic print
75 x 75 cm (about 30 x 30 in.)
Courtesy of the artist

58. *Nil, Nil #10*, 2008
Chromogenic print
75 x 110 cm (about 30 x 45 in.)
Courtesy of the artist

Gohar Dashti (b. 1980)
59. *Untitled #2*
From *Today's Life and War* series, 2008
Chromogenic print
70 x 105 cm (about 30 x 40 in.)
Museum of Fine Arts, Boston
Museum purchase with funds donated
by the Weintz Family Harbor Lights
Foundation, 2013.555

60–64. *Untitled #1, 4, 5, 7,* and *8*
From *Today's Life and War* series, 2008
Chromogenic prints
Each: 70 x 105 cm (about 30 x 40 in.)
Courtesy of the artist and
White Projects Gallery

Rana El Nemr (b. 1974)
65–68. *Metro #22, 16, 10,* and *21*
From *The Metro* series, 2003
Chromogenic prints
Each: 100 x 100 cm (39 ⅜ x 39 ⅜ in.)
Courtesy of the artist

69. *Metro #20*, 2003
From *The Metro* series
Chromogenic print
100 x 100 cm (39 ⅜ x 39 ⅜ in.)
Museum of Fine Arts, Boston
Museum purchase with general funds and
the Abbott Lawrence Fund, 2013.568

70. Metro #1, 2003
From *The Metro* series
Chromogenic print
100 x 100 cm (39 ⅜ x 39 ⅜ in.)
Courtesy of the artist

71. *Metro #7*, 2003
From *The Metro* series
Chromogenic print
100 x 100 cm (39 ⅜ x 39 ⅜ in.)
Museum of Fine Arts, Boston
Museum purchase with general funds and
the Abbott Lawrence Fund, 2013.569

Tanya Habjouqa (b. 1975)
72–74. From *Women of Gaza* series, 2009
Chromogenic prints
Each: 50.8 x 76.2 cm (about 20 x 30 in.)
Museum of Fine Arts, Boston
Museum purchase with general funds
and the Horace W. Goldsmith Fund for
Photography, 2013.565–67

75–77. From *Women of Gaza* series, 2009
Chromogenic prints
Each: 50.8 x 76.2 cm (about 20 x 30 in.)
Courtesy of the artist and East Wing
Contemporary Gallery

Rula Halawani (b. 1964)
78. *Untitled V*, 2002
From *Negative Incursions* series
Chromogenic print
90 x 124 cm (about 35 x 49 in.)
Courtesy of the artist and
Selma Feriani Gallery, London

79. *Untitled I*, 2002
From *Negative Incursions* series
Chromogenic print
90 x 124 cm (about 35 x 49 in.)
Courtesy of the artist and
Selma Feriani Gallery, London

80. *Untitled XVII*, 2002
From *Negative Incursions* series
Chromogenic print
90 x 124 cm (about 35 x 49 in.)
Courtesy of the artist and
Selma Feriani Gallery, London

81. *Untitled XIII*, 2002
From *Negative Incursions* series
Chromogenic print
90 x 124 cm (about 35 x 49 in.)
Courtesy of the artist and
Selma Feriani Gallery, London

82. *Untitled X*, 2002
From *Negative Incursions* series
Chromogenic print
90 x 124 cm (about 35 x 49 in.)
Courtesy of the artist and
Selma Feriani Gallery, London

83. *Untitled VI*, 2002
From *Negative Incursions* series
Chromogenic print
90 x 124 cm (about 35 x 49 in.)
Courtesy of the artist and
Selma Feriani Gallery, London

84. *Untitled XIX*, 2002
From *Negative Incursions* series
Chromogenic print
90 x 124 cm (about 35 x 49 in.)
Courtesy of the artist and
Selma Feriani Gallery, London

SUGGESTED READING

Ali, Wijdan. *Modern Islamic Art: Development and Continuity.* Gainesville: University Press of Florida, 1997.

Amirsadeghi, Hossein, ed. *Different Sames: New Perspectives in Contemporary Iranian Art.* London: Thames & Hudson, 2009.

——, Salwa Mikdadi, and Nada Shabout, eds. *New Vision: Arab Contemporary Art in the 21st Century.* London: Transglobe, 2011.

Ankori, Gannit. *Palestinian Art.* London: Reaktion Books, 2006.

Bailey, David A., and Gilane Tawadros, eds. *Veil: Veiling, Representation, and Contemporary Art.* Cambridge, Mass.: MIT Press, 2003.

Brodsky, Judith K., and Ferris Olin, eds. *The Fertile Crescent: Gender, Art, and Society.* New Brunswick, N.J.: Rutgers University Institute for Women and Art, 2012.

Daftari, Fereshteh. *Without Boundary: Seventeen Ways of Looking.* New York: Museum of Modern Art, 2006.

Downey, Anthony, and Lina Lazaar, eds. *The Future of a Promise.* Tunis: Ibraaz Publishing, Kamel Lazaar Foundation, 2011.

Eigner, Saeb, ed. *Art of the Middle East: Modern and Contemporary Art of the Arab World and Iran.* London: Merrell Publishers, 2010.

Ghabaian Etehadieh, Anahita. *La photographie iranienne: un regard sur la création contemporaine en Iran.* Paris: Loco; Tehran: Silk Road Gallery, 2012.

Golia, Maria. *Photography and Egypt.* London: Reaktion Books, 2009.

Graham-Brown, Sarah. *Images of Women: The Portrayal of Women in Photography of the Middle East 1860–1950.* New York: Columbia University Press, 1988.

Issa, Rose. *Iranian Photography Now.* Ostfildern, Germany: Hatje Cantz, 2008.

——, and Michket Krifa, eds. *Arab Photography Now.* Heidelberg: Kehrer Verlag, 2011.

——, Ruyin Pakbaz, and Daryush Shayegan. *Iranian Contemporary Art.* London: Barbican Art Gallery/ Booth-Clibborn, 2001.

Jouannais, Jean-Yves. *Topographies de la guerre.* Göttingen: Steidl; Paris: Le Bal, 2011.

Khatibi, Abdelkebir, Nabil Naoum, and Brahim ben Hossain Alaoui. *Regards des photographes arabes contemporains.* Paris: Institut du monde arabe, 2005.

Krifa, Michket. *Femmes d'images, fragments d'intimité.* Paris: AFAA, 2006.

——. *Regards persans: Iran, une révolution photographique.* Paris: Paris Musées, 2001.

——. *Women by Women: Eight Women Photographers from the Arab World.* Frankfurt: Fotographie Forum International, 2004.

Lloyd, Fran. *Contemporary Arab Women's Art: Dialogues of the Present.* London: Women's Art Library, 1999.

Melis, Wim, ed. *Nazar: Photographs from the Arab World.* New York: Aperture, 2005.

Mori Art Museum. *Arab Express: The Latest Art from the Arab World.* Tokyo: Heibonsha, 2012.

Naef, Silvia. *Y a-t-il une "question de l'image" en Islam?* Paris: Téraèdre, 2004.

Poignet, Sylvie. *L'Orient des photographes arméniens.* Paris: Institut du monde arabe, 2007.

Porter, Venetia. *Word into Art: Artists of the Modern Middle East.* London: British Museum Press, 2006.

Rieffel, Véronique. *Islamania: De l'Alhambra à la burqa—histoire d'une fascination artistique.* Paris: Beaux Arts Editions, 2011.

Saatchi Gallery. *Unveiled: New Art from the Middle East.* London: Booth-Clibborn, 2009.

Sloman, Paul, ed. *Contemporary Art in the Middle East.* London: Black Dog Publishing, 2009.

Van Leo; Armand; and Alban. *Portraits du Caire.* Preface by Mounira Khemir. Arles: Actes Sud / Fondation arabe pour l'image, 1999.

Weiss, Marta. *Light from the Middle East: New Photography.* Göttingen: Steidl; London: V&A Publishing, 2012.

Jananne Al-Ani
Artist's website:
   janannealani.net
Doherty, Claire, et al. *Jananne Al-Ani.*
   London: Film & Video Umbrella,
   2005.

Boushra Almutawakel
Artist's website:
   boushraphoto.com

Gohar Dashti
Artist's website:
   gohardashti.com

Rana El Nemr
Krifa, Michket. *Women by Women:
   Eight Women Photographers
   from the Arab World.* Frankfurt:
   Fotographie Forum International,
   2004.

Lalla Essaydi
Artist's website:
   lallaessaydi.com
Essaydi, Lalla. *Converging Territories.*
   Brooklyn: powerHouse Books,
   2005.
——. *Les femmes du Maroc.* Brooklyn:
   powerHouse Books, 2009.

Shadi Ghadirian
Artist's website:
   shadighadirian.com
Issa, Rose, ed. *Shadi Ghadirian:
   Iranian Photographer.*
   London: Saqi Books, 2008.

Tanya Habjouqa
Artist's website:
   tanyahabjouqa.com

Rula Halawani
Gallery website:
   selmaferiani.com
Halawani, Rula. *Palestine.* Brussels:
   La Lettre Volée, 2008.

Nermine Hammam
Artist's website:
   nerminehammam.com
Issa, Rose, ed. *Nermine Hammam:
   Cairo Year One.* London:
   The Mosaic Rooms, 2012.

Rania Matar
Artist's website:
   raniamatar.com
Matar, Rania. *A Girl and Her Room.*
   New York: Umbrage Editions, 2012.
——. *Ordinary Lives.* New York:
   Quantuck Lane Press, 2009.

Shirin Neshat
Gallery website: *gladstonegallery.com*
Brownson, Ron. *Through the Eyes of
   Shirin Neshat.* Auckland: Auckland
   Art Gallery, 2004.
Danto, Arthur C., and Marina
   Abramović. *Shirin Neshat.* New
   York: Rizzoli, 2010.
Gagnon, Paulette, Shoja Azari,
   and Atom Egoyan. *Shirin
   Neshat.* Montréal: Musée d'art
   contemporain de Montréal, 2001.
Hart, Rebecca, Sussan Babaie, and
   Nancy Princenthal. *Shirin Neshat.*
   Detroit: Detroit Institute of Arts,
   2013.
Morin, France, and Catherine Choron-
   Baix. *Shirin Neshat: Games of
   Desire.* Milan: Charta, 2010.
Neshat, Shirin. *The Book of Kings.*
   Paris: Galerie Jérôme de
   Noirmont, 2012.
——. *Women Without Men.* Milan:
   Charta, 2011.
——. *Shirin Neshat: 2002–2005.* Milan:
   Charta, 2005.

Newsha Tavakolian
Artist's website:
   newshatavakolian.com
Tavakolian, Newsha. *The Fifth Pillar:
   The Hajj Pilgrimage.* London:
   Gilgamesh Publishing, 2012.

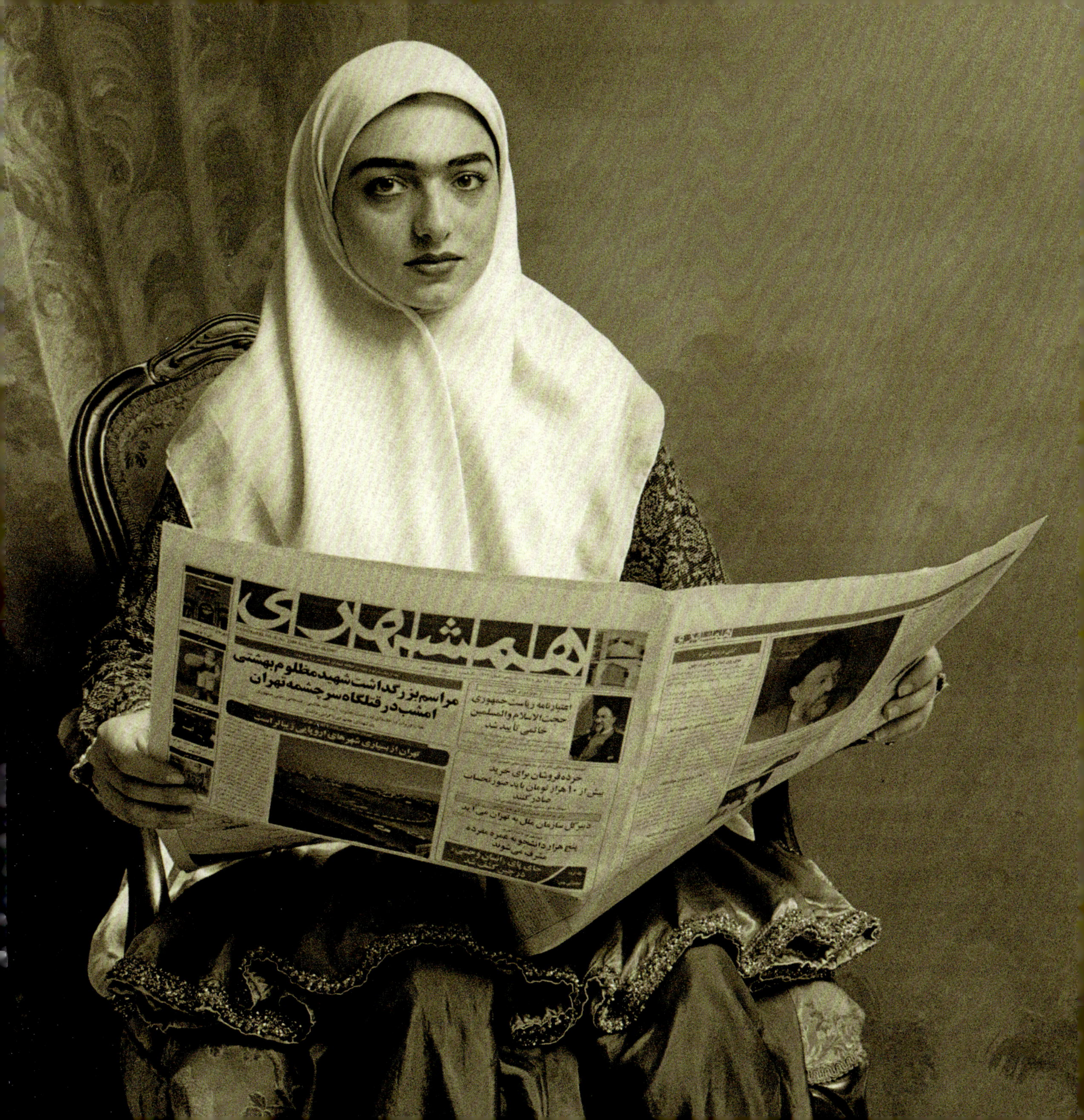
همشهری
مراسم بزرگداشت شهید مظلوم بهشتی
امشب در قتلگاه سرچشمه تهران
گران از بهای شربت های اروپایی زیاد است
اعتبارنامه ریاست جمهوری
حجت الاسلام والمسلین
خاتمی تأیید شد
خرده فروشان برای خرید
بیش از ۱۰ هزار تومان باید صورتحساب
صادر کنند
دبیر کل سازمان ملل به تهران می آید
پنج هزار دانشجوی عمره مفرده
مشرف می شوند

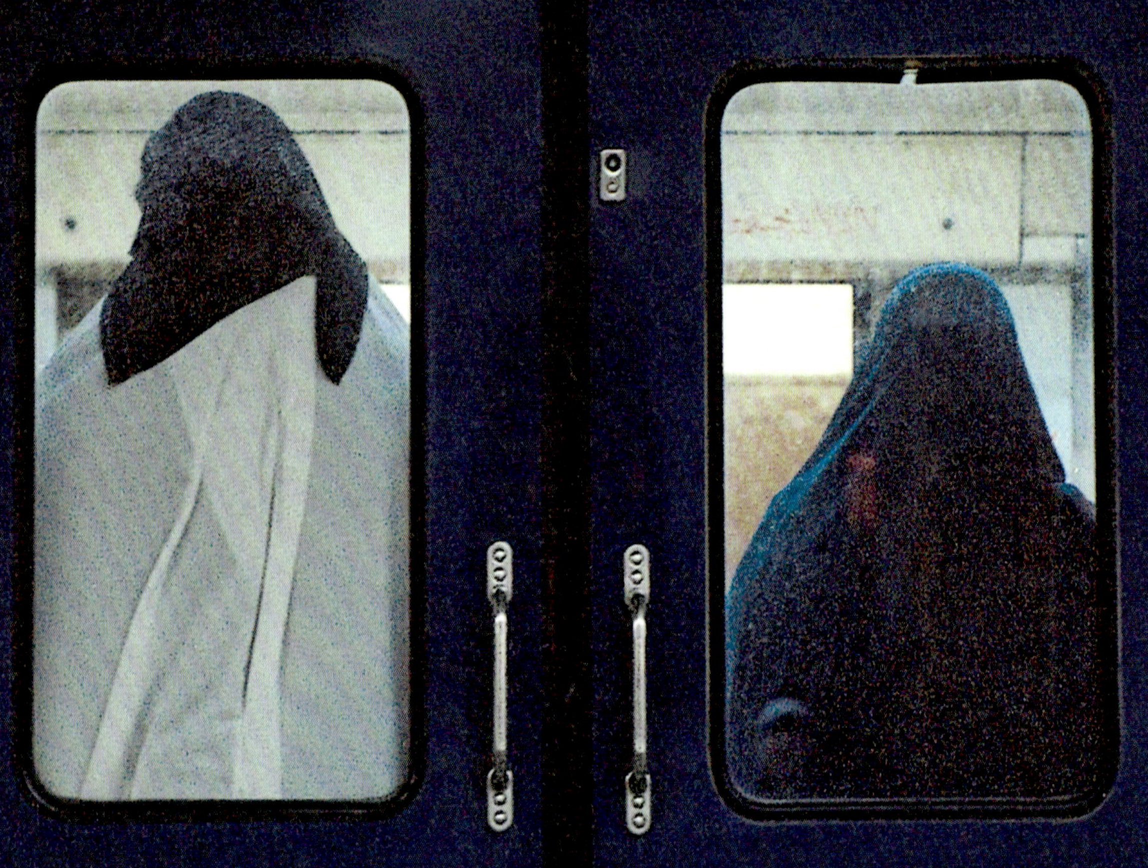

للصعود فقط

ACKNOWLEDGMENTS

She Who Tells a Story was made possible thanks to the help of many individuals and organizations to whom I am extremely grateful, including the lenders and supporters acknowledged in the Director's Foreword.

I would like first to extend my gratitude to the twelve photographers, for the stories told through their thought-provoking work and for their participation in this project: Jananne Al-Ani, Boushra Almutawakel, Gohar Dashti, Rana El Nemr, Lalla Essaydi, Shadi Ghadirian, Tanya Habjouqa, Rula Halawani, Nermine Hammam, Rania Matar, Shirin Neshat, and Newsha Tavakolian. I am grateful for their enthusiasm and for the many conversations that helped to inform and enrich this exhibition and catalogue. I am also indebted to the artists' galleries and representatives for their generosity, assistance, and support in this endeavor: Barbara Gladstone Gallery (Molly Epstein), Carroll and Sons (Joseph Carroll), East Wing Contemporary (Elie Domit and Hester Keijser), Galerie Jérôme de Noirmont (Jérôme de Noirmont, Jérôme Pauchant, Anais Ferrier), Galerie White Project (Camille Bayser and Nathalie Charriton), Howard Yezerski Gallery (Howard Yezerski), Rose Issa Projects (Rose Issa), Selma Feriani Gallery (Selma Feriani and Javier Robledo), Silk Road Gallery (Anahita Ghabaian Etehadieh), and Townhouse Gallery (William Wells, Mina Noshy, and Dina Kafafi). Special thanks go to Marc Elliott of Color Services

LLC. I am grateful to the private collectors who have lent significant work to this exhibition, including Michael Mattis and Judith Hochberg, and Lucille and Richard Spagnuolo, with special thanks to the Spagnuolos and to Teryn and Karl Weintz for their contributions toward acquisitions related to the exhibition.

I am also very grateful to Estrellita Karsh for her passion for photography and in particular for her vision of the place of photography at the MFA. With her late husband, the photographer Yousuf Karsh, she has made significant contributions to photography initiatives at the Museum, both in relation to this exhibition and beyond.

For her contribution to this book and for her pioneering role in exhibiting Middle Eastern photography, I would like to thank Michket Krifa, who has generously shared her expertise. I am also grateful to several other individuals who have shared their opinions, thoughts, knowledge, and time throughout this project: Mitra Abbaspour, Lara Baladi, Sam Bardaouil, Elie Domit, Anahita Ghabaian Etehadieh, Till Fellrath, Darine Flefel, Johnny Hazboun, Carol Huh, Rose Issa, Corey Keller, Linda Komoroff, Dalia Linssen, Farida Marei, Ellen McBreen, Kathy McMann, John G. Morris, Serge Plantureux, Venetia Porter, Nasser Rabat, Elmar Seibel, Guido Vitti, and Marta Weiss. My appreciation also goes to the staff of the Rare Books and Special Collections Library at The American University in Cairo. And for their support and hospitality during my research trips, I thank Barbara Montefalcone and Thomas Olivier, Heloise Petit and Antoine Reberioux, Marie and Marius Piciu, Diana Burnham and Mitch Reznik, and the Tawfik family.

At the MFA, I extend my deep gratitude to several key individuals for their support and commitment to this project, in particular to Malcolm Rogers, Ann and Graham Gund Director; Katie Getchell, Deputy Director; Edward Saywell, Chair, Linde Family Wing for Contemporary Art and Arthur K. Solomon Curator of Modern Art; and Patrick McMahon, Director of Exhibitions and Design. I owe a very special thanks to Anne E. Havinga, Estrellita and Yousuf Karsh Senior Curator of Photographs, for her enthusiasm, confidence, and invaluable support. I am also very grateful for Director of Publications Emiko Usui's vision and encouragement for this book.

The entire MFA Publications department has been a pleasure to work with, and I thank Jennifer Snodgrass for being an attentive, meticulous, and thoughtful editor. I also extend my gratitude to Lucy Flint for her careful editing of the text. I am grateful to Terry McAweeney for her visual sense and attention to detail throughout the production process and to Anna Barnet, Chris DiPietro, and Anne Levine for their help. And